# MVS Performance Management

# Other McGraw-Hill Books in Mini and Mainframe Computing

| ISBN | AUTHOR | TITLE |
|---|---|---|
| 0-07-056578-3 | Sherman | *The CD-Rom Handbook* |
| 0-07-039006-1 | Lusardi | *Database Experts' Guide to SQL* |
| 0-07-039002-9 | (softcover) | |
| 0-07-016609-6 | DeVita | *Database Experts' Guide to FOCUS* |
| 0-07-016604-8 | (softcover) | |
| 0-07-036488-5 | Larson | *Database Experts' Guide to Database 2* |
| 0-07-023267-9 | (softcover) | |
| 0-07-000474-9 | Adrian | *The Workstation Data Link* |
| 0-07-057336-0 | Simpson, Casey | *Developing Effective User Documentation* |
| 0-07-007248-5 | Brathwaite | *Analysis, Design, and Implementation of Data Dictionaries* |
| 0-07-035119-8 | Knightson | *Standards for Open Systems Interconnection* |
| 0-07-044938-4 | McClain | *VM and Departmental Computing* |
| 0-07-044939-2 | (softcover) | |
| 0-07-046302-6 | Nemzow | *Keeping the Link* |
| 0-07-038006-6 | Lipton | *User Guide to FOCUS* |
| 0-07-003355-2 | Baker | *C-Tools for Scientists and Engineers* |
| 0-07-057296-8 | Simon | *How to Be a Successful Computer Consultant* |
| 0-07-052061-5 | Rhee | *Error Correction Coding Theory* |
| 0-07-016188-7 | Dayton (Ranade, Ed.) | *Integrating Digital Services* |
| 0-07-002673-4 | Azevedo (Ranade Series) | *ISPF: The Strategic Dialog Manager* |
| 0-07-050054-1 | Piggott (Ranade Series) | *CICS: A Practical Guide to System Fine Tuning* |
| 0-07-043152-3 | Morgan, McGilton | *Introducing UNIX™ System V* |
| 0-07-050686-8 | Prasad (Ranade Series) | *IBM Mainframes* |
| 0-07-065087-X | Towner (Ranade Series) | *IDMS/R Cookbook* |
| 0-07-062879-3 | Tare (hardcover) | *UNIX™ Utilities* |
| 0-07-062884-X | Tare (softcover) | *UNIX™ Utilities* |
| 0-07-045001-3 | McGilton, Morgan | *Introducing the UNIX™ System* |
| 0-07-062295-7 | Su | *Database Computers* |
| 0-07-041920-5 | Milenkovic | *Operating Systems Concepts and Design* |
| 0-07-010829-3 | Ceri, Pelagotti | *Distributed Databases* |

*For more information about other McGraw-Hill materials,*
*call 1-800-2-MCGRAW in the United States. In other*
*countries, call your nearest McGraw-Hill office.*

# MVS Performance Management

## Mechanisms and Methods

Stephen L. Samson

**Executive Consultant**
**Candle Corporation**

**McGraw-Hill Publishing Company**

New York   St. Louis   San Francisco   Auckland   Bogotá
Caracas   Hamburg   Lisbon   London   Madrid   Mexico
Milan   Montreal   New Delhi   Oklahoma City
Paris   San Juan   São Paulo   Singapore
Sydney   Tokyo   Toronto

To the memory of my father,
William Samson,
who showed me the pleasure of writing.

**Library of Congress Cataloging-in-Publication Data**

Samson, Stephen L.
  MVS performance management.

  1. MVS (Computer system)   I. Title.
QA76.6.S255   1990         005.4'429        89-14013
ISBN   0-07-054528-6

1234567890   DOC/DOC   96543210

ISBN 0-07-054528-6

*The editor for this book was Theron Shreve and the production supervisor was
Richard Ausburn.*
*Printed and bound by R. R. Donnelley & Sons Company.*

*For more information about other McGraw-Hill materials,
call 1-800-2-MCGRAW in the United States. In other
countries, call your nearest McGraw-Hill office.*

# Contents

# PURPOSE OF THIS BOOK

By the simple act of starting to read this book, you have expressed your interest in the idea that IBM's MVS[1] operating system is amenable to a discipline of performance management. What we will attempt to do in these pages is to define that discipline, to build on that interest and turn it into a solid commitment, and to describe and illustrate the means of implementing MVS performance management.

On the other hand, this book is not an introduction to MVS structure and function[2], nor a treatise on MVS system programming. No knowledge of MVS internals is assumed or required for understanding. We deal with MVS's external controls and with the workloads found in most MVS installations. Some knowledge of application programming is useful.

## What is performance management?

MVS is an operating system of great functional richness and correspondingly great complexity. Much of that complexity is devoted to routines that seek to manage the allocation of resources to workloads according to the expressed desires of the installation's management. These desires are expressed to the system through numerous parameters that control parts of MVS's operation, and through decisions affecting the hardware configuration.

MVS performance management may be defined briefly as:

---

1  "IBM" is a registered trademark of the International Business Machines Corporation. "MVS" (the name is a trademark of the International Business Machines Corporation) was originally a short name for an IBM operating system, "OS/VS2: MVS", meaning "Operating System/Virtual Storage 2: Multiple Virtual Storage." MVS currently exists in several variants: MVS System Product Version 1 (MVS/370), MVS System Product Version 2 (MVS/XA), and MVS System Product Version 3 (MVS/ESA). Except as noted, the content of this book applies to all recent and current MVS levels. The name OS/VS2 is rarely seen today.

2  Another book in this series, *MVS: Concepts and Facilities*, by Robert H. Johnson, meets the need for such a work exceptionally well.

- acquiring the knowledge necessary to specify MVS control parameters and to make configuration choices

- translating service objectives into appropriate control parameters and a suitable physical configuration

- monitoring and measuring the system to verify compliance with service objectives and to assess the efficiency and effectiveness of the system

- dealing (with appropriate timeliness) with incidents of performance which is inefficient, ineffective, or inadequate to meet service objectives

This definition will be refined and elaborated throughout the course of the text.

## AUDIENCE

Those whose jobs include accountability for MVS performance are the primary audience for this book. Many others (the direct users of system services above all) are affected by the performance of the operating system and its workloads, and should derive some benefit from this book. Some of those include:

- operations production specialists

- operations managers

- "help desk" staff

- MIS application developers

- MIS managers

- MVS system programmers

- CICS system programmers

- IMS system programmers

- technical support managers

- managers of end-user organizations

- capacity planners

- resource usage accounting and chargeback staff

## OVERALL APPROACH

It is easy to be put off by the sheer size and complexity of MVS and to conclude that the most effective management strategy is that of leaving the system in its default configuration until specific problems arise, and then solving them in turn. This book expresses a different approach: MVS responds well to informed planning, and installation policies can be implemented through MVS's control mechanisms. Our purpose is to demystify those mechanisms and show how MVS can become a well-behaved **managed** system. Adding to the motivation, MVS in its default configuration (as in CBIPO, CBDPO, or MVS Express) is simply not suitable for production use. Initial performance management actions are necessary to prevent the initial production experience from being a bad one.

Irrational fear of MVS's complexity is to be avoided, but wary respect for that complexity is necessary. The saving grace of most of the actions recommended in this book is that, if done as recommended, they are reversible should problems arise. Those actions that require more care and planning are so identified.

## ORGANIZATION

In the first chapter, we examine the history of MVS, from predecessor systems through MVS/ESA (Enterprise Systems Architecture) and the beginning of Systems Application Architecture (SAA). Emphasis in these sections will be on developments important to control and performance management. The history ends with some speculation about the future of MVS.

Chapter 2 examines the physical resources managed by MVS. These include the physical elements of the computing system: CPUs, storage, and Input/Output (I/O) devices, with emphasis on direct-access storage devices (DASD).

In Chapter 3, the actual working objects of MVS are considered. These are the *virtual* resources, which stand in for and rename physical resources, and the *logical* resources, which serve as the control focus for MVS's resource management functions.

We next consider the workloads managed by MVS. In Chapter 4, the workloads are classified and characterized according to their patterns of resource use and their performance management challenges.

Chapters 5 and 6 introduce the often confusing concepts and terminology of the System Resources Manager (SRM).

Chapters 7 and 8 describe the controlling parameters of MVS. In general, these influence the operation of SRM and are materialized as members of SYS1.PARMLIB. Other parameters controlling MVS's subsystems exist in other data sets, and some of the parameters having occasional use still hide in the dark recesses of control blocks and need to be adjusted when necessary through the use of SUPERZAP or a similar mechanism. In these chapters we suggest a set of standard parameters going beyond the IBM-supplied defaults. Some configuration guidelines are given in these chapters.

In Chapter 9, we examine performance problems, how they manifest themselves, and the kind of information that will be needed to expose such problems and their causes.

We turn next in Chapter 10 to a discussion of monitoring and measurement methods, considering the specific need for, and contribution of, each type of measurement technique in facilitating or simplifying performance management. Chapter 10 also includes the details of DASD modeling introduced in Chapter 2.

In Chapter 11, we apply all the foregoing material in covering the solution of performance problems, both chronic and acute. The emphasis in this chapter is on dealing with applications and subsystems, jobs and TSO users as they are, rather than as we wish them to be.

Chapter 12 pursues that ideal, considering the often controversial subject of application tuning. The specialized application of monitoring tools to this task can often be more effective in relieving system problems than the most concerted and protracted "system" tuning efforts.

The book concludes with an extensive annotated glossary of MVS and performance management terms. New terms are generally *italicized* at the point of first use. If a definition is not contextually obvious, it should be found in the glossary. Other stylistic conventions include:

- names of hardware instructions and their operation codes are shown in SMALL CAPITALS (LPSW or LOAD PROGRAM STATUS WORD)

- macro-instruction names are shown in *UPPER-CASE ITALICS* (*RESERVE* macro)

- System data objects and states are shown in UPPER CASE (RESERVE of a device, ENQ lockout)

# MOTIVATION

For four years or more, before I was approached by Jay Ranade to write a book on MVS performance management, I had speculated about such a possibility. The speculation began when I first became responsible for the MVS portion of Candle Corporation's old Fall Performance Seminars. It occurred to me that a solid 14 hours of lecture and supporting materials might form the nucleus of a book. In the intervening years, I wrote several series of MVS articles for the Candle Computer Report and observed the emergence of MVS/XA, the 3090 (and its follow-on models, now designated as Enterprise System/3090) and expanded storage,

DB2, and the announcements of Systems Application Architecture and Enterprise Systems Architecture. Thus the time is much more ripe now for a book on MVS than it was several years ago.

As MVS systems have become more affordable (MVS may yet become viable on the IBM ES/9370), the base of experienced MVS system programmers has had to stretch thin to match the demand. System programmers' lives become more complicated as they respond to conflicting inputs about the care and feeding of MVS. Some say, "MVS is so fiendishly complicated that you should leave it alone .... You need special knowledge to change SRM parameters .... Trust us to guide you .... MVS defaults are OK ...." Others (usually technical support managers) demand that the system be made to perform well as workloads change, and demand an explanation of each episode of poor performance. Certainly (they say) the knowledge necessary to manage MVS well, and to know why it's not well when it's not, should be sufficient to take on as simple a job as setting up a sound IPS.

# PERSONAL BIASES AND MATTERS OF STYLE

MVS, its predecessors, and its successors are IBM-developed control programs intended to run on IBM systems. Several other manufacturers produce systems that are capable of supporting various levels of MVS, and manufacturers other than IBM have produced operating systems that are compatible with MVS in some respects. To the extent that the observations and advice in this book are valid for MVS and System/370 look-alikes, I am delighted to be of some assistance. However, my own experience and knowledge are focused on MVS and the systems for which it was developed. I make no claim of accuracy or insight for similar but not identical environments.

My own accuracy and insight are limited, in any event. All I promise is to communicate the lessons of my experience and to give advice that has worked in most cases. Neither I nor the publisher can in any way claim that the observations and advice contained herein are universally applicable. Before you commit hardware, software, or human resources to implement the ideas presented in these pages, make sure that your situation matches that of the given example or scenario in all crucial respects, or that you have made due allowances for essential differences.

Writing style has received unusual attention in recent years, especially in one specific area: pronouns. To the greatest extent possible, I have tried to avoid the use of gender-specific pronouns. When the syntax gets too convoluted, I use the masculine form with its generic connotation.

## TRADEMARKS AND REGISTERED TRADEMARKS

This book could be cluttered with footnotes at the first mention of each term that is a trademark or registered trademark if each citation were to be given in full. Instead, I give full credit here to the commercial and intellectual property of the trademark holders whose products are mentioned in this book, and I apologize to those whose trademarks might have been inadvertently omitted. IBM has recently begun showing trademark notices in announcements, presentations, and other materials relating to MVS. ES/3090$^{TM}$, MVS/ESA$^{TM}$, Enterprise System/3090$^{TM}$, Hiperbatch$^{TM}$, Hiperspace$^{TM}$, MVS/370$^{TM}$, MVS/XA$^{TM}$, DFSMS$^{TM}$, DFP/370$^{TM}$, and DFP/XA$^{TM}$ are examples of recently asserted IBM trademarks. Many of these names now claimed as common-law trademarks may eventually become registered trademarks.

Candle Corporation's trademark product names are mentioned in the text. These trademarks include OMEGAMON®, EPILOG®, DEXAN®, DELTAMON®, and PRO/MVS®. The name "Candle" preceded by a stylized representation of a flame is also a registered trademark.

Boole and Babbage's RESOLVE and CMF; Computer Associates' CA-LOOK, CA-EXAMINE, ACF2, and Top Secret; Landmark's The Monitor for MVS (TMON/MVS); and SAS Institute's SAS are other commercial software packages mentioned in the text, whose names are trademarks or registered trademarks of the respective vendors. Storage Technology Corporation's ALB™ is a trademark hardware feature. Again, if any other trademark is not properly identified, the omission is unintended.

## ACKNOWLEDGMENTS

None of the events that led me to write this book would have been possible if Tom Apple and Hernan Reyes had not chosen me for a special assignment while I was at IBM in San Jose in 1980. I was privileged to work with Tom Beretvas and Ron Clark on a series of measurement experiments with what became both the Extended Swap Installed User Program (IUP) and the extended swap algorithm in MVS/SP 1.3.0. My association with Tom Beretvas has continued, even after my departure from IBM in 1983. I've learned much from Tom, in the specifics of MVS and even of VM, as well as in the discipline of performance analysis. Tom and I continue to engage in lively technical dialogue, especially on a few matters in which we have differing opinions. After that 1980 turning point, I became an MVS performance specialist, with emphasis on the paging subsystem.

I left IBM after 16 years to join Candle Corporation, the pre-eminent supplier of performance management software for the IBM mainframe environment. Tom Beretvas had a hand in that move as well, since it was Tom who introduced me to Marty Sprinzen, then the Vice-President of Candle in charge of Research and Development. Marty brought me to Candle and gave me a unique opportunity to split my time among Technical Support, R&D, teaching, and writing. This balance of tasks has kept me in touch with the "real world" as well as allowing me to influence Candle's future.

Candle started as a one-man company over twelve years ago. That man, Aubrey Chernick, still leads Candle in all ways. I greatly appreciate his support in this project, as well as that of all levels of Candle management.

Finally, a heartfelt word of appreciation to my wife, Wilma, who has supported this effort with loving encouragement mixed with bemused toleration for the occasional disruptions it has caused.

# MVS Performance Management

# 1

# MVS History and Evolution

A 21-year-old programmer may run jobs today under MVS/XA or MVS/ESA that are older than he or she is. While MVS is a modern operating system—even state-of-the-art in many ways— it is a direct descendant of the first release of Operating System/360. To a large extent, the problem program environment of MVS/ESA remains that of "OS."

We recount the history of MVS to help us understand its mechanisms and the biases implicit in them. We do this here not only to illustrate IBM's continual flow of improvement and innovation,[1] but also to note when and how constraints and limitations appeared in the MVS environment and how later changes overcame those difficulties.

The matter-of-fact appearance and subsequent relief of constraints is a natural consequence of the stair-step process of delivering improvements in hardware and in the many coordinated elements of supporting software. Yet, as many of MVS's shortcomings have appeared and been recognized by system programmers, a common reaction has been to institutionalize the deficiencies and the actions taken in response to them. In a fast-moving field, this reaction can have the effect of unnecessarily perpetuating the effect of a temporary shortcoming. In this

---

[1] IBM does not develop, test, and ship operating system improvements merely for the good of its customers. Major changes in MVS usually appear for IBM's strategic business purposes, such as to support new hardware products.

chapter, we attempt to identify such episodes of the birth of legends, or at least the lagging acceptance of good news.

## 1.1. Predecessor Systems

In this section, we look at the systems that preceded MVS, and the early releases of MVS that differed significantly from today's systems.

### 1.1.1. OS/360 MVT

MVT was the culmination of OS/360. The promises made when System/360 was announced on April 7, 1964 were kept in MVT, at least to the extent that reality allowed them to be kept. The original storage estimate—that a full-function multiprogramming operating system could exist in 64K bytes—seems ludicrous today. The original assertion—that work could compete freely for the real storage resource without the problem of fragmentation or the need for storage preallocation—never came to pass. MVT had to be modified drastically to accommodate two developments in the environment—multiprocessing and time sharing—and even the most devoted "MVT bigot" would have to admit that MVT did not handle those developments very well.

Despite all of its growing pains, MVT supported the growth of the high-end System/360 and early System/370 hardware systems for over ten years and defined an application programming interface still supported in today's MVS. Indeed, a version of MVT to support IBM's 3031, 3032, and 3033 was released as late as 1978. The following concepts were introduced or made commercially successful in OS/360 including MVT:

- *Multiprogramming* of independent workloads without the need for fixed partitioning of storage

- *Multitasking*

- *Multiprocessing* using shared main storage, directed by a single control program

- Device-independent data management without the restrictions of a limited "file system"

- *Late binding* of resources to work units

- I/O resource management across multiple users

- Main storage management across multiple users

- Preemptive multiprogramming dispatching with *priority queueing*

- Dispatching priority adaptation to workload behavior

- *Time sharing* in a full-function operating system environment with full access to that environment

## 1.1.2. SVS

As unlikely as it might seem today, "virtual storage" was regarded as a radical development in the early 1970s. At one time in the development of DOS/VS, the low-end system for System/370, a proposal for optional support of virtual storage was seriously considered. Fortunately, those with greater vision prevailed, so no system called "DOS/almost-VS" was released. Systems of intermediate size were supported by OS/VS1 (based on MFT). At the high end of the 370 line, the plan was two-pronged: A minimal extension to MVT would be released first, followed a year or two later with the system that the dynamic address translation hardware was meant for—a system to become known as MVS.

The original minimal extension to MVT was known as OS/VS2 Release 1, or SVM, for "Single Virtual Memory." Soon after its announcement, the name was changed from SVM to SVS, for "Single Virtual Storage," when it became clear that the System/370 Models 155 and 165[2] were to be the last IBM systems with magnetic core *memory*, and that models 158 and 168 signaled the changeover to semiconductor main *storage*.

SVS used virtual storage to solve (to a limited extent) the outstanding problem of MVT—storage fragmentation. Within the bounds of a single 16-megabyte address space, all SVS systems

---

2    The Models 155 and 165 were the last 370s built with magnetic core memories. They were supported by the VS operating systems only when equipped with an expensive hardware extension called the "DAT box"; DAT is the acronym for Dynamic Address Translation, the essential element needed to support virtual storage.

became equal in [virtual] storage size, if not in performance. Individual jobs ran in regions as in MVT, and the regions represented real boundaries and constraints—the subdividing of a still precious span of storage into a balanced workload such that all fit without waste. TSO still ran in multi-user regions, and each session's storage was wholly swapped out and in at the start and end of each terminal wait. Little if any "overcommitment" of real storage was attempted.

### 1.1.3. OS/VS2 Release 2, 3, ..., 3.6, 3.7, ...

The early releases of MVS from 1973 to 1975 were, frankly, exciting. MVS was described at that time much as MVS/XA was first described in a more recent time, as a special system for very large configurations needing its special capabilities. With the immediate need for support of virtual storage covered by SVS, the evolution to MVS could be allowed to proceed with cooperation and feedback between IBM and the first MVS users. (When IBM overcame MVS's early growing pains, the restraint gave way to a determined selling effort, but the early words of caution had had their effect—SVS survived far too long.) During those early years of MVS, a number of constraints began to appear. Although the constraints eventually were understood and overcome, they had an influence in the MVS environment long after they were no longer current problems, and the descriptions of the constraints became generalized and divorced from their origins. These pervasive legends included:

- **"Paging 'just happens' in MVS."** Global *least-recently-used* (LRU) management of real storage replacement was used in SVS and the first MVS release. Consequently, *demand paging* occurred everywhere in the system, limiting the ability to exploit fast CPUs given the limited amount of real storage in the early MVS machines. This problem was ameliorated with the availability of *storage isolation* in MVS/SE2, and with the dramatic increase in basic and optional real storage sizes available for more recent systems. However, there remains a persistent belief that paging is an uncontrollable phenomenon in MVS, and workloads are often managed as if real storage is severely limited, whether it is or not. Mismanagement of paging has another expression: Systems are not fully loaded to avoid incurring excessive paging delay, instead of managing the paging rate in a fully loaded system.

- **"TSO swapping is not handled well in MVS."** In early MVS, the pages of inactive TSO users were left in real storage, subject to ordinary page stealing. It soon became clear that LRU page stealing was too inefficient to handle the reassignment of large numbers of idle frames. TSO *swapping* was introduced in one of the early variants of VS2 Release 3. The hardware and software approaches to swapping and their controlling algorithms have been one of the most frequently changed (and usually improved) areas of MVS over the years.

- **"TSO and other interactive workloads don't work well together in MVS."** The utilization of page data sets, caused by TSO swapping and the large number of *page faults* due to rigorous *swap trim*, was so high that paging response time for non-TSO workloads often became unacceptable. Even though the numerous changes to TSO swapping algorithms over the years yielded significant relief as early as 1981, it has remained an enduring legend in MVS that TSO and other subsystems, such as CICS or IMS, don't coexist well. Solving the mixed-workload problem was an essential prerequisite to the effective use of large configurations.

- **"MVS needs too much real storage."** The original real storage estimates for MVS were far too optimistic; the 16-megabyte limit on real storage would be in jeopardy before a new-technology replacement for System/370 would become available. A jury-rigged solution became available when the real storage limit was exceeded with late 3033s and the original (System/370) version of the 3081. What appeared to be a long-term solution came with the MVS/XA announcement of 31-bit (2-gigabyte) real and virtual addressing. By 1989, however, the two-gigabyte virtual storage limit was routinely touched, the two-gigabyte real storage limit was only two bits away, and the need for increased real storage was being met, albeit with uneven success, by the use of expanded storage. This particular legend may remain viable for some time.

In discussing these legends, we've had to jump around MVS's history a bit. We return now to a more orderly review of successive major changes in MVS.

## 1.1.4. System Extensions (MVS/SE)

In March of 1978, MVS came to a turning point. The first implementation of MVS System Extensions (MVS/SE1) was announced. Nine years earlier, IBM had announced the "unbundling" of hardware and software. Control programs required for the operation of IBM systems were classified as "system control programming" (SCP) and were provided at no charge.

MVS/SE became the first IBM operating system for which a fee was charged, and the first to require hardware features beyond those in the System/370 instruction set. Beginning with SE1, an increasing number of MVS software algorithms have been placed in microcode, leading to both increased efficiency and to a "moving target" for other manufacturers attempting to duplicate the MVS hardware environment.

The IBM 3033 with System Extensions was the first generally available IBM system to benefit from an approach to system design based on the active consideration of operating system needs and optimization opportunities. (A less rigorous hardware-software design approach, seemingly with some isolation between engineers and programmers, had been characteristic of System/360.) An additional benefit to IBM was the beginning of what has since become substantial annual revenue from the licensing of system software products.

The success of the 3033 with MVS/SE1 led to two MVS software developments, one a dead-end for the no-fee MVS System Control Program, and the other the forerunner of the licensed-for-a-fee succession of MVS offerings that continues today.

The evolution of "free" MVS stopped with release 3.8 in 1979. Although MVS 3.8 is thoroughly out of date today, it is in the public domain, still in circulation, and still available (albeit with some difficulty) from IBM. It is used to support hardware configurations not capable of exploiting the microcode-assisted features of current levels of MVS, and continues to be the "base," at least theoretically, over which today's MVS releases (both MVS/370 and MVS/ESASA) are installed. Thus it is that an RMF report for the latest MVS/SP release may still say "3.8" in its heading. The announcement of 3.8 made it clear that there was to be no future functional enhancement of a no-fee MVS.

The other development that followed the success of MVS/SE1 was the announcement of SE2 in August 1979. In addition to more microcode assistance, SE2 introduced most of today's SRM controls for storage isolation, dispatching priorities, and domains' contention indexes.

## 1.2. MVS As We Know It Today

MVS/SE2 set the pattern for MVS as it exists today. Successive MVS releases have followed in the same mold, with growing dependency on microcode.

### 1.2.1. MVS System Product Version 1 (MVS/SP)

#### MVS/SP1

On June 11, 1980, MVS packaging, nomenclature, and direction were changed once again. Two releases of a new kind of software called "MVS System Product" (MVS/SP) were announced. What was then called SP1 was functionally little more than a repackaging of SE2. As part of the repackaging, the complex "SU" (selectable units) scheme for MVS distribution was abandoned. MVS distribution with SUs had begun in 1976, when real storage constraint was at its worst, and was based on the idea that "optional" parts of the MVS nucleus could be left out when not needed, thus saving fixed virtual storage and thereby real storage. Eventually, some priced enhancements to "free" MVS were shipped as SUs; unpriced SUs continued for such additions as device support.

SP1 provided support for a significant assortment of new hardware including:

- the Extended Addressing feature of the 3033, supporting real (but not virtual) addressing above 16 megabytes

- the 3033 Extensions feature, providing hardware support for cross-memory services, making possible the "horizontal expansion" of the MVS control program with acceptable performance

- 3375 and 3380 Direct Access Storage Devices (DASD)

- Data Streaming Channels to support the new, higher data transfer rates of the 3375 and 3380, as well as the Speed Matching Buffer for support of the new devices on processors whose channels could not be (or were not) upgraded

## MVS/SP2

The second of the two releases announced in June, 1980 was MVS/System Product Release 2, MVS/SP2. SP2 exploited the cross-memory addressing mechanism introduced in SP1 by introducing the notion of "horizontal growth" in MVS. As the need grew for enhanced function and durability in the MVS environment, more operating system code became necessary. At the same time, the encroachment of nucleus and common area code and data on each address space's private area became increasingly unacceptable.

Cross-memory services made it possible, with insignificant overhead, to pare off portions of the operating system into separate address spaces. Code and associated data were removed from the commonly addressed area, thus relieving the constraint on virtual storage addressability in the private area. A section on Virtual Storage Constraint Relief (VSCR) became a common feature of IBM announcements, dating from the SP2 announcement and continuing through the latest MVS/ESA announcements. It is also possible that when IBM changed global data areas into private areas, a change in keeping with current "software engineering" notions, MVS became somewhat less complex in its potential data flows, if more complex in structure.

*Global Resource Serialization (GRS).* The first services to benefit from this restructuring technique were the enqueue/dequeue (ENQ/DEQ) routines and console services. The ENQ/DEQ restructure made it possible for IBM to address a problem of long standing. Multi-system configurations connected through shared DASD suffered from unpredictable and often severe degradation caused by ENQ's use of the volume RESERVE function to ensure integrity of data sets shared across systems.

Although some non-IBM solutions to this problem were available, they relied on a designated shared device to maintain global ENQ data. IBM's planners and developers were motivated to provide an all-IBM solution to the global data-sharing problem, substituting the potentially higher performance of channel-to-channel adapters for the conspicuously shared device. Because of the encroachment of IBM-supplied code on the users' code and data area (the "private area") and the potentially large size of a global ENQueue manager, the solution had to wait until cross-memory services became available in MVS/SP2.

The new service and its address space were known as GRS, for Global Resource Serialization. Even in nonshared systems, all ENQ and DEQ requests, as well as all related control blocks and data areas, are respectively executed through, and resident in, the GRS address space. In shared DASD systems, RESERVEs may be "demoted" to a new class of ENQ with a scope of SYSTEMS. Data-sharing information is passed, along with a token denoting control, among systems connected by a "ring" of channel-to-channel (CTC) adapters.[3]

The CTC ring introduced some new potential performance problems. In the original SP2 implementation, restarting a broken ring was very difficult. Instead of reducing shared DASD delay, SP2 GRS could increase it, either when the ring was broken or when a slower system held the token for an excessively long time. The latter source of delay may exist in current GRS as well.

---

3  It might be that the "pass-the-buck" ring design of GRS was the first IBM token-ring network.

Some non-IBM global enqueue managers employ a "star" configuration instead of a ring. If the shared device is cached DASD or a solid-state device, the performance of such a subsystem can be comparable to that of global GRS at its best, and less susceptible than GRS to delay caused by a software problem in a single system.

*CONSOLE.* Another service address space introduced in SP2 was CONSOLE. CONSOLE provided the base for a continuing series of enhancements to the handling of the operator message stream, thus dealing with another key impediment to MVS's ongoing growth. Efficient processing of the console message stream is a prerequisite for automating the console functions and for eventually attempting unattended MVS system operation, one of the emerging trends in large data centers.

Circumstances (the announcement of SP3 in November of 1980, and the short time span between availability dates for SP2 and SP3) made SP2 something of a shadow release. Very few customers installed it, preferring to wait for the more obvious benefits of SP3. This development worked to the benefit of both IBM and its customers, since the initial GRS implementation's fragility and lack of recoverability were unacceptable to many MVS customers.

## MVS/SP3

November of 1980 brought another crop of major advances in the world of MVS. The major hardware announcement was the first 3081, later redesignated as the 3081D. To support the new capabilities of the 3081, as well as those of the 3033s (which had been further enhanced with a new feature called 3033 Extensions), a new release of MVS was announced, known at that time as MVS/SP Release 3, or SP3.

SP3 (still installed "over" MVS 3.8) brought many far-reaching changes. A year later, after MVS/XA was announced, it became clear that some of these new capabilities were in the nature of "positioning" for XA, but SP3 also became the definitive surviving version of MVS/370. The new functions and support in SP3 included:

- 3081 support

- 3033 Extensions support, highlights of which (and of the 3081) included *queueing channels* and the I/O *suspend/resume* feature, that provided the basis for *seldom-ending channel programs (SECP)*. Both of these hardware extensions facilitated the offload of high-priority processor cycles to the I/O subsystem, foreshadowing the much more significant I/O overhead reduction that accompanied Extended Architecture and MVS/XA. Another element of the new hardware was very efficient support of cross-memory services.

- Extended Swap. As MVS evolved, TSO swapping and its management were revised often. The original VS2-3 version imposed unacceptable loads on the paging subsystem as the pages held by idle address spaces were stolen. Physical swapping made management of the swap paging load somewhat more efficient, and the introduction of swap data sets brought a modest amount of page data set relief. As real storage sizes began to increase, the introduction of logical swap in SE1 unloaded the page (and swap) data sets still more, but only when the real storage resource was already underutilized.

With all of these changes, it was still not wise to mix a TSO workload with a multi-user online system, such as CICS, on the same MVS system, because the appearance of real storage constraint led to the degenerative reinforcement of both TSO and CICS response time. As one got worse, so would the other. Single-task subsystems such as CICS are much more profoundly affected by paging delay than is TSO, so even storage isolation was not very effective in shielding interactive subsystems from the long delays associated with heavily loaded page data sets. A new approach to the paging problem was needed.

Other manufacturers attempted to deal with paging performance problems by using fast solid-state paging devices. These devices first appeared to the system as IBM 2305-2 fixed-head files (also known as "drums" because of they performed very much like genuine drums with a single cylindrical recording surface and one head per track). IBM had stopped making 2305s, and the solid-state devices (SSDs) filled the gap with better performance and reliability. Eventually, the storage capacity increased, the simulated device became the IBM 3380, and some provisions were made for nonvolatile storage. In light of subsequent developments, it becomes clear that any long-term success of the SSD approach would have inhibited migration to the 3090s with their expanded storage.

IBM's paging solution was an algorithmic invention. The nature of TSO swapping was changed, making the speed of mass data transfer much more significant than that of fast single-page retrieval. Before extended swap, the set of pages swapped out did not match the swap-in group, or swap group. Changed (but not necessarily recently referenced) pages were written out, while recently referenced (but not necessarily changed) pages were swapped in. The profound invention in extended swap was to recognize that a swap group with the same population for swap-in as for swap-out could be moved intact via blocked I/O. The introduction of extended swap had several benefits to IBM:

° The local page data sets could be significantly unloaded by moving swap groups to and from swap data sets. This in turn meant that demand paging response time would improve, facilitating the efficient combining of workloads on larger systems.

° The swap data sets could be placed on 3380s with their 3 megabytes-per-second data transfer rate. Solid state devices were of little benefit in this application because data transfer time (rather than page-finding time) for the first time dominated the swap-in delay.

° Use of storage isolation along with extended swap eliminated more than half of TSO page faults and thus made consistent subsecond response time possible for TSO, leading to greater user productivity. Storage-constrained systems achieved higher levels of CPU utilization as an inhibition on servicing pent-up demand was eased.

° In systems without swap data sets, *contiguous-slot allocation*, a new approach to constructing paging channel programs, brought "blocked"[4] paging I/O to local page data sets. Since most of the device-busy time on the paging devices was related to per-page overhead, contiguous-slot made the benefits of extended swap available on systems with locals-only paging configurations. Because the size of a block on a 3380 was larger than the swap set size of 12 slots, efficiency was potentially higher than with swap data sets. Two factors held back the full adoption of locals-only: the need for storage isolation of TSO along with locals-only was not appreciated at first by IBM advice-givers and the initial implementation of contiguous-slot was flawed.

° Most important for IBM's large systems strategy, the value of "drums" or their solid-state replacements was largely nullified in the TSO environment.

• A special form of Virtual I/O (VIO) known as Virtual Fetch was implemented as a set of MVS primitives and used in a new release of IMS. Virtual Fetch helps reduce IMS delays due to repeated loading of non-reenterable[5] programs.

• Although it was introduced in SP1, extended real addressing above 16 megabytes was not well-used before SP3. As SP3 could support many more TSO users and more VIO than prior releases, the added storage was used as a reservoir of pageable frames, thus avoiding paging I/O. Real storage sizes through 64 megabytes

---

4   Contiguous-slot I/O is not blocked in the sense of supporting multiple logical records per physical record, but command chaining of successive READs or WRITEs within the same cylinder produces a similar level of efficiency.

5   The term "reentrant" is sometimes used as a synonym for "reenterable." "Reentrant," and related barbarisms such as "reentrancy," should be avoided, regardless of common usage, since "reentrant" (a word whose only merit is a smaller number of syllables) has the plain meaning of "a program that re-enters itself"—in other words, a loop! The essence of the correct term, *reenterability*, is the suffix *-ility*, correctly suggesting the ability to be re-entered or reactivated while a previous activation had not yet concluded.

were eventually supported in SP3, although little benefit could be derived from real storage sizes in excess of 32 megabytes.

SP3 is the last major release of MVS/370, athough it eventually acquired a different name. Seven modification levels of SP3 have appeared to date, introducing new device support and new releases of the two alternative MVS job entry subsystems, JES2 and JES3.

## 1.2.2. MVS System Product Version 2 (MVS/XA)

### MVS/SP 2.1.0 and MVS/370 redesignation

Less than a year after the SP3 announcement, IBM dropped an even bigger shoe. The 3081 was revealed as a machine with a dual personality. In addition to the System/370 instruction set (augmented with a great deal of specialized MVS microcode), the 3081 also had another mode of operation: System/370 Extended Architecture, "XA."

For years it had been apparent to IBM's product and marketing planners that System/370 and MVS on System/370 had architectural limits that could no longer be tolerated. The limits included only 16 megabytes of virtual addressability, no more than 30 high-speed channels, central processor complexes with no more than two CPUs,[6] real storage limited to 64 megabytes, and an I/O subsystem that made continual disruptive demands on the CPU and the operating system to drive I/O and deal with the ensuing interrupts. Carryovers from System/360 defined many of the 370's limitations. A new system architecture was needed, but the customers dependent on the System/370 and its operating systems could not be expected to convert their applications to a new hardware and operating system architecture.

From its inception, XA had two principal objectives: to overcome the architectural limitations of System/370, and yet to allow the vast majority of System/370 programs to run without change.

6    Although the architecture of MVS/370 could theoretically have supported up to 16 processors, no System/370 processor exceeded a two-way configuration due to engineering constraints in the basic designs. Could $n$-way MP have worked on MVS/370? The testing effort alone could have been a lifetime career.

MVS/SP 2.1.0 accomplished both these purposes, although not without some often-confusing retroactive changes in nomenclature. The new operating system was called "MVS System Product Version 2." The prior version was obviously Version 1, although it had never been called that before. SP3 became known as SP1.3; its third modification level was, for example, SP1.3.2. (Versions and releases are numbered from 1; modification levels begin at 0.)

SP2.1.0 was functionally equivalent to SP1.3.0. As part of establishing the change of direction attendant to the release of a new operating system, the operating system was split into two parts. SP2.1.0 proper was only the Base Control Program, or BCP. The collection of "Data Facility" products, developed in IBM's Santa Teresa Laboratory in San Jose, was gathered together as one product and merged with the formerly "free" data management portion of the operating system and sold as Data Facility Product/XA, or DFP/XA. A DFP/370 was announced shortly thereafter. The BCP/DFP structure has since become standard in MVS. IBM followed the same pattern in creating another broad-function licensed program: several network control, debugging, and measurement products were gathered together as the first version of NetView.

In most cases the conversion to MVS/XA appeared to be less disruptive than the move from "SP1" to "SP3." The easy conversion in terms of system programmer effort was often followed by a nasty shock when the production workload was moved to the new XA system. The surprise was reminiscent of the one experienced when an SVS system was converted to MVS. XA is built on a much larger scale than that of MVS/370, similar to the relationship of MVS to SVS. A workload requiring 16 megabytes of real storage on MVS/370 might have needed 18–20 megabytes on XA. Storage increment sizes on the first 3081s were 8 MB, so an upgrade to 24 MB was required. The real-storage shock wore off in time as later machines were announced with larger minimum and maximum sizes, at a smaller cost increment per megabyte.

## Subsequent SP2.1 releases

Following at regular intervals after SP2.1.0 came several additional XA announcements:

- SP2.1.1 added support for cache DASD controllers.

- SP2.1.2 brought a revised Auxiliary Storage Manager that removed inefficiencies introduced with SP1.3.0. The same changes were also made available for retrofit to MVS/370, SP1.3.1 and above.

- SP2.1.3 added support for the 3090-200 and expanded storage. Interim packages (an echo of SUs) added to the SP2.1.3 base supported vector processors on the 3090s and availability enhancements, on a mutually exclusive basis.

- SP2.1.5 added support for the 3090-400.

- SP2.1.7 integrated the interim packages based on SP2.1.3 and introduced dispatcher improvements.

## MVS/SP2.2.0 and 2.2.1

MVS/XA evolution continued with two releases of "SP2.2": SP2.2.0 and SP2.2.1. They differed only in that 2.2.0 had a new JES2 component, while 2.2.1 included a new level of JES3. Changes introduced in the 2.2 level of XA include a vastly simplified system customization procedure, removal of miscellaneous functional constraints dating back to the first release of OS/360, and a new kind of data object called Data in Virtual (DIV). DIV has the potential of providing efficient support for very large data base applications with sparse reference patterns. DIV is supported by a new kind of VSAM data set called a Linear Data Set, which is also used directly by IBM's relational data base subsystem, DB2.

## MVS/SP2.2.3

On June 20, 1989, IBM announced the last release of MVS/XA, JES2 and JES3 versions of MVS/SP2.2.3. These releases are equivalent to SP2.2, except that they operate with the Data Facility Product of MVS/ESA, DFP 3.1, and a subset of its system-managed storage features. The purpose of these final releases is to allow ESA-capable systems to migrate to MVS/ESA even though older XA systems, not capable of running ESA, coexist in the same data center.

### 1.2.3. Enterprise Systems Architecture and MVS/SP Version 3 (MVS/ESA)

On February 16, 1988, IBM announced a series of far-reaching extensions to MVS. A new hardware architecture, Enterprise Systems Architecture (ESA), was announced, along with a new version of the MVS System Product. ESA is an evolutionary extension of XA. New extensions to data addressing introduce the idea of *data spaces* which are data-only counterparts of address spaces that enable application programs and subsystems to address essentially unlimited amounts of data.[7] MVS/ESA also includes the notion of *hiperspaces* (high performance [data] spaces) that can substitute an area of expanded or auxiliary storage for a data set in pursuit of a prime ESA objective: avoiding I/O on the critical performance path.

## 1.3. Extrapolation

MVS/ESA can be expected to evolve until the full functional potential of the 3090 and contemporaneous IBM hardware, such as the 3990 storage control unit, is supported. When the 3090 has a successor, MVS/ESA will likely be supported on that system even as MVS/370 was supported on the 3081. Just as ESA is a superset of XA, possible future systems will be likely to include ESA as a subset.

The size and importance of the Data Facility Product (DFP) component of MVS/ESA can be expected to grow significantly as system-managed storage (supported as DFSMS) matures and

---

7 The introduction of data spaces in ESA seems to represent the end of at least one aspect of Von Neumann architecture in the systems that originated with System/360. One basic characteristic of a Von Neumann architecture (named for John Von Neumann, an early pioneer of computer designs) is the equivalency of programs and data. A program could branch to any arbitrary address subject to boundary constraints, and the hardware would dutifully attempt to execute the bit strings found there as "instructions." Such potentially harmful operation is not possible when data is segregated from code in a data space.

becomes accepted. That maturity will be achieved when the full capability of the 3990 storage control is matched with a post-3380 generation of DASD.

In the short-term evolution of MVS/ESA, it is safe to predict the appearance of new MVS/ESA interfaces and services based on IBM's Systems Application Architecture (SAA). One such SAA-influenced change is the introduction of REXX as an alternative to TSO's traditional CLIST language in an ESA-specific version of the TSO Extensions licensed program.[8]

While SAA is designed to provide "consistent" interfaces for application programs across the IBM product line, those interfaces are usually provided by operating system primitives. The relation of Data in Virtual to the Structured Query Language (SQL) of DB2 is illustrative: SQL is an SAA interface, but several layers of operating system and subsystem support are necessary to make it run efficiently in MVS/ESA. DIV and hiperspaces should improve the performance of SQL in DB2 for some classes of queries.

In contrast to MVS/ESA, MVS/370 is essentially at a dead end. The only current IBM systems that support MVS/370, but not ESA, are the top models of the 9370 midrange line. The 9370, however, is primarily a DOS/VSE- and VM-oriented system. If heavy demand for MVS on the 9370 appears, it is likely that the microcode will be made ESA-compatible, or that an ESA-capable successor system will be announced. It is not likely that IBM will maintain parallel support for MVS/370 and MVS/ESA for as long as SVS and OS/VS1 coexisted with MVS.

MVS/XA, in turn, will become obsolete as well, probably more rapidly than MVS/370 did, since an explicit announcement of a "last XA release" has aleady appeared. An announcement of "functional stabilization" for MVS/370 has not yet been made and probably will not be as long as the 9370 line is not ESA-capable.

---

8   REXX was best known in the past as the VM/370-CMS counterpart of TSO's CLIST control language, with a reputation for superior function and performance. REXX was selected as the control language for SAA.

MVS/ESA has been designated by IBM as the vehicle for major enhancements in the large systems environment such as SAA and image processing, and is a prerequisite for new releases of major IBM subsystems such as IMS and CICS. ESA's potential for performance improvement over that which is achievable in XA will hasten the economic erosion of systems that are not ESA-capable.

Migration of application programs from XA to ESA is relatively simple, since the XA environment is a proper subset of the ESA environment. Anything that runs in XA without dependency on internal structures may be moved to ESA without change. The qualification is essential. Converting performance monitors and other system programs dependent on internal interfaces from XA to ESA is no trivial exercise. Many internal data areas changed significantly in the cleanup and relief of constraints accompanying the implementation of MVS/ESA.

## Update

IBM announced significant extensions to MVS/ESA and the 3090 processors on October 24, 1989. Some high points of the announcement are summarized here, and a few pages were revised elsewhere in this book to reflect the new features and capabilities. A full treatment of all that was in the announcement could not be included because of production schedule considerations.

New "J" and "JH" models of the 3090 feature reduced cycle times and larger maximum storage sizes. PR/SM in the new models now supports VM/XA in a logical partition, as well as dynamic storage reconfiguration.

In MVS/ESA, new facilities are provided for I/O avoidance, especially in heavy batch environments. A new function called Hiperbatch™ places sequential and VSAM data sets in hiperspaces to reduce I/O delay. The new I/O avoidance measures are available in general without the need to rewrite programs or even to restructure complex JCL streams.

# 2

# Physical Resources

MVS has no work of its own to do. Everything it does, it does on behalf of the workloads that run under its control. What, then, does it do? **MVS manages resources and the access of workloads to them.** Of course, an operating system does far more by providing services and handling exceptional conditions, including error recovery. In our concern for the performance management aspect of MVS, we'll ignore those functions for the most part. In this chapter we examine the physical (hardware) resources that MVS manages.

The end result of MVS's management of workloads is the interaction of those workloads with the physical resources of the system. We shall examine those resources and some of the difficulties workloads can encounter in trying to use them. In doing so, we will become aware of the need for the more abstract kinds of resources—virtual and logical—that MVS creates and supports in order to manage the physical resources.

## 2.1. CPU or Processor

Every program executes *some* instructions. The essence of a work unit such as a batch job, CICS transaction, or TSO command is the set of instructions to be executed. The work unit begins when the first instruction is executed, and ends (normally) when it executes a final instruction to return control to the operating system or the subsystem under which it runs.

MVS chooses a work unit to receive access to the CPU and dispatches it by issuing a LOAD PROGRAM STATUS WORD (LPSW) instruction with the address of the first instruction of the work unit specified in the *program status word* (PSW) to be loaded. In the case of a subsystem like CICS, MVS dispatches the subsystem, and the subsystem's own internal dispatcher selects an internally known work unit to be given control of the CPU. Directly or indirectly, a productive work unit begins using a CPU by executing instructions.

To be useful, however, any program needs more than just the CPU. It must communicate in some way with the outside world, and ultimately with the human being who is using it. It usually needs data from some device in the input/output configuration or from some other work unit in the operating system environment. It may need some information known to the operating system, such as the time or date. Finally, it almost always requires working virtual storage, in addition to the storage needed for the program itself. (A well-written program in MVS does not alter its own storage. This discipline is the basic criterion for *reenterability*, an attribute identifying a program of which a single copy may be used by more than one work unit at a time.)

Each of these requirements is satisfied by some kind of interaction, outside of the current instruction stream, which is handled by MVS. With some exceptions, the way in which a program requests an MVS service is to issue the SUPERVISOR CALL (SVC) instruction. This instruction causes an interruption and causes an MVS service routine to be executed. When some of these service routines complete their work, and upon the occurrence of certain other interruptions, the MVS dispatcher gets another opportunity to choose the next work unit to be dispatched (by performing the same operation as at initial dispatching, but with a restart address denoting the instruction following the SVC), and thus to receive more CPU service. (The dispatcher does not get to make the choice of who is to get the CPU next if an MVS service routine returns control of the CPU directly to its invoker.)

Many of the service requests (such as for an unbuffered I/O operation) cannot be completed immediately, so the requesting work unit is placed in a WAIT state pending completion of the request. The dispatcher is invoked again to ensure that the CPU does not go idle if any other work unit is ready to run.

I/O operations take hundreds to thousands of times as long as CPU instructions to complete, and the execution of I/O operations does not require the CPU except at initiation and completion. A substantial opportunity exists during an I/O WAIT period to dispatch a different unit of work and keep the CPU as busy as possible. (We have just defined *multiprogramming*. Of course, there is also the little matter of deciding which work unit gets the CPU now.)

The simple proposition of putting work into the CPU and letting it run to completion becomes complex in a modern multiprogramming operating system. MVS must have a way of knowing which work units are ready to receive service and which are waiting for the completion of some activity asynchronous with the CPU. The operating system must also determine, at each time that the dispatcher has a chance to choose a work unit, which one is the most appropriate to dispatch next. This kind of decision is made hundreds or thousands of times per second. The lists of different kinds of work, and the rules for choosing the next dispatchable unit of work, are the objects and parameters of CPU performance management.

Before CPU management can be fully covered, an understanding of CPU configurations is necessary. We shall look now at the various types of CPU configurations supported by MVS. The treatment is in roughly historical order.

## 2.1.1. Uniprocessors

The simplest CPU configuration is the uniprocessor. As denoted by the name, there is one PSW, one set of registers, one set of input/output connections, and one active instruction stream. Thus there is no simultaneity in processing, except what might go on beneath the "Principles of Operation" interface. Fast uniprocessors, beginning with the System/360 Model 91 and continuing through most current large systems, have always had some level of overlap in their operation, such as between the instruction fetch operation and the execution of those instructions. What distinguishes a uniprocessor from a multiprocessor is the single set of architecturally defined resources, as opposed to those included in the engineering embodiment of the architecture.

MVS in a uniprocessor does not need to do those extra things we will see to be necessary in a multiprocessing environment. Thus the throughput of a fast uniprocessor (assuming no constraint in other resources) can be higher than that of a multiprocessor built to the same architecture, using the same basic technology, and processing instructions at the same overall rate.

Uniprocessors under a given machine architecture can only become faster in two ways: (1) the basic technology (typified by machine cycle time) gets faster, and (2) the engineering designs get to be more efficient. An example of the latter might be to reduce the number of cycles needed to execute a commonly used instruction. The historical trend in uniprocessor speed improvement is about 15 to 20 percent per year. Unfortunately, the historical trend in demand for CPU cycles shows an increase of 30 to 50 percent per year. The gap is bridged by the use of multiprocessor configurations.

## 2.1.2. Multiprocessors

The word "multiprocessor" covers many different kinds of system configurations. IBM has employed the term "loosely coupled" multiprocessing to describe a JES3 configuration, in which several MVS CECs[1] are interconnected through channel-to-channel adapters. One might also extend the definition to encompass JES2 multi-access SPOOL—CECs interconnected with shared DASD— and to even more tenuously interconnected configurations.

Here, however, we shall use a more restrictive definition of multiprocessing—the kind originally named Tightly Coupled Multiprocessing, or TCMP. In TCMP, at least two "processors" similar to

---

1  Since in this discussion, the term "system" might refer to an extended configuration and the term "processor" is part of the subject, we will sometimes use "CEC" (for Central Electronic Complex) or "processor complex" to denote the set of hardware associated with a single copy of the MVS control program.

uniprocessors share the same real storage and are controlled by a single copy of an operating system such as MVS.

## System/360 Model 65MP

IBM's first production MP system of interest in the evolution to MVS was the MP65, a system using two System 360 Model 65s, modified to include some essential MP functions and "bolted together" via an "MP box" to operate under control of a modified version of OS/360 MVT.

What are those MP functions? In a two-way MP system, each processor knows of only one other. If some significant event occurs that one processor does not know about, there is only one other processor that might be responsible. It may appear sufficient in two-way systems such as the MP65 to provide a simple "shoulder tap" instruction, such that each processor can cause an interrupt to the other. In practice, however, the interprocessor signaling mechanism is also a convenient alternative to normal operating system communication conventions, and the processor may issue a shoulder tap directed to itself. The SIGNAL PROCESSOR (SIGP) instruction introduced the notion of *processor address*, so that the interrupted CPU can learn the identity of the interrupter.

In every System/360- or System/370-based MP system, each processor must have its own copy of the byte address range 0–4095. This "low storage" area had unique architecturally designated functions in System/360: All old and new PSWs, the Channel Address Word (CAW), Channel Status Word (CSW), Interval Timer (obsolete in System/370), and Machine Check Logout Area are all assigned fixed addresses in low storage. Many of those functions continued in System/370, and later in Extended Architecture (XA) and in Enterprise Systems Architecture (ESA).

To maintain the independent operation of each processor, each needs its own image of low storage. This need is met through the addition of a new register, the *prefix register*, to each CPU, and of two new instructions. These two instructions were the first in the System/360 instruction set to break the solid bond between the addresses that programs use and the physically fixed order of an array of some storage (memory) device. SET PREFIX designates an address (divisible by 4096) in *absolute* storage[2] that will subsequently be known as real byte 0 for the current processor. The address translation covers real bytes 0–4095. The reciprocal translation is also done. Real storage references to the prefix page are translated to absolute page 0.

STORE PREFIX stores the address from the prefix register in the word of main storage denoted by its operand address.

## System/370 Multiprocessors

In contrast with MVT, MVS was designed with multiprocessing support included from "day one." Access to unique but unsharable system resources was serialized through several software *locks*. (MP65 support had only one lock, thus spending proportionally more of its time than MVS "under lock" and appearing at those times like a uniprocessor. The indifferent MP performance of the MP65, in the range of 1.6 to 1.7 times that of a UP, led to another legend—that MPs were inefficient. MP efficiency has increased steadily since that time through both hardware and software improvements.) System/370 (and thus MVS/370) was still limited to two-way MP. Although prefixing, SIGP, and the MVS/370 locking structure could handle up to 16 CPUs, the System/370 engineering designs and the channel subsystem could not accommodate more than two.

The first System/370 MPs were the System/370 Models 158MP and 168MP. The 158MP employed cycle-stealing internal channels, while the 168MP had external channels. In each case, each set of channels was associated with a single CPU, eventually (in an early MVS enhancement) becoming known as a *channel set* and supported by a system availability feature known as *channel*

---

2  An absolute address is the address the CPU and channels ultimately use for storage access. A real address is converted to absolute by means of prefixing, and a virtual address is converted to a real address by dynamic address translation.

*set switching.* Such a feature was necessary because many I/O control units (for instance, the IBM 3705 communications processor) could be attached to only one channel. If a CPU failed, its uniquely attached devices became unreachable, and the availability benefit of the MP hardware was diminished. With channel set switching, *asymmetrically*[3] attached devices with unique addresses could be reached from either CPU, keeping the system up and running instead of requiring an IPL when a CPU failed.

Considerations of channel set switching are typical of the painstaking configuration analysis and specification necessitated by the architectural bonds among CPUs, channels, I/O control units, and devices in System/360 and System/370. In our consideration of the CPU resource, it is sufficient to note that MVS/370 was barely able to cope with two CPUs and their channels. XA with its independent channel subsystem was needed to simplify the connections and thus make MP beyond two-way feasible.

Succeeding the 158MP and 168MP were MP versions of the 3031 and 3033. In all of the System/370 MPs, an essential characteristic was *reconfigurability.* Each CPU, with its channels, could operate as an independent system under a separate control program (*physically partitioned* mode), or they could be combined as an MP under a single control program. The "MP box" that joined the CPUs performed an active function in *single image* (MP) mode, handling prefixing, timer synchronization, and inter-processor signaling. In *partitioned* mode, its function was limited to handling the apportionment of the main storage.

The MP configuration provided added CPU capacity with a single control program, configuration flexibility, and availability. These advantages came at the cost of expensive MP features on both CPUs, additional switching features on I/O controllers, and the "MP box," which provided no functions of its own. System/370 multiprocessing provided no added I/O addressing capacity because of the limitations of symmetrical attachment, but when

---

3  Symmetrical attachment uses the two-channel switch feature of an I/O control unit or the string switching feature of some I/O devices to make the control unit address (and thus the addresses of the attached devices) the same on each channel set of an MP. With more complex switching options, alternate (symmetrical) paths could be provided on each channel set. Asymmetric connection results when these features are not used or are unavailable.

the number of channels and their aggregate data transfer rates were a system throughput limitation, MP systems, with a full complement of channels and sufficient control units, provided some relief from that constraint.

*System/370 Attached Processors.* In an effort to provide some of the benefits of an MP configuration at a lower price, IBM developed a type of processor complex called an *attached processor* (AP). In an AP (made available on the 158, 168, and 3033), there are two processors, but they are not partitionable. In most of the AP configurations, the secondary processor (the APU) has no channels, but the final version of the 3033 AP did have channels associated with the APU. (We shall consider the AP in its original concept, without channels.)

The AP configuration had virtually no availability advantage but did provide added processor power for workloads that were CPU-intensive with less-than-typical I/O needs. When APs were installed for general purpose use, it soon became clear that I/O was a significant bottleneck. The APU could not issue the START I/O FAST (SIOF) instruction. The I/O supervisor (IOS) on the APU had to SIGP to the CPU to initiate the I/O. System/370 architecture required that the (main) CPU take all of the I/O interrupts. In today's terms, the AP was inherently incapable of being a "balanced system."

## Dyadic and Triadic Processors

Recall that the 3081 was initially announced as a System/370. In that context, its configuration was yet another multiprocessor variation. The new term was *dyadic*,[4] denoting two processors in a single box with two associated channel sets. The System/370 appearance of the 3081 was similar to that of a 3033 AP with channels on the APU: an "MP" that was not separable into two UPs, but with a full MP complement of channels organized as two channel sets, permitting symmetrical configurations to be moved intact from 3033 MPs.

---

4 Webster's New Collegiate Dictionary defines "dyad" as "**1:** PAIR specif : two individuals (as husband and wife) maintaining a sociologically significant relationship **2:** a meiotic chromosome after separation of the two homologous members of a tetrad...."

When the (true) Extended Architecture nature of the 3081 was made known, the overly complex System/370 structure could be swept aside. There were simply two CPUs, each equally capable of using the independent channel subsystem. The association of channels with CPUs was discarded, and there was no reason why a third or fourth CPU could not be added to the dyadic configuration. Such an addition was made in the generation following that of the 3081 in the 3090-300E. Conceptually, the triadic is no different from a dyadic. If storage and channels are added in balance, evolution of the 3090 "side" to a tetradic configuration would be similarly uneventful; indeed, the continued absence of such a system would be the surprise.

## Dual Processors

In the intermediate range of processors smaller in capacity than the 3081, another multi-CPU variation appeared. The largest models of the IBM 4381 are *dual* processors. They are similar in concept to dyadics, but the channels are associated with CPUs, as are System/370 channel sets, and are cycle-stealing ("integrated") channels. The XA requirement of independence (of channels from CPUs) is met with additional microcode, indicating potential inefficiency of the original 4381 design in XA mode. The ESA models of the 4381 continue the "integrated channels" approach. A successor to the 4381 more optimized to ESA would seem to be a likely later development.

## 3084 and 3090 Multiprocessors

Prior to the announcement of the 3081, the biggest MVS systems were always "full" MPs. They had two CPUs, two channel sets, and were partitionable into two independent quasi-uniprocessors. With the 3081 such an arrangement was not possible, since the dyadic already had two CPUs and two channel sets. After XA was announced, it became possible to announce the 3084. A 3081 was one side of a 3084; the other side was originally a spectacularly expensive "upgrade kit," but eventually two 3081KXs could be fused into a 3084QX. (Perhaps as important, they could be unfused as well. Many installations made successful and nondisruptive migrations from MVS/370 to MVS/XA by exploiting the ability to partition the 3084 into two 3081-equivalents.)

The designs of successor systems have built on the two-sided model of the 3084. The 3090-280E, -250S, and -280S are basic MPs like the 3033MP, composed of two partitionable "sides," each equivalent to a 3090-180E, -150S, or -180S, respectively. The 3090-400, and later the 400E, 500E, and 600E (and their S-series counterparts) are composites of dyadics and triadics, as indicated by their model numbers. The 3090-380S is a composite of a uniprocessor and a dyadic.

Each two-sided system retains the physical partitionability of the 3084, but that might become a less important attribute as a hardware feature IBM calls PR/SM (Processor Resource/Systems Manager, pronounced "prism") comes into common use. Similar in purpose to Amdahl Corporation's Multiple Domain Facility (MDF) and National Advanced Systems' Multiple Logical Processor Facility (MLPF), PR/SM allows logical partitioning of a processor complex into as many as seven independent system images per side. Thus a hardware configuration can support multiple operating systems running concurrently without the need for a software *hypervisor* such as VM/XA.

### 2.1.3. CPU—Summary

In every MVS system, regardless of the CPU configuration, there is only one dispatching queue. Whenever an MVS routine that exits *via* the dispatcher completes execution, the dispatcher is invoked on that CPU. In Chapter 6 we'll examine dispatching priority and its control, as well as the elements that make up the dispatching queue.

## 2.2. Real Storage

In many of the older CPU configurations, it was nearly impossible in practice to use all of the CPU power productively. The bottleneck most likely to have inhibited full CPU productivity was that of insufficient real storage.

Real storage in MVS is organized into page frames of 4096 bytes each. Programs in MVS refer, not to real storage, but to virtual storage addresses. (An exception occurs in the input/output subsystem: I/O data addresses are absolute, and access method routines translate virtual addresses to absolute addresses as part of channel program construction.) Hardware translates the virtual references to real addresses through dynamic address translation. MVS manages real storage on the basis of demand; the Real Storage Manager assigns frames from an available frame queue (AFQ) when they are needed. Frames are reassigned (stolen) when the AFQ length falls below a threshold, or when a need for frames cannot be met from the current AFQ.[5]

To understand the great importance of carefully planned real storage management in MVS, consider some of its uses:

- Residence for pages of the system with virtual addresses the same as their real addresses ("V=R").

- Residence for pages of programs that need to run in V=R mode. V=R programs and system routines were prevalent in the early days of SVS and MVS. As fear of the unknown diminished, dynamic address translation was recognized as innocuous (if not beneficial), and V=R strictures were removed as code was rewritten from the MVT base.

- Residence for fixed pages. Pages are fixed (removed unconditionally from eligibility for reassignment) because addresses within them must be invariant across I/O operations that work with real addresses and usually take long to complete. The short-term page fixing associated with I/O need not be expensive in real storage. Only buffers associated with an I/O currently in progress need be fixed.

  Pages are also fixed for other reasons. To enhance performance in one part of the system, usually at the expense of performance elsewhere, pages may be long-term fixed. Unless done with great care and with full analysis of the process whose pages are to be fixed, including its other re-

5 As we'll see in later chapters, control of the Available Frame Queue through page stealing is inefficient. When the workload permits such a choice, the primary control of AFQ should be through swapping.

source needs, such page fixing often produces little benefit at great cost. (Storage isolation is usually a more appropriate technique for this purpose.)

- Residence for system data. The control blocks and data queues through which MVS manages resources are in this category. Some are fixed, but many simply remain resident because of their high activity.

- Residence for the working sets of active address spaces. "Working set" is a difficult term to define, because it varies depending on the time span of interest. In any time interval of interest, it is the amount of real storage (usually denoted in pages) a program needs to complete the current activity without adding another page frame. At the lowest (instruction) level, this amount is often a single frame, but one might imagine a worst case in which eight frames are needed. A single TSO transaction may need 50–200 frames.

"Working set" is a concept that maps well to the behavior of a single program. Most programs have the property called *locality of reference*—instructions executed later are not far in virtual storage from those executed earlier, and the data they access lie within a small span of virtual addresses. Consequently, they make reference to only a few real page frames as well.

As subsystems such as CICS, serving many on-line users, became the norm in MVS, the working set concept became less useful. Successive requests are likely to be unrelated, so there is little continuity of virtual or real storage reference from instant to instant. Consequently, we cannot speak of a "working set" for a CICS subsystem in the strict sense. Rather, we regard the working set for such a subsystem as the number of pages it needs to have bound to real storage frames to avoid sustaining a damaging page fault rate. This is not a crisp definition, but rather one element in a series of tradeoffs between the (resource or dollar) cost of providing service and the effect of a particular level of service on the larger business. In a later chapter we'll discuss storage isolation, an MVS service that allows such storage binding to be selected and controlled.

- Residence for the working sets of inactive address spaces. As MVS evolved, there were several time periods in which the focus of interest swung between saving real storage and exploiting it, between using the paging subsystem heavily and avoiding its use, and between throughput and response time. MVS today retains traces of the extremes of those swings—in default parameters that oppose each other, and in basic mechanisms that are equally in conflict. It appears that real storage constraint (at least in many 3090s) is not a current problem, so the mechanisms encouraging real storage residency for inactive address spaces, as well as for inactive pages of active address spaces and system data areas, are now dominant.

This use of real storage began in MVS/SE1 with the introduction of logical swapping. In that time frame, 168MPs with 16 megabytes of real storage started to become available. The full real storage complement was often more than the system could use, and the chronic problem of TSO's paging conflicting with the response time needs of other workloads was solved by exploiting the surplus real storage to maintain inactive TSO users in real storage.

## 2.2.1. MVS/370 and the "16 megabyte line"

In System/370, 16 megabytes was the architectural upper limit on both virtual and real storage addressing. As the 3033 replaced the 168 at the high end of the line, and as MVS's internal constraints were gradually eliminated, systems started to become unbalanced again, this time with real storage in short supply. The problem was particularly acute in 3033MPs. Two 16-megabyte 3033UPs could be made into a symmetrical MP limited to only 16 megabytes, leading to a drastic real storage shortage. The difficulty was temporarily overcome with the "extended addressing" feature on the 3033 using a previously reserved bit in a dynamic address translation table entry to double the size of real storage to a maximum of 32 megabytes.

Easing the real storage constraint led to a new class of problem in MVS/370: Which pages could go to page frames in the extended addressing range? In System/370, the Channel Command Word (CCW) format was limited to a 24-bit real address, so normal I/O access methods could not exploit real storage "above the line." (The operating system made use of the Indirect Data Address Word [IDAW] to address upper real storage, so paging I/O could exploit extended addressing.) Consequently, MVS/370 beginning with SP1.1 had to move pages from frames above 16 megabytes to frames below the line when those frames contained buffers for active I/O. This added system overhead, prominently reported in monitoring programs such as RMF, became significant as systems were loaded to full capacity with TSO users and interactive subsystems. As with many other System/370 growth limits, the partial benefit of added real storage became more complete only with Extended Architecture.

## 2.2.2. Real storage in MVS/XA and MVS/ESA

In System/370 Extended Architecture and Enterprise Systems Architecture (and therefore in MVS/XA and MVS/ESA), the real storage limit was extended to two gigabytes. The XA compatibility goals required that System/370 channel programs operate unchanged in XA mode. However, System/360 and System/370 channel command words are limited to real data addresses of 24 bits. XA and ESA thus have two CCW formats; the original 24-bit CCW is denoted format 0, and the newer 31-bit version is called format 1.

Several MVS/XA and MVS/ESA access methods, as implemented in the Data Facility Product (DFP) portion of the operating system, have already been reimplemented to create format 1 channel programs, and more will likely follow. Therefore, the corresponding I/O operations are not restricted in the real storage areas used for input or output. Antique MVT or MVS/370 programs that build their own CCWs still need to place those channel programs and buffers below 16 megabytes (real), or the operating system must move pages above and below "the line" as MVS/370 had to.

## 2.2.3. Central storage and expanded storage

As we have considered the uses of real storage, it becomes clear that much of it is occupied by relatively inactive pages. The alternative, to place those pages on auxiliary storage, leads to significant delay from the paging subsystem when those pages are needed later. However, the demand for such standby storage increases greatly as CPUs grow more powerful and become capable of supporting much larger workloads.

When System/360 was first announced, and even when System/370 was first announced, the storage limit of 16 megabytes seemed more than generous. However, the explosion of growth facilitated by MVS soon made it clear that 16 megabytes was not enough. When XA was announced, the two-gigabyte real storage limit was welcomed, but with fewer predictions of its being excessive. Some 3090 models, with real storage approaching one gigabyte, are already testing that limit.

To provide a means of accommodating inactive pages without the reactivation delay of auxiliary storage or the cost of "real" storage, a new solution was devised for the 3090 line and eventually added to the CPU architecture in Enterprise Systems Architecture (ESA).

The solution is called *expanded storage* (ES).[6] Once again, the introduction of a new element added complexity and caused nomenclature to be changed. IBM stopped using the term "real storage" and has substituted *processor storage* for it. In systems with expanded storage, processor storage is now divided into *central storage* and expanded storage. Central storage is, of course, what we used to call real storage.

Expanded storage is not accessible to the I/O subsystem or to normal instructions in the CPU and is addressable only as pages, not as bytes. Expanded storage is large and fast. Sizes of up to two gigabytes are already available. It performs at about half the speed

---

6   Some IBM publications and products (in their output) use the name "extended storage." The more correct term (based on precedent and even on current usage in the personal computer field) seems to be "expanded storage," and we shall maintain that usage. The word "extended" has two other prior and conflicting uses in the MVS environment: "extended addressing" was the name for real addressing above 16 megabytes in MVS/370, and the virtual areas of MVS/XA above 16 megabytes are denoted as "extended CSA," "extended private," and so forth.

of central storage, but that figure is very dependent on technology. The only expanded storage operations supported are "page in" and "page out," instructions to transfer pages synchronously between expanded and central storage.

In MVS/XA, expanded storage is managed by the Real Storage Manager (RSM) with guidance from the System Resources Manager (SRM). In contrast, VM/SP manages expanded storage as a fast paging device, and VM/XA simply apportions expanded storage to the virtual machines to use as the operating systems in those machines direct. MVS/ESA adds *hiperspace* services providing additional direct and explicit access to expanded storage by application programs and subsystems.

Expanded storage meets the need for standby storage of inactive address spaces or of individual pages without devoting full-function central storage to that purpose. Consequently, the central storage resource can grow at a slower rate than previously, and the two gigabyte limit is safe for a few more years. The architectural limit of expanded storage is $2^{32}$ pages, or $1.76 \times 10^{13}$ bytes (16 terabytes). It is with and because of expanded storage that chronic real storage shortage in XA and ESA is being called "a thing of the past." Unfortunately, not all 3090s have ES, and it is just becoming available on the "E" models of the 4381. Older systems, notably the 308X generation, have no such relief of real storage constraint available.

As MVS/ESA replaces MVS/XA as well as MVS/370, ESA's options for replacing I/O operations with the use of real storage may well bring back real storage constraint unless careful planning (including generous real storage contingencies) is done. The widespread use of "multiple image" options, such as IBM's PR/SM and Amdahl's MDF, will further engender real storage (central and expanded) constraint.

We will therefore consider the problems of real storage constraint in detail throughout this book.

## 2.3. Input/Output Resources

We turn now from real storage as a source of performance problems to the second most likely source in MVS/370, and probably the main tunable problem in XA and ESA. That source is inefficiency, contention, or a simple lack of resource in the I/O subsystem. MVS/ESA has several mechanisms designed to lessen vulnerability to I/O contention and delay, but the vast majority of MVS systems today do experience I/O problems.

Several kinds of I/O-related delay affect MVS workloads:

- direct delay in waiting for I/O completion. Such "active I/O" delay is often a sign of inefficient I/O: too few buffers, extended use of the DASD SEARCH command, fragmentation of data on devices, or failure to use more efficient alternatives to conventional I/O.

- delay waiting for access to devices. "Queued I/O" delay is most often caused by poorly planned sharing of direct-access devices, either between systems, between workloads, or within a single workload.

  If one of the workloads sharing a device is much more important to the installation's business than the others, its data sets may need to be moved to a device less susceptible to contention. Such "I/O tuning" should take place in conjunction with responding to a service discrepancy for the workload, rather than being based on a search for "problem" devices. Often, devices that look "troublesome" on the basis of utilization or queue length are serving workloads designed for just such efficient I/O, or workloads with less stringent service needs, and are not causing unacceptable levels of delay to more important workloads.

- CPU delay caused by the I/O. CPU cycles are used to set up each I/O and to deal with the hardware interrupt that marks its end. In certain processors, such as the IBM 4381 family, the channel subsystem is not wholly separate from the CPU. In such "integrated" or "cycle-stealing" channel configurations, CPU cycles are not available while the channel is accessing storage.

Regardless of whether CPU cycles are stolen to use for the I/O operation itself, "front-end" and "back-end" activities occur at the highest dispatching priority in MVS (global SRBs) and thereby interfere with CPU access for all workloads. A general goal of minimizing the number of avoidable I/O operations is one of the few MVS performance management absolutes.

We shall divide I/O into several classes and concentrate on only a few of them:

- *Source/sink devices*. These are devices that bring simple input to the system, take output from the system, or both. Printers and card readers and punches are examples. These used to be called *unit record* devices, the unit being a card or a line of print. Today's printers scarcely fit in this mold, being high-speed, all-points-addressable page printers; very few systems now have card I/O. Locally attached terminals fall into this category as well, but we choose to regard them as communications devices because of the human user.

  Source/sink devices are usually managed by the Job Entry Subsystem (JES) and are rarely a source of system performance problems.

- *Console devices*. These are (usually) locally attached devices for use by the operations staff, and are limited to terminals and printers. Variations today include pseudo-devices managed by automated operations packages, personal computers emulating consoles, and systems with only remote consoles, following the trend to unattended operation. We shall again dismiss or ignore the performance problems of console devices only because such problems are rare and of little general interest. The system service address space (CONSOLE) that drives consoles runs at a very high dispatching priority; console performance problems are either a symptom of a very sick system or indicative of a hardware or configuration problem.

- *Communications devices.* Terminals, printers attached to terminal control units, and devices masquerading as these are in this class. Many people regard the terminals they work with as "the computer." In many systems, response time at the terminal is the essence of the service level agreement. We will touch on only a few aspects of communications devices in this book, since our focus is on MVS, not networks. We will consider MVS's telecommunications access method (VTAM) and the ways in which problems with VTAM affecting response time may be managed. Problems affecting the portions of the network outboard of the processor complex are beyond the scope of this book.

- *Secondary storage devices.* Here resides the data[7] that justifies the term *data processing.* We call Direct Access Storage Devices (DASD or disks) and tapes "secondary storage" to distinguish them from processor storage, but the terms are usually implicit. In the near future, optical storage devices may join the magnetic devices in this category. When a system programmer complains about a "storage shortage," processor storage is usually meant. When an MIS manager uses the term, it is almost always secondary storage that is in short supply. (It was easier in the old days, when processor storage was called "memory.") Our consideration of the I/O subsystem focuses on secondary storage for several reasons:

  - It's where the money is (Willie Sutton's Rule). In many installations, the "DASD farm" is comparable in cost to the processor complex. Because each device is rather expensive but unspectacular, it is often more difficult to upgrade secondary storage than to get a new CPU.

  - It's where the data is. The value of what resides on secondary storage far exceeds the value of the medium or the supporting hardware. It's not expensive to acquire raw computing power. Today's personal computers can

---

7   "Data" will be considered a singular collective noun. If there is a reason to consider an elementary item, "datum" will be used.

serve individual users for prices comparable to those of "dumb" terminals. Why, then, connect them to a large central system? The data is the reason. The value of a centralized system derives from the value added by the sharing and centralized management of the data resource.

- It's where the problems are. Because data has value depending in part on the complexity of its use, conflicts are inevitable. Picture an enterprise in which all employees and many customers are on-line to all of the business's data. The need for controls and discipline is apparent. Problems that can arise are those of access control, integrity, and performance. We will examine the resulting performance problems in detail in later chapters.

- It's where the labor is. The next manifestation of a "black hole" for human labor, akin to "every person a telephone operator," solved in the early decades of the 20th century with the introduction of automated telephone exchanges, is "everybody into storage management." Storage management is an error-prone, under-recognized, and labor-intensive business. Until IBM's plans for "system-managed storage" with DFSMS in MVS/ESA materialize into a comprehensive automated system, the need for people and for data processing efforts to be devoted to managing the data resource will continue to grow with the size, complexity, and importance of the resource itself.

- *Auxiliary storage devices.* Part of secondary storage is set aside for system purposes. Examples include the devices housing page data sets and the JES SPOOL and checkpoint data sets. Because problems surrounding these devices, particularly those used for paging, can have profound effects on system performance, we consider auxiliary storage apart from the rest of secondary storage.

## 2.3.1. IBM's I/O architecture

In systems that can run MVS, several different hardware elements together constitute the I/O subsystem. We examine each of them in turn, from the CPU outward to the device.

### CPUs

In System/360, I/O involved the CPU a great deal. The original START I/O (SIO) instruction, for instance, did not *release* the CPU (complete execution) until the path through the channel, control unit, device controller, and device had been secured. Only then could an independent channel operate concurrently with the CPU. As CPU speeds grew rapidly, with I/O speeds trailing along behind, relatively more CPU time would be spent waiting for I/O connections to be established. This same pattern was repeated at the channel level.

Beginning with the replacement of the START I/O instruction by START I/O FAST [RELEASE] in System/370, the trend of development from System/360 through System/370 to XA and ESA was to push I/O activity outward from the CPU and the channels, tying up hardware in the processor complex only when it was necessary for information transfer.

In Extended Architecture and in Enterprise Systems Architecture, the CPU's role in initiating I/O is diminished, and the CPU impact of I/O completion is reduced as well. I/O path selection is done by the channel subsystem, so a complex section of MVS's I/O Supervisor (IOS) code is not needed. Restarting channel programs that have not been able to run is also a function of the channel subsystem, thus eliminating much I/O exception-handling code.

I/O interrupt control in XA and ESA has a finer structure than in System/370, so each CPU in a CEC can be disabled for such interrupts entirely, or enabled only for selected classes of interrupts. In systems sustaining high I/O interrupt rates, a new instruction, TEST PENDING INTERRUPT (TPI), allows a CPU to stay in I/O interrupt handling code to "pick off" the next candidate interrupt instead of allowing the interrupt to disrupt some other process.

The XA and ESA approach to the CPU's role in I/O setup is to "throw it over the wall" to the I/O subsystem. Upon completion of the I/O, a CPU is again involved to deal with the consequences of completion.

## Channels and the Channel Subsystem

The invention of the I/O channel in the mid-1950s was one of the key developments that made today's operating systems possible. Before the time of the IBM 709, I/O was executed as an instruction in the CPU. The notion of *wait state* was equivalent to the idea of an idle system. With the I/O channel (and later with several channels), the former longest-running (I/O) instructions were transformed into simple control operations to manage the channel. The channel did the I/O "dirty work." While I/O proceeded in the channel, the CPU did not have to wait for the I/O operation but could execute other instructions that were not dependent on the I/O in progress. When the overlapped instructions were in a different program, what we now call multiprogramming was the result.

A channel is an independent processor, often as powerful as a CPU. It has read/write access to the same [central] storage as the CPU. The channel responds to a small set of instructions that control its operation. One of those instructions, START I/O or START I/O FAST, directs the channel to perform a series of activities:

- Obtain from known places the address of the beginning of a channel program and the identity of the I/O device to be selected.

- Establish the connection to the device.

- Process the control words that constitute the channel program. These channel control words (CCWs) specify the operation to be performed (read, write, or non-data "control") and the address and extent of the data or control information to be transferred.

- Handle exceptional conditions that might arise during execution of the channel program.

- Signal the CPU when the channel program has completed execution.

The details differ from System/360 through ESA. As processing power has dropped in cost and increased in speed, more of the detail work is done by the channels and less by the CPU. In turn, intelligence and function have migrated further outward—to the control units and device clusters.

During the transition from System/360 to System/370, channels were expensive and few in number, even on large systems. Functional enhancements such as *disconnected command chaining* (DCC), *rotational position sensing* (RPS), and *block multiplexing* provided ways to increase channel productivity. During operations that did not involve the transfer of data, the channel could be disconnected from the control unit.

The control unit and device, acting on their own, would complete the operation (such as a seek to a different cylinder) and then reconnect to the channel. While one or more devices were executing disconnected commands, another could use the same channel path to transfer data. Block multiplexing was the corequisite feature needed to keep track of multiple disconnected high-speed operations.[8]

The throughput benefits of block multiplexing, DCC, and RPS were realized, but at the expense of considerable performance degradation for less-busy devices when the channel paths were kept busy by active devices. In XA and ESA, the portion of DASD I/O time potentially spent waiting for channels to reconnect is reduced by the dynamic path reconnect feature, which allows the completion of an I/O operation on any channel connected to the device.

In System/370, reconnect must take place only on the initially selected path, leading to significant delay when that path is kept busy by other devices. XA and ESA eliminate most path delay,

---

8 System/360 channels were either selector channels, allowing only one channel program to proceed at a time, or byte multiplexor channels, interspersing the data transfer of low speed devices byte by byte.

with support for up to four data paths per device adding to the benefits of dynamic path reconnect.

## Control Units

A control unit (also known as a *storage director* for disk devices) is needed to synchronize I/O operations between channel and device, to handle routine error recovery, to translate I/O requests conveyed in CCWs into *orders* that devices can execute, and to handle path selection and the establishment of data transfer connections. These functions were handled in the past by dedicated hardware with all logic hard-wired in the circuits, much like CPUs of the past. As microcoded CPUs and channels became the norm, so did microcoded control units.

The cost of semiconductor storage continued to decline in the 1980s, and it became possible for IBM to introduce a new class of control unit for high-speed disk devices, one that had storage as well as logic. The first such device for general-purpose systems was the IBM 3880 with the speed matching buffer (SMB) feature. SMB made it possible to hold a track's worth of 3380 data in a storage director, allowing the 3380 with its 3.0 megabytes-per-second data transfer rate to function on standard System/370 channels rated at 1.5 megabytes per second. SMB was a transitional feature, needed only until 3 MB/s "data streaming" channels came into general use.

The next way in which storage was used in disk control units came in the initial generation of cache control units. In these devices the storage was used not just to buffer between differing device and channel speeds, but to enhance the performance of disk devices. The IBM 3880 Model 11 was optimized as a paging subsystem, permitting obsolescent 3350 devices to function with greatly reduced apparent rotational delay and at effective data transfer rates greater than that offered by the device. Its companion Model 13 enhanced the response time of 3380s used for general data.

The first-generation cached IBM 3880 Models 11 and 13 were superseded by the Models 21 and 23, offering more cache storage at lower cost per megabyte and other improvements. The next generation of cache devices arrived with the IBM 3990 Model 3, offering very large cache sizes as well as 4-path support. The 3990-3 also performs a speed-matching function (opposite in sense to that of the Speed Matching Buffer) along with its cache function; data can be transferred to and from cache storage at 4.5 megabytes per second on channels supporting that data rate. It is likely that this approach will become the norm for increasing channel speeds. Device characteristics (other than average access time, gigabytes per cubic foot, square feet of floor space per gigabyte, and cost per gigabyte) may become less important than cache capacity and cache data transfer rate.

## Device controllers

Some devices require an additional level of control. Most disk devices, for instance, are organized into *strings*, with a *string controller* needed to mediate the connections between devices and control units, and to translate the native physical characteristics of the device into the architecturally specified count-key-data (CKD) format used with all MVS-supported DASD. The controller's logic is shared among all the devices in a string, but is not associated with any single device in the string. A common misconception is easy to understand, however. Because the string controller is often packaged with the initial device or cluster of devices on a string, some special preference is incorrectly attributed to the "head of string" device.

Because the string controller is needed for the full duration of data transfer operations (including SEARCH), a bottleneck can develop at this place on the I/O path. Just as multiple channel connections to multiple storage directors reduce bottlenecks at the inboard part of the I/O path, so multiple connections between devices and controllers can reduce the obstacle at the outboard interface as well. IBM was not the first with such connections; other manufacturers' versions of 3350s had a feature usually known as *dual port*, providing two independent data transfer paths per string of devices. IBM supported two data transfer paths per pair of devices[9] on its 3375, and later two transfer paths per cluster of four devices on its initial 3380 model AA4. IBM eventually provided true dual port capability on its second-generation 3380 models AD4 and AE4. IBM's third-generation 3380s, models AJ4 and AK4, extended connection capabilities to four paths when used with IBM 3990 Model 2 or 3 control units.

## Devices

The standard DASD in today's systems is the IBM 3380 or some other manufacturer's functional equivalent. Several IBM variations exist:

- Model A04—two logical drives of 630 megabytes' capacity each, on each of two head-disk assemblies (HDAs); one internal data path connecting to one storage director; and attachment capability for up to three Model B04s. Strings of 3380s headed by the A04 have substantial inherent contention. Few A04s were sold.

- Model AA4—two logical drives of 630 megabytes' capacity each, on each of two head-disk assemblies (HDAs); two internal data paths connecting to two storage directors (with two more paths in reserve for added B-boxes); and attachment capability for up to three Model B04s. The AA4 has dynamic pathing, including dynamic path selection in both 370 and XA or ESA, and dynamic path reconnect in XA and ESA.

  These advanced features are balanced against a substantial drawback. The 3380-AA4, with its maximum complement of three 3380-B04s, has 16 logical devices but only four internal data paths. Contention for the internal data paths can cause serious performance degradation in "standard" 3380s (AA4s with B04s)[10] unless extremely careful data set

---

9  Because device controllers are not sold apart from devices, the distinction is hard to maintain. In IBM DASD nomenclature, the "A-box" of a string (as in 3380-AJ4) contains the (first) device controller. "B-boxes" are pure storage modules. The "C" designation was used for 3350s with alternate controllers and has been brought back for the low-entry 3380-CJ2. The second controller in the not-quite-dual port configuration of the IBM 3375 was a "D" model.

10  The IBM 3380-A04 was not sold in sufficient quantity to be considered "standard."

placement planning is done. Initial planning is not enough; continual monitoring and adjustment is necessary as well.

The first-generation 3380 B-box was the B04. The B04 took on the attachment characteristics of the A-box to which it was connected—either the A04 or the AA4—and it could be connected to only these A-boxes. (Second- and third-generation B-boxes are covered in passing in the discussion of their respective A-boxes below.)

- Model AD4—two logical drives of 630 megabytes' capacity each, on each of two head-disk assemblies (HDAs); one internal data path per logical device in the string, connecting to two storage directors; and attachment capability for any combination of up to three Model BD4s and BE4s. The AD4 has all of the benefits of the AA4, but with true dual port capability (called by IBM *device level selection*) replacing the restricted internal data paths of the AA4 string.

- Model AE4—two logical drives of 1.26 gigabytes' capacity each, on each of two head-disk assemblies (HDAs); one internal data path per logical device in the string, connecting to two storage directors; and attachment capability for up to three Model BD4s and BE4s. The AE4 is very much like the AD4 with twice the capacity per logical volume. AE4s and BE4s are often called "double-density" 3380s. The AE4 has a faster-moving seek actuator than the AD4; seeks over the same number of megabytes are faster on the AE4, but the maximum seek time is greater on the AE4. IBM refers to the D and E models as "extended function" 3380s.

- Model AJ4—two logical drives of 630 megabytes' capacity each, on each of two head-disk assemblies (HDAs); one internal data path per logical device in the string, connecting to up to four storage directors; and with attachment capability for up to three Model BJ4s and BK4s. The AJ4 has all of the benefits of the AD4, but with four-way connectivity, faster seek times, and installability improvements. Four paths are supported with two AJ4 or AK4 A-boxes connected to a 3990 Model 2 or 3. Each substring may contain up to three BJ4s and BK4s, freely intermixed, for an overall string maximum of 32 logical drives. Any four of the devices may be connected at a time.

- Model AK4—two logical drives of 1.89 gigabytes' capacity each, on each of two head-disk assemblies (HDAs); and one internal data path per logical device in the string, with the same attachment capabilities as the AJ4. The AK4 is very much like the AJ4, with three times the capacity per logical volume. AK4s and BK4s are often called "triple-density" 3380s. The AK4 has a faster seek actuator than the AJ4; seeks over the same number of megabytes are faster on the AK4, but the maximum seek time is also greater on the AK4. IBM refers to the J and K models as "enhanced subsystem" 3380s.

All 3380s share the same track format. Data on a 3380 track is organized into 32-byte groups. There are 1499 such groups to a track, excluding track control information. For each record on the track, 15 groups are used for the count field and its gap, and seven groups for the gap preceding the optional key field. Twelve bytes of ECC (error-correcting code) are added to each key field, if present, and to each data field. Each of these areas occupies some number of full 32-byte groups. Simple calculations show that each unkeyed record has an overhead of 492 bytes.

A consequence of this track layout (shared by the IBM 3375) is that small physical records (blocks) on 3380s are extremely inefficient. Space utilization efficiency of 80 percent or more is attained only with blocks of at least 2000 bytes. Eighty-byte blocks, still common in many installations as a legacy of punched cards, use only about 14 percent of the maximum capacity of a 3380 track. Space inefficiency is also speed inefficiency; while each 80-byte record moves at three megabytes per second, the 83 records on a track can't be transferred in less than a full device rotation of 16.56 milliseconds. The maximum effective data transfer rate for 80-byte physical records is thus just 392K bytes per second.

## 2.3.2. Modeling I/O operations

Understanding I/O operations can be aided through modeling. An analytic model of a typical I/O operation is relatively easy to construct, given the published facts about devices and their connections to systems. The technique is described in Chapter 10.

## 2.4. Summary

We have reviewed the physical resources to be managed by MVS, with particular emphasis on CPUs or processors, real storage (both central and expanded), and DASD input/output resources. In the next chapter, we'll look at how MVS organizes these resources into objects and structures that it will then manage.

# 3

# Virtual and Logical Resources

*Things are seldom what they seem*
*Skim milk masquerades as cream*

—*W. S. Gilbert*

Little Buttercup must have been an MVS designer. In MVS systems, things are often not what they seem. Let's consider a simple assembly language program that will read a sequential text data set, change all occurrences of the characters "3090F" to "3090S," and write it back in place. As this program executes, the objects it deals with are hidden from direct view by a number of translations and indirect references. We refer to the direct translations or mappings as *virtual* counterparts of real objects, while the composite structures and indirect namings define *logical* resources. These are not firm distinctions or standard terms. They may prove useful in understanding the pervasive nature of renaming in MVS.

## 3.1. Virtual Resources

In our hypothetical program, the initial need is to acquire a quantity of storage for buffers, work areas, control information, and save areas for general registers and other status information. The storage is virtual and is acquired from the private area of the current address space.[1] If, say, 64K bytes is required, a *GETMAIN* or *STORAGE* macro-instruction in the source program is translated by the assembler to several instructions that place parameters in registers and then issue the SUPERVISOR CALL (SVC) instruction to invoke the appropriate service routine of MVS. That routine, part of the Virtual Storage Manager component of MVS, will allocate a 64K block of virtual storage from the private area and return the starting address to the program.

No *real* resources have been given to the program yet. The first instruction in the program that attempts to store data in the acquired storage will cause an *address-translation exception*,[2] a type of hardware-defined program check. The *page fault interrupt* caused by that exception will eventually be passed back to the Real Storage Manager of MVS, so that a page frame (real), initialized to binary zeros, may be assigned to the page (virtual). This process will occur up to 16 times as the program executes and "touches" (makes reference to) each page in the acquired space.

All of this activity is transparent to the programmer and not important to an understanding of the program's logic. However, it is clearly relevant if we wish to understand the performance of the program and of the system in which the program runs.

We'll return to this example when we examine logical resources in the second part of this chapter.

### 3.1.1. Calling something by another name

Resources in MVS are made virtual ("virtualized") so that the same set of objects and addresses may be used in many address

---

1 The address space is little more than what the name denotes: a linear space of contiguous byte addresses in which a unit of MVS work executes. An essential attribute of an address space is its size, the total amount of storage that may be allocated implicitly (as by causing a program to be loaded) or explicitly, by requesting storage through the GETMAIN service. Each address space is divided into a common area, shared with all other address spaces, and a private area, unique for each address space.

2 An attempt to read data from this area of storage would make no sense; nothing has been put there yet. If such an attempt were to be made, the same page fault would take place, whereupon a page frame full of binary zeros would be found.

spaces concurrently, independent of the physical resources that will ultimately be used. Another benefit of virtualization is that the virtual resources can have standardized attributes (such as the range of usable addresses), regardless of the amount of physical resource available. Because most workloads other than batch jobs do not demand service continuously, many virtual resources are usually not needed full-time. Thus a scarce real resource may be shared among many virtual entities with performance often approaching that of a 100 percent real system. This benefit becomes very significant when the virtual resource is of much greater aggregate size than the supporting real resource.

Storage is the best-known of these virtualized resources, but external data may be made virtual using the *VIO* (Virtual Input-Output) service, or through the exploitation of hiperspaces in MVS/ESA for storage of performance-critical data objects directly in expanded storage.

IBM's 3850 Mass Storage Subsystem (MSS) was installed in many early MVS systems. The virtualized entity in the case of MSS was an entire IBM 3330 or 3330-11 device, simulated with a combination of a 3330 or 3350 real device and the data contained on one or more strips of magnetic tape, rolled up in cartridges when idle, stored in a honeycomb-like repository, and brought to the read-write mechanism by robotic arms.

With logical partitioning implemented by IBM's PR/SM feature or NAS's MLPF (or as separate domains with Amdahl's Multiple Domain Facility), whole systems are virtualized. With PR/SM in LPAR (logically partitioned) mode, a single CPU complex (or "side" of a multiprocessor) can look like as many as seven separate virtual instances, with each CPU in a multi-engine configuration having up to seven "logical" appearances.[3] Each virtual instance or system is independently initialized (IPL'd) and has a defined complement of central storage, optional expanded storage, and channel paths.

3   The treatment of CPUs in PR/SM and MDF is a classical virtual treatment, but IBM and NAS chose to call the virtual CPUs *logical partitions*. Amdahl chose to call them *domains*. The distinction may be useful; use of these terms helps to distinguish these hardware virtualizations from those provided with software assistance by VM.

IBM's Virtual Machine (VM) family of operating systems virtualize systems through software—also making use of specialized hardware features that were forerunners of PR/SM, or of PR/SM itself—in the various levels of System/370.[4] Each user of a VM system can be presented with the appearance of a complete System/360 or System/370 hardware configuration, ranging from a basic model to an ESA system, depending on the VM variant and the requested options. Although VM systems, most notably VM/XA System Product, can support "guest" operating systems including MVS/ESA, within virtual machines, the typical VM end-user does not start up arbitrary systems, but uses program development tools and other application interfaces built on CMS (Conversational Monitor System[5]) as a time-sharing user.

## 3.1.2. Physical backing of virtual resources

Virtual resources are useful abstract entities, but to get work done they must be backed up by appropriate real resources at the time of use. It is a major purpose of operating systems such as MVS to manage the real resources and to control assignment of those resources to the virtual objects and work units that the operating system supports.

## 3.1.3. Virtual storage and the paging subsystem

Because the aggregate size of virtual storage in a typical MVS system is very large compared with the amount of real storage resource, the data in virtual storage pages must be stored somewhere else when real storage frames are not available. A moderately large system might have 800 active address spaces, requiring on average 175 pages each. The 140,000 page frames needed to "map" all of this virtual storage to real are not found in any single system available at the time of this writing. Even if that much storage were to be available, it would be extravagant to

4   VM/XA System Product (SP) uses the PR/SM hardware to support multiple preferred virtual guest operating systems; such use is mutually exclusive with LPAR mode.

5   This incarnation of CMS is based distantly on the original Cambridge Monitor System, a simple single-user operating system very similar to PC-DOS in power and ease-of-use. CP/67, the forerunner of VM/370, was originally intended to be a simple "hypervisor" providing multiple CMS virtual machines to time-sharing users.

install it to support such a workload. Experience shows that 80 to 90 percent of interactive users are idle at any given time. Real storage of 30,000 to 40,000 frames should be sufficient to support the workload with acceptable response time.

Pages not currently mapped to real storage must be kept elsewhere. In systems with expanded storage, processor storage is divided into *central storage*, similar in concept to the older undivided real storage, in which instructions and data may be accessed by the CPU, and *expanded storage*, which holds data not accessible to the CPU except as page-sized objects to be exchanged to and from frames of central storage. In such systems, expanded storage is the first choice for storage of pages not currently needed by the CPU but likely to be needed soon.

With or without expanded storage, all pages of all virtual storage in an MVS system must be backed by *slots* of *auxiliary storage*. Each slot is the size of a page (4096 bytes), and the Auxiliary Storage Manager is the MVS component that manages the assignment of pages to slots and initiates the input/output operations needed to move pages between central and auxiliary storage. This resource is organized into *page* (or *paging*) *data sets*. Collectively, the set of page data sets, along with any optional *swap data sets*, is known as the *paging subsystem*.

Before large real storage sizes (and the use of expanded storage) became common in MVS systems, the paging subsystem was often the single most critical performance management challenge. Factors to be considered included number, size, and placement of page data sets, the degree of interference from and to other I/O, the use (and then the number) of swap data sets, the size of real storage, and the interaction of MVS's internal workload management controls with paging performance.

IBM speakers at user-group meetings have recently begun to suggest that the days of storage constraint may be at an end, and that tuning the paging subsystem may be of less importance in the future. Acknowledging that there is now a trend away from real storage constraint, nevertheless we recognize in this book that not all systems are the latest, not all budgets are the most generous, and that those who pay for and use MVS systems are

very ingenious in devising ways to exploit the real storage resource. We also note that MVS/ESA is a relatively new system
with the capability of enabling a new generation of applications
implemented in a storage-rich environment. Whatever temporary
ease there may be in real storage may well become constraint
again as those new applications come into full production and
maturity. In short, we will assume that optimizing paging subsystem performance to control paging delay remains a worth-
while concern.

## Virtual Storage in MVS/370

The layout of virtual storage in an MVS/370 system is shown in
Figure 3-1. Each address space is 16 megabytes and includes all of
the MVS *nucleus, common storage area (CSA), link pack area
(LPA),* and *system queue area (SQA).* The remaining space, below
a 64-kilobyte *segment boundary* defining the limit of the *system*

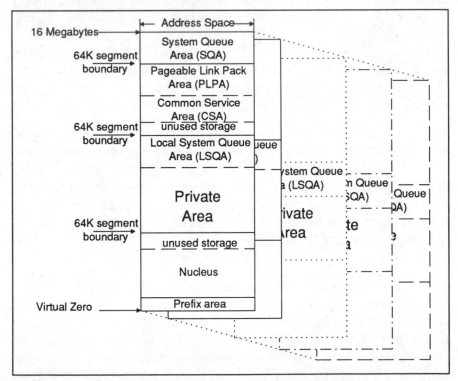

Figure 3-1. MVS/370 Virtual Storage Layout

*area,* and above the segment boundary defining the nucleus, is the *private area.* From that area is deducted the *local system queue area (LSQA),* containing control information (such as *page-translation tables*) required by the address space.

What is left is the available area for the real business of the address space. This area was originally to have been guaranteed as no less than eight megabytes. In many MVS/370 systems, it is less than six megabytes. For a program package to be portable across most MVS/370 systems, it must fit into the smallest available private area in any of those systems. The phenomenon of limited virtual storage leading to program design compromises was dubbed *"virtual storage constraint."* Successful efforts to roll back the system area boundary and make more private area available were and are announced by IBM as *virtual storage constraint relief* or *VSCR.*

***Splitting large programs across address spaces.*** Many programs, particularly subsystems like IBM's Customer Information Control System (CICS) and Information Management System (IMS), frequently cannot fit in the limited confines of a single address space. The MVS versions of IMS (IMS/VS) are designed to use at least two address spaces, a Control Region and one or more Message Processing Regions.[6] More recent versions of IMS can use additional address spaces to manage data base I/O and recovery management functions.

CICS is less formally structured than IMS.[7] Multiple address spaces in CICS may each perform a full range of functions with little or no intercommunication, or they may be organized into specialized terminal-owning, resource-owning, and application-

---

6  The "region" designation is a leftover from MVT and SVS. Each such region is an independent address space.

7  The informal structure of CICS appears to be becoming less so in the MVS/ESA release of CICS, Version 3. This version, not yet available at the time of this writing, will exploit MVS/ESA features such as data spaces, and will incorporate multitasking internal structures to ensure that it can take full advantage of multiprocessor configurations.

owning address spaces. Again harking back to MVT terminology, the structuring of CICS into multiple cooperating address spaces is known as Multiple Region Operation, or MRO.

*Interaddress space communication.* Programs that communicate across multiple address spaces do so through a variety of means. The earliest one used, before *Cross-Memory Services* (CMS)[8] became available in hardware, was an indirect discipline involving the scheduling of dispatchable work units to run in the target address spaces. These work units, *Service Request Blocks* (SRBs), are preferred by the dispatcher above all tasks in the address space when it is selected for dispatching. The task in the address space that asked for the service needs to wait for the SRB's completion, often signaled by a complementary SRB scheduled in the caller's address space by the server.

Asynchronous cross-memory communication via SRBs has several drawbacks. The use of SRBs involves extra overhead and potential delay. The *SCHEDULE* macro's SUPERVISOR CALL (used to create SRBs) could be issued only by an address space running in authorized state, and any data required for communication needed to be passed in common storage so that both communicating address spaces could have addressability to it. This use of CSA contributes to the very virtual storage constraint that the communication across address spaces attempts to relieve.

With the support of CMS hardware by MVS/SP Version 1, a much more efficient means of communication became available. After required control structures had been set up, an address space could transfer control synchronously to another address space, resuming operation following the synchronous return. No supervisor services are needed after initialization. Data can be moved directly between address spaces known to each other, and the address spaces need not run in the authorized state.

8   This CMS has nothing to do with the CMS of VM/370. Some writers prefer to use "XMS" to denote cross-memory services, but this choice has been pre-empted; "CMS" has been institutionalized as an MVS lock name. The term "cross-memory" itself is another throwback to MVS prehistory. Because the original name of MVS was MVM, for Multiple Virtual Memories, terms like "memory create" and "cross-memory" are deeply ingrained in the internal literature of MVS (for instance, the comments embedded within the source code) instead of more accurate and less confusing terms referring to address spaces.

The "horizontal splitting" made possible and efficient by using CMS helped MVS/370 to remain viable long after its 16-megabyte virtual addressing capability had become inadequate.

### 3.1.4. Virtual Storage in MVS/XA and MVS/ESA

The virtual storage layout of MVS/XA and MVS/ESA is shown in Figure 3-2. Note that data spaces are available only in ESA.

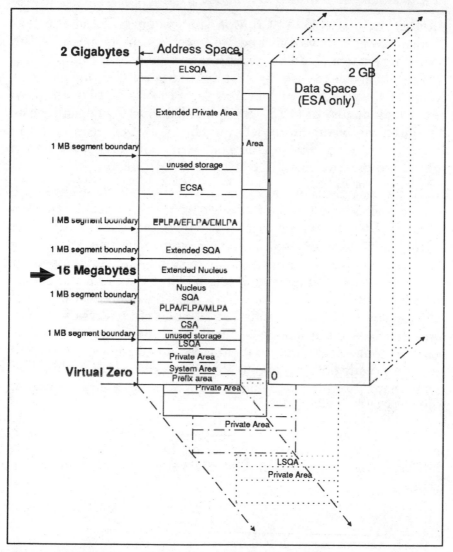

Figure 3-2. MVS/XA or MVS/ESA virtual storage layout

A major objective of System/370 Extended Architecture (XA) was substantial VSCR. Certainly this was a possibility; the virtual address range of XA is 128 times as large as that of MVS/370. However, many key subsystems did not make use of the private area above the 16-megabyte "line" for years after the original release of MVS/XA. VSCR came from the operating system itself as more system address spaces were split out of nucleus functions. The historical details are provided in Chapter 1.

Another part of XA's VSCR was the system's use of the "extended" areas "above the line." As soon as major parts of the operating system could be rewritten to exploit 31-bit addressing and reside above 16 megabytes, those parts could be moved from Nucleus to Extended Nucleus, or from PLPA to EPLPA. Because of the long history of MVS, which has led to many dependencies on system data remaining where it had "always" been, and the important goal of release-to-release compatibility, this was a protracted process and still continues in MVS/ESA.

In Enterprise Systems Architecture (ESA), another hardware change makes new forms of addressing growth possible. Sixteen *access registers* (ARs) correspond to the 16 general registers. For each general register used as a base register,[9] a new addressing mode uses its paired access register to supply indirectly a pointer to an individual segment table origin. Thus data (but not executable instructions) may be found in a separate address space. That address space may be specified as a data-only address space, or *data space*. A data space's segment table does not include the common area's segments, so it provides a full 2-gigabyte address span for private data, and up to 15 of them (one per access register other than AR0) may be active in support of an address space at any time.

Using data spaces, subsystems may be restructured to gain new levels of performance (by minimizing the need to store active data on external devices) and integrity (by separating code from data).

---

9   Access register 0 has no defined use as yet, since general purpose register 0 cannot be a base register.

## Hiperspaces in MVS/ESA

Another mechanism in MVS/ESA to save input/output operations is the high performance space, or *hiperspace*.[10] Note that hiperspaces are *not* shown on the virtual storage layout illustration. Hiperspaces reside outside the virtual addressing structure, although each hiperspace is visualized as a byte space of up to two gigabytes in size, but with an addressing granularity of a page (4096 bytes.) The data within a hiperspace may be examined or manipulated only when it is brought into an address space or a data space by operations analogous to data set *READ* and *WRITE*.

The performance advantage of a hiperspace is achieved by materializing a "data set" in it and letting the paging subsystem do the I/O for only those portions that are read or written. A high-performance type of hiperspace is defined to reside only in expanded storage, and is called ESO, for Expanded Storage Only. More mundane hiperspaces may reside in a combination of expanded and auxiliary storage. Hiperspaces never reside in central storage. For response-critical applications requiring very large data structures with low access density, hiperspaces can provide nearly unlimited definable storage. Unlike data spaces, limited to 15 active at any time by the number of base/access register pairs, the number of simultaneously active hiperspaces is limited only by address space limits in the IEFUSI SMF exit. The maximum combined size of data spaces and hiperspaces owned within an address space is $2^{24}-1$ *megabytes;* the maximum number of such objects is $2^{32}-1$.

Since application programs need to be conceived, designed, and implemented to take advantage of such potential, it may be some time before the potential of hiperspaces is fully realized. More likely, the MVS/ESA Storage Management Subsystem (SMS) could use hiperspaces in automatically staging performance-critical data sets to expanded storage at the time of need. If that

---

10 Hiperspaces do not depend on access registers or on any other hardware features of ESA. They are an example of system improvements implemented only in ESA since IBM has announced the last version of XA and therefore its *de facto* "functional stabilization."

occurs, old applications will be able to exploit new facilities with simple redefinitions of storage classes for key data sets.

## 3.2. Logical Resources

Going back to the example that introduced this chapter, our simple editing program has established its environment by acquiring its own working virtual storage; it has saved the caller's registers; and it is now ready to get to work. Remember, we were going to read a text file, look for a particular character string, replace the string with another of the same length, and write the changed information back to its original location.

To perform a data-editing operation that is very simple to do in a high-level language, our assembly language programmer must deal with a formidable series of structures interposed between the program and the data "out there" on a device.

### 3.2.1. Logical I/O Resources

Data recorded on a track of DASD such as the IBM 3380 is written as a series of 32-byte groups, regardless of the data organization we see at a higher level. The device is at its most efficient if all the groups are written at once; only one instance of overhead is needed if only one *physical record* is written per track.

Physical record? What happened to 32-byte groups?

The 32-byte groups are not visible to the operating system. A virtual structure is superimposed on the track organization by microcode in device, string controller, and storage director. The virtual picture is that of a *count-key-data* (CKD) device, differing only in quantitative physical details from the first DASD on System/360. In the CKD architecture, each track is organized into physical records, and these records correspond to the data moved by a single READ or WRITE CCW.

## Data Organization on DASD

MVS supports several logical organizations of the data contained in the physical records of I/O devices. Of interest in the current example is the *physical sequential* organization. In this type of *data set organization*, (DSORG) the operating system, through an *access method*, recognizes that the data exists in order, and that a request for the "next" block or record does not require positioning information.

## Data Sets

The aggregate of data which is commonly called a *file* in the jargon of other systems is known as a *data set*[11] in MVS. The data set in our example is a *sequential data set*, and our program will read and update it by means of the queued sequential access method, or QSAM.

The data set is the fundamental unit of data management in MVS. It corresponds to a label entry (known as a *data set control block*, or *DSCB)* in the area of each disk volume that is reserved for such entries. Most permanent data sets are also *catalogued;*[12] such a data set can be found and retrieved by name only, without knowing which volume it is on.

## Late Binding

The previous discussion may seem a bit vague, but it was meant to be. MVS has a deliberate amount of vagueness built-in. In systems less sophisticated than MVS, a file might be found in a *directory* of a specific disk device, and all of its attributes would be either implicit or specified directly in its directory entry. A strength of MVS is the idea of *late binding*; data set attributes may be specified or amended at the time of use. This is accomplished by a multiple level of specification. In the case of a batch job, the chain of specification begins with the job control language for the job step in which the program will be executed. In turn, data set information is specified in the following layers:

---

11  This term is sometimes spelled as a single word, "dataset."

12  In the system-managed storage (SMS) environment of MVS/ESA, *all* permanent data sets are catalogued.

- **DD Statement.** The DD, or data definition, JCL statement has a name specified in the program. (In the interactive TSO environment, an ALLOCATE command is the counterpart of the DD statement, and the term *file name* is used as a synonym for DD-name as a tag to denote the program's view of the data set.) The idea of the DD was the key innovation of late binding. A program needs to have some way of identifying the data it will use or create, but if a data set name is embedded in a program, the program will have little general usefulness. The DD provides a layer of insulation. The program refers to a constant DD name, but the DD or ALLOCATE can name any data set meeting the needs of the program The data set's attributes may be specified at the time of its creation and some of those attributes can be amended at each time of use.

- **Data Set Control Block (DSCB).** For a preexisting data set, the DSCB (a more complete version of the *file label* in earlier systems) records the attributes with which the data set was created or last updated. Some of these attributes (such as the data set organization) cannot be overridden by DD specifications or from within the program; others, such as the physical record size (known in MVS as *block size*), can be overridden.

- **Data Control Block (DCB).** The DCB is both an MVS control block and the macro-instruction that generates it. In a program prior to its execution, the DCB contains, at minimum, the view of the data set required for the successful resolution by a compiler or assembler of references to it within the program. Those references to the DCB are as targets of I/O macros or corresponding higher-level statements within the program. In our example, we would expect these macros to be *OPEN, GET, PUTX*, and *CLOSE*.

- ***OPEN* Macro.** *OPEN*ing a DCB binds dynamically the program's view of a data set to the real data set. In the original concept of OS/360, *OPEN* would complete the fields of the DCB, dynamically load the appropriate *access method* modules, create or update the DSCB for a data set on a direct-access device, acquire storage for buffers, and, for a sequential data set to be used for queued input or update, "prime" the buffers in anticipation of the first *GET* request.

This set of functions has been resilient over the years. The only major difference in an MVS/XA or MVS/ESA system of today is that the access method code does not need to be physically loaded; it is likely to be already resident in the pageable link pack area (PLPA). As ESA's new capabilities are exploited, this, too, may come full circle. It may become more appropriate to load some access method modules from libraries maintained in data spaces by the Library Lookaside Facility than to take up virtual storage for them in PLPA.

An even more flexible set of late-binding primitives exists in the *dynamic allocation*[13] service introduced as a matter of necessity when TSO was added to MVT. With dynamic allocation, a data set name and its attributes can be elicited interactively from the terminal user, placed in a DCB by dynamic allocation services, and allocated to the TSO session. The DCB can then be *OPEN*ed, and the data set created, or otherwise manipulated, without the need for even a DD-name as a fixed external reference.

## SYSIN, SYSOUT, and Terminal Processing

Most batch jobs and many subsystems produce printed output. A DD statement as simple as

```
//SYSPRINT DD SYSOUT=A
```

and corresponding program statements such as

```
          ...
PUT       PRINTIT

...       ...
PRINTIT DCB ...DDNAME=SYSPRINT, ...
...
```

---

13 MVS's *allocation* component handles the assignment of physical resources (devices) and logical resources (data sets) to address spaces. In OS/360, allocation was part of the *scheduler*, the set of services responsible for sequencing batch jobs through the system. With the coming of TSO, the need for dynamic allocation forced changes in venerable OS/360 allocation code. We might view allocation today as a structure built on dynamic allocation as a basic set of primitives. Most current MVS subsystems use dynamic allocation rather than relying on static JOB step allocation.

direct the desired output to the Job Entry Subsystem (JES; either JES2 or JES3) to place on its Class A queue for output. The details of how it will be printed are left to the JES. SYSOUT processing is an extreme example of late binding.

If the same program is run in TSO, the user probably won't want printed output, but output displayed on the terminal. Without a program change, the TSO user need only enter

```
alloc f(sysprint) da(*) reus 14
```

or accept the same default allocation, found in most TSO LOGON procedures, to direct SYSPRINT output to the terminal.

The Job Entry Subsystem can manage input streams as well as output streams. Batch jobs can obtain control information or low volume data input from the JCL itself; the method of doing this is to use the "DD *" or "DD DATA" option:

```
//SYSIN DD DATA
```

This command will associate what follows that statement in the JCL data set with the SYSIN DD-name. The input ends when the MVS reader-interpreter encounters an input record beginning with the characters "/*". The TSO counterpart for input from the terminal is:

```
alloc f(sysin) da(*) reuse
```

## 3.2.2. Other logical resources in MVS

A data set OPENed for output is an example of a *serially reusable resource* (SRR), so named because only one work unit can use such a resource at a time. There are many other such resources in MVS. Depending on the nature of the SRR, different kinds of damage may result if several work units (tasks) attempt to use one concurrently. A mechanism is needed to protect SRRs from such damage.

---

14 In the command, **alloc** is an alias for **allocate**; **f** is the minimal abbreviation for **filename**; **da** is the minimal abbreviation for **dataset**, the * denotes the terminal, and **reus[e]** makes the allocation independent of whether the filename had been previously allocated. The last option is available only with IBM's TSO Extensions Licensed Program. Note also that the entire command is case-insensitive.

At least two such mechanisms are available. For SRRs that are used frequently and have consistently fast service times, hardware-assisted *locks* are used. An example is the SALLOC lock, used to ensure that only a single process is allocating virtual storage at a time. Locks are generally used by "system programs," *i.e.*, those that call on or provide low-level services.

For more ordinary resources, the GRS (Global Resource Serialization) address space in MVS provides ENQ (enqueue) and DEQ (dequeue) services, invoked by similarly-named macro-instructions and their generated SUPERVISOR CALLs. Like locks, ENQs and DEQs are usually concealed by higher-level services. When a data set is *OPEN*ed, for instance, the OPEN service routine will issue an *ENQ* against a major resource name of SYSDSN and a minor name identical to the 44-character data set name. The *ENQ* macro will specify the EXCLUSIVE attribute if the data set is to be used for output or update, or SHARED if the intent is input only. If a task requests an ENQ when another task has an EXCLUSIVE ENQ for the same resource, the requesting task will be notified of the condition in a return code or will wait until the resource is available.[15]

Contention for real resources is held off by the ENQ/DEQ mechanisms. Instead, contention is transferred to the logical objects represented by ENQ resource names. When programs are sloppy in either securing or releasing ENQs, contention between address spaces can arise.

One of the most frequently seen performance-killing conditions, especially in the TSO environment, is "ENQ lockout." ENQs are requested one at a time. Thus it is possible to secure some but not all of the logical resources needed for a program. Tasks that do not release ENQs if not all required resources are available can "fight" with other tasks and cause system productivity to suffer. The culprit may well be a program that retains an EXCLUSIVE ENQ after the need for exclusive access (such as a data set update) has passed. As we'll see in Chapter 10, performance monitors can detect such slowdowns and often offer a means to cancel the address space holding the blocking ENQ.

---

15 Notice how easy it is to confuse the logical gatekeeper for a resource with the resource itself. The resource may be no longer in use by the other task; GRS will not know until a *DEQ* is issued for the correct resource name.

## 3.3. Summary

MVS operates through virtual and logical resources to:

- protect critical system information from damage

- facilitate resource sharing

- insulate system users and program designers from the complexity of the real system resources

- project an appearance of resources better suited to the needs of an operating system, its subsystems, and its workloads than the bare hardware

The cost of these protections and flexibilities is system overhead. The overhead is usually far outweighed by achieving the ability to make effective use of a vast array of system resources. The performance management challenge is to understand the nature of the resources and to be able to look beyond them to solve underlying problems.

# 4

# Workloads

MVS has three categories of address spaces:

- Batch jobs—the common workload of earlier operating systems. The normal purpose of a batch job is to perform some data transformation task without human interaction during its execution. In the past, a batch job came into the system on punched cards, and its output left the system on printed paper, on cards, or on both. A job does not run continuously but starts and ends, leaving behind some change in the data left in the system, or creating output data that leaves the system.

  Although a job may be divided into individual steps, the job as a whole is usually thought of as a single transaction with a single purpose. The name of the job is specified as the first token on the "JOB card," the first 80-byte card image that constitutes the job. The remainder of the job control language (JCL) that defines the job may be supplied wholly or partly through one or more *catalogued procedures* contained in libraries known to the job entry subsystem (JES).

- Started Tasks—address spaces that provide some kind of operating system or subsystem function. Started tasks (called "system tasks" in MVS's predecessor systems) normally run continuously. The name derives from the usual means of activating these address spaces. The START operator-command designates a catalogued procedure, and the program executed by the procedure remains active in the system, usually until the next time the system is initialized. The name associated with the started task is typically the name of the catalogued procedure.

- TSO sessions—the system-level means of enabling users at terminals to gain access to most of MVS's functions in the same manner as a batch job, but with an increasing number of TSO-specific productivity tools as well. A TSO session starts at LOGON and ends at LOGOFF, but a session may comprise many unrelated transactions. The name of a TSO session is the *user-ID* specified in the LOGON command.

We'll consider each of these address space types in turn, characterizing the resource usage pattern and performance demands of each. We might, however, find a different classification useful as well. Another way of regarding MVS workloads is to look at two less precise categories:

- Subsystems—address spaces (or related sets thereof) that serve the needs of other workloads or directly support their end-users at terminals. IBM's DB2, CICS, and VTAM, and Computer Associates' ROSCOE are such subsystems. Subsystems are usually started tasks, but they sometimes masquerade as batch jobs.

- Individual address space workloads—ordinary batch jobs or TSO terminal sessions. In a loose sense, these are the direct end-users of the system, as distinguished from those served indirectly through subsystems.

## 4.1. Batch

A batch job comes into the system by one of several different means, each of which leads to its placement on a *job queue*. Each job on the job queue is in a *job class* and has a *selection priority*. The selection priority affects a job's placement only within its own class on the queue.

Removing jobs from the queue and placing them into execution is done by the *job entry subsystem* (JES). Two such subsystems exist, JES2 and JES3[1]. They differ in details of job management and in the services they provide, but both perform the same basic functions with respect to job selection and initiation. The JES also manages SYSIN and SYSOUT, standard data streams for job input and output. SYSIN forms part of the job queue along with the statements in Job Control Language (JCL) that define the job. SYSOUT collectively constitutes the output queue. The term *SPOOL*[2] is applied to the collection of JES queues. SYSIN is usually associated with the images of 80-column punched cards, and SYSOUT is usually destined for printers, but other options are available.

The image from which many terms describing MVS job entry and scheduling services are derived is that of a card reader whose input is transcribed to the job queue. There are few card readers in today's MVS systems, but a common means of placing jobs on the queue is to direct the card images that constitute a job to a SYSOUT facility called an *internal reader.*

## 4.1.1. Types of Batch

In many MVS installations, batch comprises two distinct workloads. The more traditional kind of batch is *production* or *scheduled* batch, standard jobs or series of jobs that perform work essential to the business that the installation serves. The other is *nonproduction* or *unscheduled* batch. This type of batch represents test runs of production jobs, test versions of subsystems that normally run as started tasks, work submitted by TSO users for almost any conceivable purpose, system maintenance tasks—in short, anything that can run in MVS as a batch job other than production.

Production batch may seem boring—the same jobs running the same programs every day, week, or month—but it is often the lifeblood of the enterprise.

1    There is also a JES1, part of the now-defunct OS/VS1 operating system.
2    SPOOL is an acronym for Simultaneous Peripheral Operations On-Line, a primitive form of multiprogramming found in early operating systems.

The importance of production batch is such that whole *production control* departments exist to watch it, to help it, to restart it after problems occur, and generally to escort its jobs and output safely through the system to the ultimate user. Production batch workloads are usually very predictable in timing, dependencies, and resource requirements. Also, production batch classically runs during the hours when online service is either suspended or has low demand. Thus, system operators and performance management personnel are not usually concerned with acute contention problems or other symptoms of unpredictability in the production batch workload, except when the production workload is the victim of some other workload's bad habits.

In contrast, nonproduction batch often does intrude on other workloads, and its management may influence profoundly the performance of the online subsystem, or of production batch. The burden of exercising that management falls heavily on the system's operators, unless the system programmers and service planners have designed a resilient and responsive set of system parameters and operational procedures to manage the batch workload.

## 4.1.2. Job Classes and Initiators

Batch jobs enter an MVS system through JES-controlled queue servers called *initiators*. Each initiator occupies and serves a single address space. An initiator is assigned to one or more job classes; the classes are in the order specified in the initiator's JES definition. The dequeuing of jobs is sequential by class order whenever an initiator is idle, and by priority order within class. For example, if an initiator is "open" for (serving) classes B, J, X, and T in that order, a job in class B with selection priority of 1 (the lowest) will be selected ahead of a job in class J with a priority of 15 (the highest).

### Job Classing Schemes

Job classes may be assigned for various reasons. Because classes interact with initiators, the classing scheme and the number of initiators and their class assignments must be considered together.

*Serialization approach.* In some instances, production jobs must be run in a strict sequential order. The simplest method for ensuring such processing is to place all such jobs in a single class, to start exactly one initiator for that class, and to make sure that the JES reader processes each sequential stream of jobs in the correct order. A common technique to guarantee that order is to place the JCL for the entire jobstream in a sequential data set or in a member of a partitioned data set, and to start an *internal reader* with the desired set of jobs as its input, thus placing the jobstream on the job queue.

One or more unique job classes may correspond to one-class initiators for managing production batch jobs. Such a rigid structure is not responsive to even the relatively slow rate of change possible in a real-world workload or to the need for adjusting parameters or dealing with recovery situations. Large data centers with extensive batch production work rely on more flexible control schemes. An extensive example of such a scheme is the job-dependent scheduling feature of JES3, in which jobs are *held* until *released* by the successful completion of a designated predecessor. A supplementary IBM-licensed program is available to provide some of the same capability in a JES2 installation. Independent vendors also offer production batch control packages.

Statically sequenced batch jobstreams are not the last word in dependency scheduling. Many modern production systems do not use canned JCL at all, but include *JCL generators* to build and submit[3] successor jobs when predecessor jobs reach the earliest point at which all dependencies are satisfied. Such systems allow more sensitive dependency control than that available in JCL. To take full advantage of large multiprocessor systems, they may also permit "fork" and support "join" of parallel threads. Since scheduling systems can enforce sequential scheduling and also support multiple parallel jobs, reserved classes and initiators for production batch jobs may not be necessary.

*Operator involvement.* Another basis for setting up classes reflects the degree of operator involvement needed for a job in its execution

---

3   *SUBMIT* is a TSO command that uses an internal reader to place a job on the job queue. The term is used in a loose sense to describe any process that places jobs on the input queue.

stage. By placing a job in a "hold-for-setup" class, the submitter is relieved of the need for the TYPRUN=HOLD or TYPRUN=JCL-HOLD parameter in JCL. JES holds the job automatically, but most installations still require SETUP or MESSAGE JCL statements for quick and accurate determination of the job's setup needs.

The most usual example of setup is tape retrieval and mounting. As the use of automated tape libraries and very-large-capacity online storage devices grows, the need for this kind of hold processing will diminish. The Storage Management Subsystem (SMS) of MVS/ESA should also contribute in two ways to the reduction of tape setup jobs. First, by making better use of different generations of DASD, SMS might use lower-performance DASD, such as last year's model, for data sets that formerly might have resided on tape. Second, many tape jobs are *backups* of key DASD or *archives* of disused data sets. SMS, by making backups and archive jobs more selective and efficient, will minimize the need for tape.

A remaining use for an automatically held job class is to allow submission of jobs that are to be explicitly held, irrespective of resource availability, and run at a later time, perhaps to take advantage of a favorable off-shift billing policy.

***Service expectations.*** If job classes need not be related to production job status or dependencies or to setup requirements except in unusual cases, what is an appropriate basis for establishing job classes? A common choice is to relate classes to service expectations. In many cases, expected levels or rates of resource consumption are included in the determination of classes. A possible scheme including resource requirements and service expectations, as well as production status and setup needs, might be:

| CLASS | CPU-sec. | Priority | Comment, other attributes |
|-------|----------|----------|---------------------------|
| A | any | low | default class |
| B | 0-2 | high | production class |
| C | 2-20 | high | production class |
| D | 20-120 | high | production class |
| E | 120-600 | high | production class |
| F | over 600 | high | production class |
| G | 0-2 | high | systematic class |

| CLASS | CPU-sec. | Priority | Comment, other attributes |
|-------|----------|----------|---------------------------|
| H | 2-20 | high | systematic class |
| I | 20-120 | normal | systematic class |
| J | 120-600 | normal | systematic class |
| K | over 600 | normal | systematic class |
| L | 0-2 | high | same as G with setup required |
| M | 2-20 | high | same as H with setup required |
| N | 20-120 | normal | same as I with setup required |
| O | 120-600 | normal | same as J with setup required |
| P | over 600 | normal | same as K with setup required |
| Q | over 120 | normal | long-running non-production jobs |
| R | over 120 | normal | same as Q with setup |
| S | any | normal | guaranteed serialization (single INIT) |
| T | any | normal | same as S with setup |
| U | any | normal | defer to next shift |
| V | any | normal | same as U with setup |
| 9 | any | high | emergency priority |

In this scheme, each job submitted is expected to have the
TIME= parameter specified on the JOB statement, except for
classes S-V and 9. JES, SMF, and SUBMIT exits[4] check for this
entry and substitute the appropriate "systematic" job class, according to the time specified and the presence or absence of the
/*SETUP statement or its JES3 equivalent. The absence of the
TIME parameter (or of a class exempt from TIME checking)
leads to a default assignment of class A, a low-priority class.
Special classes Q through V can be specified in JCL and cannot
be altered by the exits. Class 9 can be specified only by designated "authorized" users whose credentials are checked by exits
in conjunction with the installation's resource-access-control system. Finally, the production job classes are selected by exits
according to the TIME parameter, in conjunction with distinguished USER names or account numbers.

## 4.1.3. Batch performance considerations

The performance characteristics of batch jobs are examined here
based on the "normal" pattern of batch. That is, a job is *not* a

---

4   Exits are documented interfaces at which installation-supplied code may be
    inserted for many purposes, in this case to change control information for a job.

never-ending address space simulating a started task. A normal batch job is a voracious consumer of MVS resources, accepting CPU and I/O service and using real storage until the purpose of the job is done. It may wait for the availability of resources it needs or for services it requires, but there is no limit to the rate at which it can consume service other than that imposed by the hardware and the operating system.

Once a job enters a JES input queue, there are several factors that can delay both its initiation and its execution. These factors include:

- No initiator is open to the job's class.

- The open initiators are serving other classes specified ahead of this job's class.

- Other jobs may have higher selection priorities within the class.

- The job has requested the allocation of devices or data sets that are not available, and the JES is not screening for allocation dependencies. In JES3 systems, allocations may be checked before job initiation. If this option is not selected in JES3, and in all JES2 systems, a job may be started and immediately go into "allocation recovery," with MVS's allocation recovery function prompting the operator to substitute available devices for unavailable ones. This is a decision the operator is unlikely to be prepared for, so the job fails on a time-out or by explicit operator option.

- JES3 is not allowing new jobs, or this job in particular, to start.

- The job's dispatching priority may be low, and the CPU at or near saturation. Time spent waiting for the CPU may become a significant execution state for the job.

- The job may use resources in such a way as to cause significant operator intervention delays. Placing intermediate data sets on tape rather than on DASD (or on VIO), for instance, may lead to excessive delay for tape mounts. Such data sets are often used in large linked jobstreams to pass data from job step to job step or from job to job.

- The SRM has reduced the system's multiprogramming level (MPL), this job's domain has had its target MPL reduced, and its composite recommendation value (RV) is among the lowest in the domain. The job is thus unilaterally swapped out, and "SRM Delay (MPL)" may become a significant execution state[5] for the job.

- The job uses I/O devices inefficiently. Inappropriate block sizes, multiple data sets on the same device, and fragmented data sets with long SEEKs between extents may all lead to "active I/O" becoming a significant execution state for the job. Applications that perform I/O to repeatedly reread unchanging data, instead of using virtual storage in the address space or, in MVS/ESA systems, in data spaces, to retain that data are simply wasting I/O when a more appropriate resource is readily available.

- The job may use sharable I/O devices that are already in use by other address spaces. I/O queuing may thus become a significant execution state for the job. If the devices are shared with another system, the queuing due to intersystem contention appears as "RESERVE delay" in MVS/370. In an MVS/XA or MVS/ESA system, intersystem device contention appears to be the same as genuine active I/O time, because the queuing and redriving of the I/O is handled by the I/O subsystem. The impact of queuing on the same system can be altered if I/O priority is specified for the job independent of dispatching priority, but the contention is only displaced somewhat to other work, not eliminated.

- The job suffers from significant real storage contention. A sloppy storage reference pattern in conjunction with some

---

5 Performance monitors such as Candle Corporation's degradation analysis products (DEXAN for MVS and EPILOG for MVS) show the distribution of execution states adding up to a job's elapsed time. When a nonproductive execution state accounts for a large percentage of the job's duration, a tuning opportunity may exist. Such a condition may also indicate a successful resource management policy; for instance, batch should incur heavy paging or MPL delay before TSO is affected by real storage constraint.

level of real storage constraint may cause page-in delay to become a significant execution state for the job.

Real storage contention (page-in delay) can be a highly variable factor in determining the elapsed time of a job. When the job is run at an otherwise idle time, there may be virtually no page-in delay. On the other hand, if the job is run at a prime-shift peak time, page stealing may repeatedly strip the job's address space of all but the most recently used page frames and lead to very long aggregate page-in delay. The increased paging rate should trigger MPL reduction, leading to unilateral swapping; otherwise the increased activity on the local page data sets leads to slower paging response times and a general slow-down of the system.

We've seen that the number of initiators, along with the selection and order of the classes they serve, is a more significant delay factor than is selection priority. Selection priority is specified by the PRTY parameter on the JOB statement or in the separate PRIORITY statement. It is usually destructive to orderly system management to allow users to specify job selection priority. JES parameters provide for the adjustment of selection priority as jobs age on the selection queue. If control of access to the job classes (as by exits) is sound, such management of selection priority is very effective.

## Initiators as a Resource

In JES2 environments, initiators are set up in the JES2 parameters and may be altered by operator action. JES3 may alter initiator settings on its own, according to the policies represented in its parameters as they interact with the workload. We will disregard such dynamic adjustments in discussing initiators. We shall regard initiators as specific (named) resources, one of which must be acquired by each batch job before it may proceed.

Each initiator may be set to one or more classes, up to the full complement of 36 classes. The number of defined initiators (including both "active" and "drained" ones) may range from zero up to the maximum number of address spaces allowed for the current IPL, less the total of started tasks and logged-on TSO users.

## Delay Caused by Initiator Settings

Since an initiator is coterminous with an address space, it serves only one job at a time. The interplay between jobs waiting for execution and the availability of initiators is a crucial factor in determining the length of "on-queue" delay for a job. A tactical position that may have had some value in the past may increase this delay, namely, the avoidance of "over-initiation," defined simply as admitting more batch jobs to the system than real storage can accommodate.

In older MVS systems, the physical swapping load required to manage a large number of batch jobs through a smaller MPL had a severe impact on the performance of TSO and online subsystems. Since that time, the "extended swap" algorithm along with "contiguous slot" blocked swap paging was introduced in MVS/SP 1.3.0, significant improvements in paging and swapping were shipped in subsequent MVS/370, MVS/XA, and MVS/ESA releases, and maximum real storage sizes have increased dramatically. Over initiation is now a disease with few symptoms.

## The Need for Over-Initiation

*Under*-initiation is a far greater source of inefficiency than over-initiation. Once jobs are in the system, they are managed by the System Resources Manager. The SRM can select jobs to be swapped in or out to ensure maximum throughput, as well as to respond to the installation's priorities. The SRM responds dynamically to load-balancing opportunities. For instance, it might swap in a few more batch jobs when 30 TSO users go to a meeting, and swap the jobs (or their successors) back out when the TSO users return. This opportunity is lost if a stingy initiator configuration is selected to avoid "over-initiation" at peak load time. A great deal of system capacity can be wasted in a mixed-workload system when jobs reside out of reach on the job queue rather than close at hand on the page data sets.

It is necessary, of course, to ensure that the swapped-out jobs resulting from planned over-initiation are not holding specific resources needed for other work. The preinitiation allocation screening done by JES3 eliminates this problem to a large extent, and real-time monitoring of ENQUEUE contention can detect such problems and facilitate corrective or (future) preventive action.

## Initiator Classes

Because of the great variability of workloads and installation service policies, it is impossible to prescribe an "ideal" initiator lineup. Let's study a hypothetical example based on the job classes listed above. We'll state some facts, assumptions, observations, and rules and indicate how a selection of 20 initiators may support them. We assume that the relative priority specification applies to both selection priority and dispatching priority.

- Classes B-H, L, M, and 9 are shown as "high" priority.

- Class A is "low" priority.

- All other classes are "normal" priority.

- No initiators for classes U and V may be active on prime shift

- Classes D-F, I-K, and N-R have substantial resource requirements. Capacity studies at our example installation indicate that only four jobs in these classes should be active at any given time on prime shift. Up to seven jobs may be run off-shift.

- Only one initiator may be active at any time for classes S and T. Batch jobs requiring serialization are in these classes until the jobstreams are brought up to date with dynamic job submission into classes with open initiators.

- Classes B, C, G, H, L, and M are the classes accounting for the bulk of jobs. They should be accommodated with minimum delay. Ten times as many "0-2" jobs run as "2-20," but the "2-20" jobs may be slightly more important than the shorter ones. Average execution times for "2-20" jobs are five times as long as for "0-2" jobs.

  If the number of short jobs submitted per hour is 100, the number of longer jobs per hour is 10. Execution time for short jobs is 100 relative time units, and for longer jobs, 50 such units. Execution resources are tied up twice as long for short jobs as for longer ones, so we conclude that the shortest jobs need twice as much preference for initiators as the next longer running class.

- Production jobs rank ahead of nonproduction jobs with identical attributes.

- Setup is irrelevant once a job is released.

In the initiator setup shown below, all class-S jobs are selected by initiator 5 before that initiator (and only that initiator) can select a top-priority class-T job. Note that no initiators are defined for subsystems such as IMS or CICS; these are best run as started tasks. Additional initiators or classes may be needed for IMS batch message processing jobs (BMPs).

| Sample Initiator Settings | | | |
|---|---|---|---|
| **No.** | **Classes** | **Status** | **Workload Type** |
| 1 | 9DEFINJOQRKPBCGHLMA | Active | Prime shift heavy batch |
| 2 | 9EFDINJOQRKPBCGHLM | Active | Prime shift heavy batch |
| 3 | 9FEDINJOQRKPBCGHLM | Active | Prime shift heavy batch |
| 4 | 9DEFINJOQRKPCBHGML | Active | Prime shift heavy batch |
| 5 | 9STCBHGML | Active | Serialized classes S, T |
| 6 | 9BCGHLMA | Active | High priority batch |
| 7 | 9BCLMGH | Active | High priority batch |
| 8 | 9BCGHLM | Active | High priority batch |
| 9 | 9BCLMGH | Active | High priority batch |
| 10 | 9BCGHLMA | Active | High priority batch |
| 11 | 9BCLMGH | Active | High priority batch |
| 12 | 9BCGHLM | Active | High priority batch |
| 13 | 9BCLMHG | Active | High priority batch |
| 14 | 9CBHGMLA | Active | High priority batch |
| 15 | 9CBMLHG | Active | High priority batch |
| 16 | 9CBHGML | Active | High priority batch |
| 17 | 9CBMLHG | Active | High priority batch |
| 18 | RKPBCGHLMA | Drained | Off-shift deferred |
| 19 | 9VUEFDINJOQRKPBCGHLMA | Drained | Off-shift deferred |
| 20 | 9UVFEDINJOQRKPBCGHLMA | Drained | Off-shift deferred |

Waiting times in queue by class may be studied with a tool such as Candle's EPILOG for MVS, and adjustments to the number of initiators open to a given class and the order of classes served by each initiator can be made if service targets are not consistently met.

## 4.2. Started Tasks

In the progression from MVT to SVS to MVS/370, and through MVS/XA to MVS/ESA, a dramatic growth area has been the explosion in the number of started tasks. This trend matched the evolution of IBM's high-end operating system from a batch-dominated workload to an online, interactive system vital to the business of the enterprise. It is no accident that the latest step in the progression that started with System/360 and Operating System/360 was named "Enterprise System/370."

The address spaces that run as started tasks in MVS do several different kinds of work:

- provide subsystem services to batch jobs and TSO users. The job entry subsystem (JES2 or JES3), and systems for managing the archiving and recall of data sets, such as IBM's DFHSM, are examples.

- manage terminal networks in support of TSO users or transaction-processing subsystems. The VTAM (Virtual Telecommunications Access Method) address space is the current example.

- provide data base subsystem services for appropriately connected address spaces or terminal users of other subsystem address spaces. The several address spaces that provide DB2 services are in this category, as are several data base subsystems, such as Computer Associates' IDMS, offered by non-IBM vendors, as well as the data base portion of IBM's IMS/VS.

- support users at terminals with transaction processing services. IBM's IMS/VS and CICS/VS,[6] as well as TP (telepro-

---

6   Now redesignated as CICS/ESA.

cessing) monitors from other vendors, are such subsystems. Some of them, such as IMS, have integrated (yet optional) data base facilities, while others have more or less complex file systems as part of the basic offering.

Complex interactions among such subsystems are not uncommon. In a single system, DB2 might serve IMS-supported and CICS-supported terminals, TSO users through QMF, and batch jobs executing static SQL applications. At the same time, IMS users and CICS users, as well as specially structured batch jobs called Batch Message Processors (BMPs), make use of data bases provided by IMS/VS's Data Language/I (DL/I.) Finally, CICS users may access VSAM files.

Still more complexity is found when products of other vendors, as well as home-grown subsystems, are added to the mix.

• provide services usually thought of as part of the operating system. In previous systems and earlier levels of MVS, these services were part of the operating system's nucleus or did not exist. The GRS, ALLOCAS, CONSOLE, CATALOG, and LLA address spaces are examples.

In Chapter 1 we traced the evolution of MVS to its current structure. Cross-memory services made "horizontal splitting" possible, and the exhaustion of available virtual storage through the growth of MVS complexity and services made it necessary. The trend continues through MVS/ESA.

• provide special access control and data management services. ACF2, from Computer Associates, and IBM's DFHSM are such programs. The storage management subsystem (SMS) of MVS/ESA is embodied in several such address spaces. As system-managed storage evolves, the differing needs of the several parts of SMS will almost certainly lead to splitting into additional specialized address spaces.

• receive and process measurement data for the system and its workloads. IBM's Resource Measurement Facility (RMF) and Systems Management Facility (SMF) are the best known of such data collectors. RMF data is captured, collected, and developed in the MVS nucleus, then harvested and written to the SMF data sets by the RMF started task. SMF data is created by numerous sources and funneled to buffers, then collected and written out by the SMF started task.

- collect and display (or store) performance, availability, and other data about the system and its workloads. Performance monitors, such as Candle's OMEGAMON and EPILOG, and IBM's RMF Monitor III, are in this category.

## 4.2.1. Started tasks—Performance considerations

Unlike batch jobs, started tasks are rarely non-stop consumers of resources, nor do they normally "complete" execution unless commanded to do so. Most started tasks spend the bulk of their lifetimes in the WAIT state, depending on the occurrence of some external event (I/O, timer interrupt, or supervisor call) to trigger a burst of activity, and then go back to sleep. Many don't even wake up; instead, they are invoked through cross-memory services, and the CPU usage is charged to the requester and provided at the requester's dispatching priority.

Many started tasks are key components of the operating system. As such, they have high dispatching priorities set by MVS, and special immunity from page stealing. Unless unusual workload conflicts cause unanticipated problems, these address spaces rarely have, and can rarely cause, performance problems.

Other started tasks are driven by the demands of MVS workloads through cross-memory services, via either SRB scheduling or cross-memory PROGRAM CALLs. After initialization of the started task, subsequent CPU use is at the dispatching priority of the requester, and is charged to the address space requesting service. The started tasks that act as subsystems have minimmal intrinsic resource needs but simply reflect the aggregate demand of their end-users.

## Dependencies

Started tasks on which other workloads depend for service must be more favored in MVS than the address spaces that depend on them. Otherwise, the dependent address spaces and their end-users will suffer multiple delays. Consider, for instance, a CICS service that serves 1000 terminals. There might be a CICS terminal-owning region[7] (TOR), two application-owning regions (AORs), and three resource-owning regions (RORs) communicating through cross-memory services to process transactions.

The CICS subsystem depends on other started tasks for necessary services. If the installation is in transition from older data base architecture to a relational data base, both IMS-DC and DB2 (or equivalents from non-IBM vendors) may be present. VTAM is needed to manage the terminal network. IBM's RACF or CA-ACF2 might be used to provide LOGON security, and to control individual users' access to transactions.

When a CICS transaction needs a service provided by one of the non-CICS address spaces, CICS requests it, and the transaction waits until the server signals an end to the *WAIT* by issuing a *POST* SUPERVISOR CALL. Any delay in the server address space, including that caused by the CICS address spaces as they serve other transactions, affects only those transactions waiting for the outside service. On the other hand, if a CICS address space suffers a delay, perhaps to wait for a page fault to be resolved, all transactions will be delayed.

The balancing between internal delays and external delays, between hold-ups to individual transactions and delays to the whole subsystem, is a complex part of MVS performance management. In this example, as in general, it is essential to have a good understanding of the service targets, the actual degree to which those targets are attained, and the nature of the delays causing targets to be missed in order to conduct a sound performance management strategy.

---

7   Again, the CICS "regions" are separate address spaces.

## Storage Considerations

There are few MVS systems with absolutely no storage constraint. Consequently, the need for and use of virtual and real storage by started tasks must be analyzed and understood along with such need and use in the rest of the system.

To protect an address space from paging delay, the usual method is to use *storage isolation*—specifying a target frame count in an address space—to protect it from page stealing. The target may be adjusted based on the paging rate sustained by the address space. Storage isolation will be described in greater detail in a later chapter.

Started tasks that provide critical and frequently requested services for the rest of the system must deliver their services in the least time possible. The Global Resources Serialization (GRS) address space is a good example. It runs at high dispatching priority, equal to that of the "master" address space, and it has a default pseudo-specification of storage isolation that protects an increasing number of its frames from page stealing whenever a page fault is encountered.

As we move from the unquestionably "important" started tasks to those whose services have intrinsically longer service times and are requested less frequently, protection from paging delay is less necessary. Even if a CICS terminal-owning region suffers two page faults per transaction, only about one-tenth of a second will be added to each transaction's response time. If the service target is a two-second response time and it is now three seconds, paging in the TOR is unlikely to be the most promising tuning target.

## CPU Considerations

Dispatching priority specification mechanisms will be discussed in Chapter 6. For now, let's simply examine the order in which different address spaces should have access to the CPU. There are some simple rules we can derive from the nature of each type of started task. First, remember that the dispatching priorities of several address spaces are out of reach; they are set by the operating system and can't be changed. In an MVS/SP 3.1.0 (ESA) system, these include the MASTER,[8] RASP, GRS, DUMPSRV, CON-SOLE, SMF, SMS, and CATALOG address spaces. Because the others *can* be changed, we must understand the range of possible change and the reasons for making each selection.

If we suppose that there is such an ideal as a "well-ordered CPU," a measure of that order is that high-priority started tasks are essential to other work, that they are needed frequently, that they have short service times, and that they rarely use resources subject to contention, so they rarely encounter delays. As priority for access to the CPU declines, each of these attributes moves toward its opposite extreme. Since we wish to plan such an ordering, we should look for these characteristics and arrange our priorities accordingly.

The top priorities are assigned to those auxiliary address spaces of the operating system for which dispatching priority may be assigned: PCAUTH, ALLOCAS, VLF, LLA, and TRACE, with SMS added as appropriate. Because most of the activities of these address spaces are obtained through cross-memory PRO-GRAM CALLs,[9] dispatching priority is of significance only during initialization and recovery, and for those remaining services still invoked through supervisor calls.

The next layer of started tasks includes those required for perform-ance and availability monitoring of the operating system. Those monitors that sample the execution states of other address spaces, particularly in order to measure CPU delay, must do so from the vantage point of higher dispatching priority for accurate results.

Following performance monitors in rank are enabling subsys-tems. The VTAM address space must be higher in priority than its users, and JES must be "above" address spaces that make use of its services. With JES2, these are all batch jobs and all TSO transactions but the shortest. JES3 has a more dynamic role to play in TSO systems, so its priority should be above that of all TSO work. Ranking about equal with TSO is the Terminal Con-trol Address Space (TCAS), used only for TSO LOGON.

---

8   MASTER, DUMPSRV, SMF, AND CATALOG stand outside the scope of normal started tasks as "privileged" address spaces.

9   Remember that a cross-memory PROGRAM CALL is a simple flow of control, re-taining the dispatching priority of the originating address space.

Finally, having gotten through all of the "overhead" started tasks, we get to those that actually do some work. IMS, CICS, and DB2 subsystems are at this level of priority. Again, those acting as servers to other address spaces must, in general, rank higher in priority than the users of those services. Thus the IMS Control Region is higher in priority than its Message Processing regions.

At the bottom of the ladder are test counterparts of the production subsystems—started tasks, but not of crucial importance to the main purpose for which the system is installed. Also low in priority are started tasks that are not performance-critical. Miscellaneous data collectors such as the RMF (writer) address space are in this category.

## 4.3. TSO

TSO (Time Sharing Option) became available in 1969 as an optional part of MVT. The option was a large one; a batch-only operating system had to be extensively modified to accommodate a very different type of workload. Because several TSO users had to be accommodated in a single MVT region, a form of *swapping* had to be added. Because the data set needs of TSO users could not be predicted in advance, *dynamic allocation* was a necessity. An efficient terminal access method was needed, and TCAM was the initial response.

TSO was not a notable success in MVT for a number of reasons:

- Terminals were expensive and slow.

- TSO response time in MVT was intrinsically slow.

- The alterations to MVT in support of TSO were extensive and unreliable, resulting in a system that could no longer be trusted to run the backbone batch workload, and could not support a useful number of terminal users.

- IBM offered a superior time-sharing alternative in CP/67, the predecessor of VM/370, with CMS. At the time that TSO was struggling to define itself, CP/CMS was becoming a mature system supporting far more terminals for an equivalent configuration.

From this unpromising beginning, TSO's reputation continued to suffer through later releases of MVT and into the first few releases of MVS. TSO in MVS is no longer an "option," but the name was retained. TSO's problems in early MVS were covered in Chapter 1. Let's look now at the reasons for TSO's good reputation and widespread acceptance and use in more recent versions of MVS:

- TSO was designed into the basic structure of MVS, not grafted on as an afterthought. MVS was also designed for high integrity; more recent versions have been made suitable for continuous operation. Consequently, MVS with TSO is far more reliable than was MVT without TSO.

- VTAM was far more efficient and capable than TCAM at managing large terminal networks.

- Terminals for TSO evolved rapidly from converted typewriters to alphanumeric CRT devices in IBM's 3270 line, with color and graphics being added and prices declining almost as rapidly. A TSO user today might use a personal computer, equipped with any one of several connectivity adapters, as a terminal. Such a terminal might support four simultaneously connected sessions, each emulating a full-function IBM 3179 or 3194, with full native PC functions available as well. Connection of such an *intelligent worksta-tion*, or of an ordinary "dumb terminal" to MVS through a multisession extension to VTAM can provide access to a practically unlimited number of TSO or other sessions.

- More sophisticated interfaces than the primitive TSO line-oriented commands became available, increasing the functional richness and productivity of TSO. The most successful of these is IBM's ISPF (Interactive System Productivity Facility), which has become so standard an interface that IBM has made it part of SAA.

- Most important, MVS became capable of running TSO well. The improvements in paging and swapping and the increase in real storage sizes found on MVS systems eventually overcame TSO's appetite for storage. Because TSO is a basic part of MVS, every performance improvement in MVS has benefited TSO as well.

## 4.3.1. TSO as a workload

Each interaction of a TSO user with MVS is known as a *transaction*. As we'll see in Chapter 6, transactions are distributed in size, most of them being short, or *trivial*. A trivial transaction typically executes a few thousand to about one hundred thousand instructions. It may call for some small number of I/O operations in addition to the terminal I/O that initiates it, and it may make reference to some 20 to 200 frames of real storage.

A TSO service is usually judged by the speed and consistency of its response time to trivial transactions. In recent years, behavioral research has suggested that response times under one-half second increase the productivity of TSO users. Other research indicates that consistency of response time is perhaps a more significant factor.

Longer-running TSO transactions may call on complex MVS services or may do far more I/Os than trivial ones. Experienced TSO users tend to realize it when a transaction makes unusually heavy resource demands, and they are prepared to wait a few seconds for response.

Another class of TSO users is likely to make more stringent demands and be less tolerant of response delays. These users may be using TSO as a gateway to DB2 through the Query Management Facility (QMF), or using it to access one of several fourth generation language facilities (4GLs). These users are *not* knowledgeable about TSO or MVS, and they are insulated by their application interface from an understanding of how complex their requests are. Such a workload is a great challenge to manage well, often requiring the performance analyst to exercise persuasive skills on the *ad hoc* application programmers while educating them in the realities of MVS performance. The last chapter of this book provides some suggestions for dealing with such workloads and those responsible for them.

## 4.3.2. Transaction profiles

Typical TSO transactions spend most of their time waiting to use the CPU, waiting for page fault resolution, or waiting for the completion of physical swap-in. If a significant portion of transaction time is spent using the CPU, waiting for the SRM to allow a swap-in, for I/O completion, or for ENQ conflicts, either the transaction is unusual or the system requires tuning.

A complicating factor in characterizing the TSO workload is a consequence of TSO's generality. In contrast with more rigidly structured terminal-based systems like CICS or the CMS component of VM/370, the TSO environment allows virtually any program that can operate in the MVS environment to be invoked in TSO via the CALL command or some variant thereof. If the invoked program simply performs some action and exits, no unusual behavior is evident. However, if the program does what would have been unit-record I/O if it ran in batch, the standard SYSIN DDname is allocated to the terminal, as is SYSPRINT.

Since input records are not ready and waiting for the program, the terminal user needs to enter the input. The "think time" as well as the input entry time appears to MVS as active time rather than idle time. With output to the terminal as SYSPRINT, output will be sent to the terminal until the screen is full, when three asterisks ("***") appear at the bottom of the screen and the TSO session is placed in the Terminal Output Wait state. This state, too, is considered as active time (even though the user is not attempting to do anything) and is indistinguishable from a genuine problem-related execution state with the same designation.

Systems in which many TSO users use the CALL command to invoke what are in effect batch programs will appear to have poor and variable trivial response time; in fact, the only problem is corruption of the reported numbers. In Chapters 9 and 10 we'll see how to interpret such numbers and how to correct them for reporting.

## 4.3.3. Storage considerations

In MVS systems with constrained real storage, paging delay dominates TSO transaction time. A series of actions may be taken to lessen this delay. We will look at the mechanisms by which such actions may be taken in Chapter 6, and describe those actions in Chapter 8.

A stable level of TSO storage delay may suddenly increase. A frequent cause of such an occurrence is the installation of a new release of a frequently used TSO facility such as ISPF. In such an installation, the new version is placed in a LINKLIST library, and the modules of the old version, in the pageable link pack area (PLPA), are renamed. In MVS/XA systems with the Linklist Lookaside Area (LLA) and in MVS/ESA with the extended Library Lookaside Area, I/O increase may be insignificant, but the working set (active frame count) of *each* TSO user will increase by an average of 15–30 frames.

## 4.3.4. I/O considerations

Because TSO is an online window to all of MVS's capabilities, and because batch jobs can be translated easily and exactly to TSO CLISTs or EXECs, almost any degree of I/O intensity might be encountered in a TSO transaction. It may be presumed, however, that I/O-dominated TSO transactions are atypical. If a group of TSO users do tend to be heavy I/O consumers, it might be appropriate to segregate them, manage them, and measure them apart from others with a differently distributed execution profile. In Chapters 6 and 8, we shall see how to accomplish such isolation of selected users.

An indirect and hard-to-see form of I/O delay can occur in TSO systems, largely as a result of carelessness. Every system programmer should realize that TSO is a program-fetch-intensive environment. If there are five TSO transactions per second, there are probably 10–20 *LINK*s, *LOAD*s, *ATTACH*es, or *XCTL*s executed by TSO transactions or on behalf of them by TSO application platforms like ISPF. If 95 percent of the TSO fetch activity is resolved from the PLPA, there is no significant TSO I/O impact. However, at many installations TSO LOGON procedures become modified for one reason or another. A common procedure is to use a STEPLIB DD statement in the newly modified LOGON procedure, to keep the new code out of the LINKLIST libraries until it is proven by use. If the STEPLIB is temporarily used for such a purpose, a reasonable tradeoff has occurred. If the STEPLIB is left in effect, the system will suffer.

A STEPLIB is efficient for batch or for a started task subsystem, where all (or at least most) of the program modules to be fetched will be found in the STEPLIB. It may also be efficient for a constrained application system built on TSO. It will be grossly *inefficient*, however, for an unconstrained TSO service, because each fetch operation will cause the entire STEPLIB directory to be searched, to no one's benefit, if the module is in PLPA but not in the STEPLIB.

### 4.3.5. CPU considerations

CPU delay tends to dominate TSO transaction times in systems without storage constraint. Usually, this situation is innocuous: "The CPU is the last bottleneck." Excessive or inconsistent CPU delay is almost always caused by deviation from the scheme of "well-ordered" dispatching priorities we examined in the discussion of started tasks in this chapter. Again, we examine in Chapters 6 and 8 the methods by which TSO transactions may be placed appropriately in dispatching priority order, and we show how to apply those methods in Chapters 9 and 11.

## 4.4. Summary

In this chapter we have examined the workloads of MVS, the ways in which they are brought into execution, and their dependencies and vulnerabilities.

# 5

# The Language of SRM, Part I

"When *I* use a word," Humpty Dumpty said, in rather a scornful tone, "it means just what I choose it to mean— neither more nor less."

*—Lewis Carroll*

This chapter and the next introduce SRM's concepts and terminology. This first part covers time concepts, "workload," service units, service rates, and objectives. Chapter 6 moves on to domains, performance groups, and performance periods.

Following these introductory chapters, Chapters 7 and 8 cover each SRM parameter in detail, and provide recommended settings.

## 5.1. SRM—Using Part of the System to Manage Itself

MVS may be unique among operating systems in the extent to which it uses part of the system's resources to manage the rest of those resources. It almost certainly was one of the first to do so. MVS may also be unique in the subtlety of many of its concepts and the obscurity of the language in which they are described.

The MVS component that manages the distribution of system resources to workloads is the System Resources Manager—SRM. It is often described as having two priorities: the first, to allocate resources to workloads in accordance with installation directives; the second, to maximize throughput of the system consistent with the first priority.

In that brief description is the key to the core of MVS performance management. Accurate translation of the installation's priorities to language that the SRM "understands" ensures that MVS (as directed by SRM) will operate in accordance with those priorities. Failure to do so may lead to unpleasant surprises. In the absence of correct guidance to SRM about workloads, control of the system will be dominated by SRM's second priority, that of maximizing throughput.

## 5.1.1. The danger of defaults

In new MVS systems especially, it is all too easy to be overwhelmed by the sheer volume of work needed to get the system functioning at all, and to push aside performance management considerations. This (perhaps unintentional) choice appears sound because everything appears to be working well at first. Until there is contention for one or more resources, MVS will appear to have few performance problems, and all workloads will receive adequate, if sometimes erratic, service. But as soon as a chronic constraint appears, MVS's throughput-oriented default controls take over, often to the detriment of response-critical workloads.

With some knowledge of SRM and how it is directed, the system programmer or performance analyst may conduct simple experiments aimed at improving the performance of key workloads.[1] These experiments are easy to assess and safely reversible, yet few bother to try them. The sheer size of MVS intimidates the prospective performance specialist—and so another MVS system continues to run under control of IBM's defaults.

In many systems that have numerous provisions for adjustment, the defaults might be good enough to accept for a while. However, IBM's defaults for MVS throughput management are based

---

[1]  Note that performance management deals with workloads. There are some activities, described in Chapter 11, that might properly be described as "system tuning," but performance problems and efforts to conquer them have to do with workloads.

on arbitrary limits, on extraneous considerations such as the speed of the CPU, or on unconstrained laboratory measurements. They are not related to the management of real workloads, nor are they based on typical configurations.

## 5.1.2. Management approach

To "tame" MVS is an exercise in several parts. These are summarized below as if they were sequential steps, but of course they are not. There are many overlapping cycles of activity involved in initial performance management, and in its ongoing adjustment and refinement.

The authoritative reference source for descriptions of SRM parameter sets and their values is the book *System Programming Library: Initialization and Tuning,*[2] published by IBM in individual editions for each major version of MVS, and amended for each new release of the operating system.

The steps in approximate order are:

- Make a preliminary determination of the workload mix [to be] supported by the system, and establish an order of relative importance.

- Create an initial service level target for each major workload on the system, based on prior experience or the stated requirements or expectations of the system's users. Gary King's "Workload Characterization"[3] methodology is a good starting point for predicting the performance characteristics and resource needs of each type of workload.

- Ensure that the system's hardware configuration is approximately adequate for the projected full workload. Again, King's "Workload Characterization" provides good guidance.

2  The short title *Initialization and Tuning* will be used in subsequent mentions of this publication.

3  Gary King of IBM's Poughkeepsie Laboratory has published and presented under this title and on the related topic of Processor Storage Estimation in various forms and venues, notably SHARE and CMG.

- Reconcile the hardware configuration with the service expectations, and make adjustments as needed.

- Create a set of global SRM controls in an IEAOPTxx[4] member of SYS1.PARMLIB so that SRM's ability to vary the multiprogramming level (MPL) of the system will be used effectively to control paging delay of critical workloads by in turn controlling the page fault rate. This important control, as well as others in the "OPT" member, are described in Chapter 7.

- Divide the overall workload of the system into distinct *performance groups* first, on the basis of similar types (batch, TSO, subsystem) of address spaces, and second, according to priorities established for the various workload constituents. Establish how TSO and batch may be expected to break down into short, medium, and long transactions. For each division of these swappable workloads, and for each of the nonswappable address spaces, lay out the order of dispatching priorities from the top down, according to the principle of the "well-ordered CPU" discussed in the preceding chapter. Translating these general judgments into the precise language needed for an Installation Performance Specification (IPS) is discussed in Chapter 6 and Chapter 8.

- Once the workloads have been associated with performance groups, ensure that the system enforces that association. Do this by creating an Installation Control Specification (ICS), another member of SYS1.PARMLIB. The ICS is described in Chapter 8.

- Create an overall system parameter set (IEASYSxx)[5] denoting the new OPT, IPS, and ICS, along with all the other parameters required to bring up an MVS system.

- Bring the system up with the new parameters. This may not be a simple matter if it is attempted all at once. Since

---

4   The name derives from an early version of MVS in which the predecessor of today's SRM was known as the "optimizer"—hence the customary designation of "OPT." The "xx" suffix is the name by which a particular parameter set is designated. The default designation is "00."

5   The default name for this parameter set is IEASYS00, often pronounced as "eye-easy-Sue."

the OPT, IPS, and ICS may be set and reset at will, always keep a proven older version of each SYS1.PARMLIB member as the –00 version, making and proving all changes in a member with a different suffix. When all members are functioning as planned, suitable renaming can be done. Conflict will be minimized if changes are made in the order OPT first, then IPS, then ICS.

- Measure the performance of the system and its workloads with tools that can measure service attainment against targets and identify the nature of bottlenecks if they are present. IBM's RMF Monitor I, by itself or as interpreted by IBM's Service Level Reporter (SLR), Legent's MICS, or Merrill's MXG, is one such source, Candle's EPILOG for MVS is another, and other vendors offer similar monitors and reporting programs as well.

- Continue the cycle of refining and adjusting the system parameters until all service targets are comfortably and reliably attained. If this proves impossible, targets may need to be changed or configuration changes might be necessary.

- Continue to revise and adjust the service targets until the service delivered by the data center matches what the management of the enterprise wants, needs, and is willing to pay for.

## 5.2. Introduction to SRM Concepts

The SRM is complex and often appears to be in conflict with itself. It has evolved to its current form from the first days of MVS with continuous additions and few if any deletions. To study the SRM, we need to break down its functions and perhaps oversimplify.

SRM controls several aspects of MVS, including:

- assigning and dynamically altering dispatching priorities

- controlling page stealing, including protecting pages of favored address spaces from page stealing

- responding when TSO transactions end, by determining whether the address space will be swapped out to auxiliary storage or retained in processor storage

- changing the multiprogramming level by swapping address spaces into and out of real (central) storage

- determining how tape drives are allocated

These are all essentially simple actions; the complexity is in how SRM gathers the information on which its decisions are based, and the specification of the values that guide those decisions. To explore SRM and break down its complexity, we need first to acquire its vocabulary.

## 5.3. SRM Terms and Concepts

The documentation of SRM uses what appear to be common words to describe concepts, actions, and parameters. Some of these words have uncommon meanings or interpretations in the context of SRM. In this section, we'll explore SRM terms and highlight special meanings as appropriate.

### 5.3.1. Time in the SRM

Various measures of time are used in SRM. Most of these measures are various intervals of normal clock time, but there are others whose basic unit is adjusted to represent ticks of a clock that runs faster as CPU speed increases. Some times encountered in performance management are:

- SRM measurement sampling interval(RM1)—an adjusted time based on the *SRM second*, described below

- Time Unit—a subdivision of the SRM second

- SRM measurement summarization interval (RM2)—a clock time interval, but not the same in all systems. It varies from 20 seconds in MVS/370 and in slower CPUs in MVS/XA and MVS/ESA, down to five seconds or less in larger, faster CPUs in XA and ESA

- transaction "response" (completion) time—a clock time

(real-time) interval from the time SRM recognizes the start of a transaction to the time recognized as the end of the transaction.[6] Note that transaction completion times are *not* necessarily response times. If transaction completion is signalled to SRM after the end of each terminal interaction, the difference is negligible. In TSO systems with many non-TSO programs invoked via the CALL command, the difference can be great and is usually suggested by inflated standard deviations in RMF's reported transaction completion times.

- resident-time—the time an address space spends swapped in

- out-time—the time an address space spends swapped out, although ready to run

- long-wait-time—time spent swapped out and not ready to run

- active-time—sum of resident-time and out-time

- transaction-elapsed-time—sum of active-time and long-wait-time

## SRM Seconds

It is a reasonable goal that the impact of SRM overhead be approximately equal across different processor models. Also, the timing of SRM decisions should be based on the ticks of the CPU's cycle time, rather than on those of a wall clock. Accordingly, most internal SRM timed events occur on the basis of the SRM second. The SRM second was equal to a second of common wall-clock time when MVS ran on the IBM System/370 Model 155-II.

For other CPU models, the size of the SRM second is adjusted to represent the time needed to execute approximately the same

6  SRM is notified of transaction state changes by means of SYSEVENTs. SYS-EVENT SUPERVISOR CALLS are issued by various MVS routines. Chapter 6 of *Initialization and Tuning* for pre-ESA levels of MVS describes SYSEVENTs. That material has been moved to a different publication (*Component Diagnosis and Logic: System Resource Manager* [sic]) for MVS/ESA.

number of nominal instructions as ran on the 155-II in one second. For IBM systems capable of running MVS/XA or MVS/ESA, the SRM second ranges from about one-third of a second down to less than one-twentieth of a second. Consequently, SRM collects the resource information on which its decisions will be based at an interval ranging from three to about 23 times per second as CPU speed increases. Note that the duration of an SRM second does not depend on number of processors in a multi-engine complex.

## Time Units

On slower systems, for which the SRM second is a time interval perceptible by a person, it might be inappropriate to alter dispatching priorities at intervals of one or more SRM seconds. SRM provides a way to subdivide the SRM second into up to ten *time units*. Using this capability, time slicing and the now-obsolete rotation of dispatching priorities can operate at an interval smaller than that which a human can perceive.

## 5.3.2. Service and service units

When a transaction runs in MVS, it uses the basic resources of the system: instructions in the CPU, page frames of central storage, and I/O operations. Because systems differ widely in their ability to provide these resources to workloads, standardized measures are defined to facilitate management of both system resources and workloads.

The standardized measures are *service units*, defined separately for CPU, storage, and I/O. The CPU component is further divided in two parts, for TCB time and SRB time.

## CPU and SRB service units

CPU service is accumulated in two different modes, each representing a separate count of service units. The unqualified CPU service is that which is acquired in TCB mode. (TCB is a Task Control Block, the basic unit of dispatchable CPU work.) Other service is received indirectly in SRB mode. (SRB is a Service Request Block, the means by which authorized programs can request MVS services. Global SRBs are dispatched ahead of local SRBs and all TCBs; local SRBs are dispatched ahead of TCBs in each address space.) Many SRBs are charged to the requesting address space; some are not, and represent *uncaptured time* in resource measurement.

A CPU (or SRB) service unit is an interval of CPU time differing by basic CPU model, by number of processors,[7] and by operating system environment. In early MVS systems, a service unit was defined as 10,000 instructions. The measure today is in terms of a specified number of service units per second of execution time, or its reciprocal. A second yields from less than 100 to about 1000 service units, depending on CPU model. A service unit, then, is between 1 and 11 milliseconds of CPU service.

## Main Storage Occupancy (MSO) Service Units

MSO service units are accumulated for central storage held while CPU cycles are being used. The basic unit of measure is the *page-second*, defined as a page frame held for one CPU (TCB or SRB) service unit. To make MSO roughly commensurate with CPU service units, the raw page-seconds number is divided by 50 to yield MSO service units. Storage used by cross-memory reference is charged to the target address space (but note that such address spaces do not accumulate CPU service units when accessed in cross-memory mode). MSO service is not charged for expanded storage occupancy.

## I/O Service Units

There are two alternative measures for I/O service units. In all MVS/370 systems, and by default in XA or ESA systems, each "EXCP"[8] is counted as an I/O service unit. (In XA and ESA,

---

7   The devaluation of CPU service for multi-engine configurations represents the "MP penalty." The loss of productivity from uniprocessor to dyadic, or to a two-way MP, may be calculated from the times given in the appropriate *Initialization and Tuning* book.

8   EXCP stands for EXecute Channnel Program, a basic unit of work presented to the MVS I/O Supervisor (IOS), and is also the name of a low-level I/O macro-instruction supplied with MVS. EXCP is used as a last resort when standard access methods lack necessary function or ultimate performance. EXCP has often been thought of as an interface upon which access methods are built. This was never strictly true, and it became clearly false when VSAM and later IMS (OSAM), the JESs, and DB2 supplied their own "I/O drivers."

EXCPs are replaced by a count of I/O blocks transferred, a more consistent and inclusive measure.) The second option in XA and ESA, specified by the IOSRVC parameter in the IPS, is to count connect-time, divided by a constant of .0083 to make the count roughly equal to that of blocks for half-track records on 3380s. Regardless of which IOSRVC option is chosen, the number of JES SPOOL blocks transferred is added to the IOC total.

Counting EXCPs or blocks charges fewer service units for efficient programs with large I/O block sizes. Even as data bases proliferate, most MVS I/O is sequential, and many block sizes are far below optimum. On the other hand, counting connect-time ignores VIO transfers as well as the CPU overhead associated with each I/O operation. The latter choice might be appropriate in large multi-engine systems with abundant real storage, but continuity with measurements from MVS/370 systems is lost. Hence the choice is not obvious.

## Service Definition Coefficients (SDCs)

To move from raw service units to the *service* that the SRM uses in various algorithms involves an additional scale factor for each category of service. These factors are specified in the IPS as *service definition coefficients*, and each ranges from 0 to 99.9. Thus service is the sum of the four service unit calculations, with each one first being multiplied by its respective service definition coefficient. This scaled and weighted measure of service is still denominated in service units, and we will mean this kind of service unit in the rest of the SRM discussion, unless otherwise noted.

It is tempting for those in charge of resource accounting and charge-back to use service units as a measure of resource consumption for the purpose of tracking workloads or recovering the cost of service.

As results are evaluated, those responsible for billing may alter the SDCs in pursuit of consistent billing. A common result is that some users may still continue to receive bills or usage reports that they dispute on the basis of inconsistent charges, yet the

SRM is denied the opportunity of controlling the system properly.

Altering the SDCs is dangerous and unnecessary—unnecessary because the raw components of service are reported in SMF records for each type of workload, or may be calculated by dividing each component by its SDC at the time of data collection. It may then be multiplied by any appropriate factor for billing purposes. The SDCs are available in RMF workload records.

Altering the SDCs is also dangerous because the service rates and accumulations used by SRM to manage the system's resources depend on the SDCs, and good service depends on stable controls. We might even venture to say that SDC alteration is foolish since the degree to which a resource is constrained (the basis for performance management decisions) has little correlation with its marginal cost.

## 5.3.3. Service rates

Several SRM algorithms depend on the *service rate* received by a workload. We define service rate as the service received by a workload in a time interval, divided by the length of the time interval. The unit of service rate is service units per second. Let's examine some typical examples to understand the rationale for the various ways in which service rates are calculated.

- A batch job has received some service and is now swapped out by the SRM to allow another job to be swapped in. As the job "ages" in the swapped-out state, we would like it to become increasingly eligible for swap-in.

- A TSO transaction is swapped out because it has entered a WAIT state while an archived data set is being retrieved. When the WAIT is satisfied, we would like the session to be just as eligible for swap-in as it was at swap-out time. As it stays swapped out but ready for swap-in, we would like its swap-in eligibility to increase.

- When an address space is swapped in, it may accept or *absorb* service at a high rate. Using only this high *absorption rate* to determine swap eligibility might result in unstable sequences of swapping in and out. We wish to take account of the swapped-out time, during which no service was received, as well.

Given these goals, we define various service rates as follows:

- The count of service units is reset to zero and service starts accumulating at each swap-in time. (Overall service is accumulated for a job or TSO transaction in other counters. We are concerned here only with service *rate* as used by SRM.) This count of service units is the numerator or dividend for the service rate calculation.

- For a swapped-in address space, the denominator or divisor is the sum of the most recent out-time and the current resident time. Service rate will thus start at zero (because the service unit count is reset) and increase until the out-time becomes insignificant compared to the resident time. Defining *absorption rate* as a service rate with the out-time disregarded, we see that the service rate approaches the absorption rate (if constant) over time.

- For a swapped-out address space, the denominator or divisor is the sum of the just-completed resident interval and the current out interval. Service rate will start at the value just prior to swap-out and decline linearly over time. Note that long wait time is not used in the service rate calculation.

## 5.3.4. The "workload" scale

We have examined service rates as dependent variables in examining how service rates are determined. The next step as we develop the language of SRM is to note that service rates are used in turn as independent variables in the algorithms used to manage swappable address spaces. We now consider the dependent variables in those algorithms.

When a service rate associated with all or each of the address spaces in a domain is used as an independent variable to determine the domain's ranking for raising or lowering multiprogramming levels (MPLs), the dependent variable is called a *contention index.*

When the service rate of an address space is used as the independent variable to rank the address spaces within a domain to decide which is to be swapped in or out, the dependent variable is called a [swap] *recommendation value.*[9]

Contention indexes and recommendation values are defined in the same units on a common scale. That scale is specified in the IPS, and the set of values specified is called the *workload* specification. "Workload" is one of the most confusing terms in the jargon of SRM. It has no relation to the load on the system nor to any particular segment of that load. It is simply an arbitrary scale used to make relative rankings. We shall refer to it by its IPS name of WKL, so that the word "workload" may be left with its common meaning.

WKL is specified as a monotonically increasing series of up to 32 integers in the range from 1 to 128. The WKL scale is extended to 1.5 times the last number in the series when at least one objective is defined in a certain way.

## Objectives

The function used to convert service rates to WKL values is called an *objective.* In *Initialization and Tuning,* IBM has developed a nonstandard way of representing objectives. An objective is usually portrayed as a graph in which the horizontal axis is WKL and the vertical axis is service rate. The conventional representation would interchange the axes, but we will bow to precedent and adopt the IBM convention. However, it is important to realize that WKL is always the dependent variable and service rate always the independent variable.

Objectives are hard to set up properly in MVS systems. A bit of general discussion might help to simplify the subject. Looking first at the interaction of objectives with domains, a domain

---

9 Domains are described at length in Chapter 6. For now, we note that address spaces are grouped in domains to control the resident multiprogramming set and the swap eligibility of address spaces.

might be defined in the IEAIPSxx (IPS) member of SYS1.PARM-
LIB as:

**DMN=5,CNSTR=(0,9),DOBJ=3**

The domain is named as domain 5. Between zero and nine address
spaces assigned to domain 5 may be in central (real) storage at any
time. Domain 5's contention index for increase or decrease of the
permitted number of resident address spaces is determined by the
total service rate of all address spaces in the domain, according to
the functional relationship defined by objective 3.

Suppose that the following definitions also exist in the IPS:

**WKL=(1,50,98,99,100)**

**OBJ=3,SRV=(8000,8000,4000,2000,0)**

Objective 3, shown in Figure 5-1, maps the listed service rates to
the set of WKL numbers in a one-to-one positional correspon-
dence. Linear interpolation is applied between the specified service rates. A service rate greater than 8000 SU/sec returns an
effective zero WKL number.

A contention index will be calculated for each domain in which
there is at least one ready address space, whether swapped in or

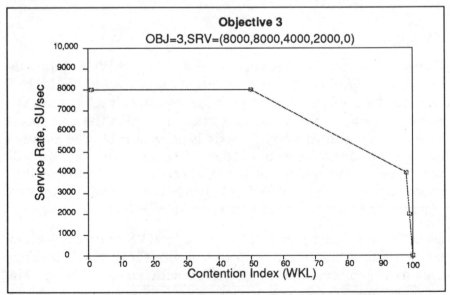

Figure 5-1. Objective as DOBJ for an ordinary domain

out. Depending on the relative contention indexes of all the domains, domain 5's target multiprogramming level (TMPL) may be increased (but not above its maximum CNSTR, 9 in this case), decreased (but not below its minimum, 0 in this case), or left unchanged each time that SRM's Swap Analysis routine is invoked.

Since the objective is named as a "DOBJ" in the domain definition, the service rate that is the independent variable in the objective is the sum of the rates for all address spaces in the domain. Using objective 3, domain 5's contention index will approach zero if that aggregate service rate is more than 8000 service units per second, and will be 100 if the service rate is zero. Between these extremes, the contention index is determined by the aggregate service rate according to the relationship in the objective, shown in Figure 5-1.

The appropriateness of this objective for this domain cannot be determined in isolation. If the address spaces in this domain are of moderate importance, then a "more important" domain might have an objective like that in Figure 5-2, and a less important

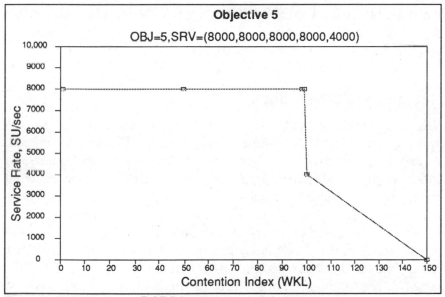

Figure 5-2. Objective as DOBJ for "important" domain

domain one like that in Figure 5-3. The ranking is according to the relative contention indexes at given service levels.

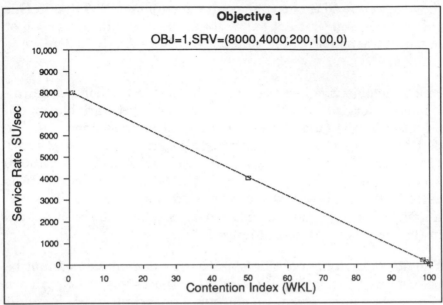

Figure 5-3. Objective as DOBJ of "unimportant" domain

Note in Figure 5-2 that the WKL scale is extended to 150% of the specified maximum value. This is because the objective's last specified service rate value is not zero.

## Recommendation Values

When a domain's target MPL (TMPL) is adjusted within its specified constraints, a change in its current MPL may be needed. A domain is selected for MPL change on the basis of its contention index (high or low according to whether the MPL is to be increased or decreased). To change a domain's current MPL, an address space must be swapped in or out. The choice of which address space is selected for swap-in or swap-out is made according to its ranking within the domain. That ranking is on the basis of another number measured on the WKL scale, the recommendation value (RV). In general, the address space with the highest RV is selected for swap-in when the MPL is to be increased; the one with the lowest RV is selected for swap-out in the opposite case.

The RV used to evaluate swap eligibility is the *composite recommendation value*, made up of four components. The component always present is the RV derived from the address space's service rate, through its objective, by SRM's workload manager. The other three components are selected when SRM's *load balancers* are invoked by selection in the IPS.

## Load Balancers

When a system resource such as real storage is fully utilized and in contention, it might be helpful to system throughput if address spaces that make unusually large demands on that resource were to be swapped out so that the possibility of acute contention may be reduced. When that choice is made, it would also be desirable to swap in the "resource hogs" preferentially when the resource in question is in a period of low utilization.

SRM offers three load balancers to assist in making such choices. The balancers are of widely differing usefulness, and each requires at least one explicit parameter specification to activate it. The three areas subject to load balancing are CPU, I/O, and main (real or central) storage.

**CPU load balancing** is based on a series of questionable assumptions:

- that the CPU can be overloaded
- that CPU absorption rates differ enough across address spaces so that useful distinctions among workloads are possible
- that swapping an address space out is necessary to deny it access to the CPU

In general, proper assignment of dispatching priorities makes CPU load balancing unnecessary. It should be reserved for the most pathological workloads, such as CPU-intensive programs that may absorb several seconds (or even minutes) of pure CPU use before incurring an I/O wait.

**I/O load balancing** may be useful occasionally for address spaces (usually batch jobs) that are unusually I/O-intensive.

With the general use of DASD without internal path limitations and with multipath connections using Dynamic Path Reconnect, I/O load balancing is rarely necessary in up-to-date systems. In MVS/370 systems, I/O load balancing may remain a useful option.

**Storage load balancing** is the remaining load balancer, and it remains useful. The appropriate way to defend the system from the storage impact of a not-very-important job with an enormous working set is to swap it out. Storage load balancing does not depend on subtle secondary denial of resources like the other load balancers. The resource with a shortage (real storage) is the one relieved directly (by swapping out the storage hog.)

To activate storage load balancing for a workload requires two overt actions: A parameter must be specified in the IPS for each period of the workload's performance group, and a parameter in the OPT must be changed from its default value. To control storage load balancing effectively, more OPT parameters may need adjustment as well. Specific parameter descriptions and recommendations are found in Chapter 7.

Each load balancer is invoked when its respective resource is seen by SRM to be underutilized or overutilized. Its effect is on the swap recommendation values for each address space defined as eligible for that class of load balancing and identified as a significant user of the resource. A positive or negative alteration is added to the RV of the address space. The amount of such alteration, as well as the thresholds used for each load balancing decision, are OPT parameters (*i.e.*, entries in the IEAOPTxx member of SYS1.PARMLIB).

## How to Set Up an Objective

The key need in setting up an objective is to understand its purpose. An objective used to control a domain's contention index does so as a piecewise linear function of the service rate in the domain (DOBJ) or of the average service rate for each address space in the domain (AOBJ). An objective used to control swap recommendation values for address spaces within a domain does so as a piecewise linear function of the service rate received by each address space assigned to the objective.

Since *service rate* is the independent variable in each case, it is essential to have an accurate picture of the service rate received by a domain or address space and the range of values it may assume. This information is available from almost any performance monitor. Suppose, for instance, that we are using the WKL specification shown earlier in this chapter,

    WKL=(1,50,98,99,100)

An objective is specified as

    OBJ=4,SRV=(8000)

and the objective is used to control swap recommendation values. If an address space receives from 0 to 7999 service units per second, it will have an RV of 150. If its service rate is over 8000 SU/sec, the RV will be less than 1. To avoid unexpected default treatment of a high service rate, the maximum service rate in each OBJ should be greater than the usual peak value of service rate for the workload being controlled.

The "slope" of the objective determines the extent to which the WKL value increases as service rate declines. A "horizontal" slope, denoting a constant service rate (as above), is the most favorable; the WKL value associated with a constant segment is that of the highest WKL value corresponding to the segment. A declining slope (this is the only other choice because the slope cannot be positive) is less favorable. Also less favorable is an objective intersecting the WKL axis at less than the maximum WKL. For an objective used for determining recommendation values, this intersection is called the *cutoff* RV. The cutoff value is important in determining the way that address spaces are managed just after swap-in.

Understanding what makes an objective more or less favorable allows us to rank objectives and to devise a new objective to fit into an existing structure, with some confidence about what the new objective might accomplish. However, we might also put the matter of objectives in perspective. Perfectly valid and serviceable IPSs may be constructed with no objectives at all; they are not needed if all workloads are nonswappable. Domain definitions do not require objectives since every domain may have an assigned constant contention index. Swap recommendation values are relatively unimportant except when a significant amount of out-and-ready work (usually swapped-out batch jobs) exists. As real storage sizes increase in proportion to CPU power, there is less out-and-ready.

# 6

# The Language of SRM, Part II

## 6.1. Application to Workloads

The concepts developed in Chapter 5 are of little use by themselves. In this chapter we examine the interaction of those ideas with the work that runs (as address spaces) in an MVS system. Address spaces are organized by the SRM in two ways:

- A *performance group* defines most operational parameters associated with each address space, including its dispatching priority, objective, and domain.

- A *domain* defines a group of address spaces to be managed for swapping according to specific rules, as directed by SRM to control system loading and apportion resources.

### 6.1.1. Performance groups

Each address space in MVS is assigned to a performance group, either explicitly or implicitly. Control performance groups (those defined in the IPS) exist for the purpose of allowing SRM to manage the attributes of address spaces. These include:

- domain
- dispatching priority and I/O priority
- objective
- storage isolation

- load balancer eligibility

- exchange swapping control

- performance period control

Each of these attributes is examined in detail in this chapter if it was not already covered in Chapter 5. The last attribute might remind us that each performance group is defined as one or more (up to eight) performance periods. Nonswappable address spaces assigned to a multiperiod performance group always stay in first period. For swappable address spaces, SRM's service accumulation usually determines the passage from period to period; a new transaction always starts in the first period.

## 6.1.2. Service intervals

SRM bases some of its actions on the amount of service an address space receives during some period of residency. All of these decisions are related to swapping decisions, so the values discussed below apply only to swappable address spaces.

### Enqueue Residence Value (ERV)

ERV is a means of ensuring that an address space, holding an ENQueue for a resource for which there is current contention, is protected from being swapped out for a specified interval. ERV is measured in CPU (only) service units, has a default value of 500, and is specified in the OPT. This parameter survives from the earliest days of MVS.

### Interval Service Value (ISV)

ISV specifies the minimum number of service units that an address space should receive during *each* interval of real storage residency. The purpose of ISV is to stabilize the system against overly frequent exchange swaps (discussed later in this chapter). ISV is reset at each swap-in, is measured in total service units, and has a default value of 100,000 SUs. ISV is an optional parameter in each performance period definition in the IPS. The default value is high enough to block most exchange swaps.

## Performance Periods

SRM can manage swappable transactions differently as they age. The measure of that aging is accumulated service, and the means of changing management parameters is the passage from one performance period to the next. The DUR parameter gives the duration of each performance period except the last in a performance group, and is usually measured in total service units (SUs). A rarely-specified UNT=R parameter in the performance period definition allows DUR to be measured in wall clock seconds.

TSO performance period DURs usually range from a few hundred SUs in first period to a few thousand in the next-to-last (third or fourth) period. (The last period is unbounded and DUR may not be specified.) A typical batch first period might be 5000 service units; the second period might be 20,000 to 50,000, if three periods are used.

Even in the case of batch, the sum of the specified performance period durations is usually less than the 100,000 SU default for ISV. Therefore, it is unnecessary and useless to specify ISV in any period but the last, unless one wishes to encourage exchange swaps with a low ISV specification.

## 6.1.3. Domains

Each address space is assigned to one domain at any time. If the assignment is omitted in the performance period definition, a default assignment of domain 1 is made for ordinary address spaces, and domain 0 for privileged address spaces. Privileged address spaces include initiators, LOGONs, VTAM's Terminal Control Address Space (TCAS), and those with an active program named in the *Program Properties Table* (PPT) with the PRIVILEGED attribute.

Each domain is defined in the IPS. Although only the domain number must be specified, two additional kinds of information are usually supplied: constraints and a means of setting the contention index.

## Constraints

Domain constraints are specified as a lower limit (minMPL) and an upper limit (maxMPL) in the range of zero through 999. The limits may be equal.

When upper and lower domain constraints are equal, control of the domain's MPL has been denied to SRM. Constraints of 0,999 allow full SRM control. A non-zero minMPL may be specified to ensure minimum swap-in delay for TSO users or swappable subsystem address spaces. A restrictive maxMPL allows the installation to control the impact of resource-intensive or contention-prone jobs.

Many installations, especially those that have had MVS for many years, tend to retain history in their IPSs. An IPS may define 10 or 20 domains, each one having had a good justification for its existence at some time in the past. The effect of having too many domains is a small increase in SRM overhead during swap analysis. With a large number of domains, too, the SRM's ability to manage swapping by selecting among address spaces within a domain is diminished. There is usually no benefit in having more than about ten domains.[1]

TSO is an important swappable workload. There is usually a separate domain for each of the first few performance periods, and another covering the last period or two. A typical specification for a domain associated with a TSO first period is to set the minMPL equal to about one-fifth of the number of logged-on users expected at an average peak period. The first-period maxMPL might be set to the approximate number of TSO address spaces that could be accommodated in real storage, assuming that batch MPLs are driven to their minimum values. (A working set of 100 page frames per TSO address space might be assumed for this calculation.) Such a maximum might be needed to deal with the aftermath of a TSO stall condition such as an ENQ lockout of a commonly used shared data set.

In general, domain MPLs should be defined to be as close to their

---

1 Before report performance groups became available in 1978, there was some justification for segregating workloads in domains for (RMF) reporting purposes.

default wide open values as possible. In other words, trust the SRM! If SRM is allowed to adjust the system-wide MPL based on appropriate criteria, distinctions among domains can be made in the selection of an algorithm for setting each domain's contention index and the particular values selected. Similarly, distinctions among address spaces are made on the basis of RVs, which are, in turn, set by objectives. It may be difficult to get it right, and somewhat intimidating to yield control to the SRM if one has not done so before, but the alternative is to remain constantly involved in trimming and adjusting inflexible domain constraints in order to keep current with workload changes.

## Contention Indexes

MVS supplies four algorithms for setting a domain's contention index. The oldest of these, *domain weight*, is obsolete, and the presence of a domain weight in an IPS rules out the use of the other three algorithms, known collectively as *target control keywords*. The algorithms are:

- **Domain weight** is specified as a third value, ranging from 1 to 255, in the domain's CONSTR (constraint) specification. If omitted (and if there is no target control keyword in the IPS), a default value of 1 is assumed. When a domain weight is specified or assumed by default, a domain's contention index (CI) depends on three variables: the specified weight (W), the current target MPL (TMPL), and the ready user average (RUA), a running average of ready address spaces in the domain[2], according to the formula

$$CI = (RUA \times W) / TMPL$$

  TMPL starts at minMPL and is increased up to, but not above, maxMPL as long as swapped-out address spaces in the domain are ready to run (i.e. out-and-ready) and the calculated CI causes the domain to be selected for MPL increase. Domain weights are generally inappropriate controls of contention index because neither the number of

---

2 RUA is recalculated at every SRM summarization interval (RM2), equally weighting the past value with the current number

ready address spaces in the domain nor the current target MPL is a good indicator of how a domain should rank against others in competition for MPL adjustment.

Domain weights were superseded in MVS/SE2 by the target control keywords AOBJ, DOBJ, and FWKL. Each of these is used to specify the contention index for the domain more directly than is done with domain weights.

- **FWKL** is the simplest of the three target control keywords. FWKL=$n$ specifies a fixed contention index directly as $n$, a value on the WKL scale in the range 1–128. FWKL=1 (the lowest fixed contention index) is the default value if any target control keyword is specified in the IPS. FWKL=1, explicitly or by default, guarantees that the associated domain(s) will always rank lowest in competition for MPL. Higher FWKLs may be used to create a constant, explicit ranking of domains according to constant contention indexes.

A high FWKL is often specified for a TSO first period domain or one serving interactive graphics users in a pseudo-batch performance group. Such address spaces make modest resource demands and are usually preferred workloads. Although the domains serving these address spaces usually have generous minMPLs, occasional stall conditions can lead to a pile-up of ready address spaces when a stall is relieved, and thus a need to increase the domain's MPL. The MPL increase should be independent of the number of ready address spaces, and of the service rate in the domain, up to the max-MPL. A high FWKL ensures that the preferred domain will be selected for MPL increase at each swap analysis cycle, up to its maxMPL.

- **DOBJ** is used to adjust the domain's contention index as a function of the total service rate received by all address spaces in the domain, according to the objective designated by the DOBJ parameter. DOBJ is most often specified for domains serving latter periods of batch performance groups and for last period TSO. Since the resource demand of batch jobs can vary widely, DOBJ serves to regulate the total impact of the domain's address spaces irrespective of the resource demand of each address space.

- **AOBJ** is similar to DOBJ except that the domain's total service rate is divided by RUA before the objective is used to derive the contention index. Specifying AOBJ tends to regulate the service rate received by the average address space in the domain.

## 6.1.4. MPL adjustment

The principal reason for swapping out an address space in MVS is to ensure that sufficient central (real) storage is available to service page faults and swap-ins. Swapping may be regarded as the *macro* control of the available frame queue. Page stealing is the *micro* control. Since swapping is less disruptive and usually more efficient than page stealing, a goal of performance management should be to minimize the incidence of page stealing.[3]

In a system with a significant swappable workload (such as TSO), most swap-outs are of inactive address spaces. The physical swap-outs occur (in systems without expanded storage) when the criteria for logical swap are not met. With expanded storage, physical swap-outs go to expanded storage as central storage frames are needed, or to auxiliary storage when the relation between migration age and workload-related criteria (specified in the OPT) indicates that expanded storage should be bypassed.

SRM initiates swap-outs or swap-ins of active address spaces when its system measurements indicate that one or more controlled variables is out of the desired range.[4] By computing several measures of system activity each SRM second (RM1) and summarizing them at a longer interval (RM2), SRM decides how to adjust the system wide multiprogramming level (MPL) and recalculates the target MPL (TMPL) of each domain.[5] Target MPLs for the domains are recalculated based on current domain

3 Swapping affects only one address space at a time; page stealing may cause deferred damage to many address spaces as page faults later occur. In a system with expanded storage, there is less need to choose between swapping and page stealing unless the amount of expanded storage is inadequate.

4 A simplistic view is that the resources are "over-" or "under-utilized."

5 At the completion of each *RM2* interval, SRM makes a simple decision about system MPL: up one, down one, or remain as is.

MPLs and contention indexes. The set of TMPLs is one of the inputs to the swap analysis process that is at the heart of SRM-directed swapping.

Swap analysis also regulates swap-ins, both those initiated by SRM's resource-management actions and those needed to reactivate previously inactive address spaces. Active address spaces swapped out by SRM and newly ready address spaces, swapped out when inactive, all compete for admission to the multiprogramming set. Each competes only in its own domain, so the more important initial Swap Analysis decisions deal with domains.

## The Swap Analysis Cycle

Swap[6] Analysis is initiated each SRM second, at the completion of each swap-out, and whenever a swapped-out TSO address space becomes ready[7] (i.e. the user hits ENTER.) At each activation, the following actions take place, subject to the usual caution that IBM does not guarantee not to change MVS (and swap analysis in particular) at each release or even with each maintenance update:

- Swap Analysis retries swap-ins previously deferred for lack of frames.

- It then swaps out address spaces in each domain currently exceeding its TMPL. Enough address spaces are chosen (those with the lowest composite RVs) to make the current MPL in the domain equal to the TMPL. If any such *unilateral swap-outs* are initiated, Swap Analysis exits at this point.

- If an address space holding an ENQueue is swapped out, Swap Analysis swaps it in. (Only one such *ENQueue swap-in* may be done per swap analysis cycle.) If its domain is at its TMPL, the domain's swapped-in address space with the

---

6   It should be noted that swapping does not and never did require swap data sets. As suggested in the discussion of MVS evolution and history in Chapter 1, swap data sets are obsolete and should not be used except as a last resort or in very unusual circumstances. An extended discussion may be found in Chapter 11.

7   The SRM reacts to the USRREADY SYSEVENT issued by the TSO Terminal Monitor Program.

lowest composite RV is swapped out to maintain the domain's MPL. If an ENQueue swap-in, with or without such an *EN-Queue exchange swap-out* is initiated, Swap Analysis exits at this point.

- Swap Analysis swaps in address spaces in each domain having at least one out-and-ready address space, and currently at an MPL less than its TMPL, up to the number needed to restore the TMPL for each domain. If any such *unilateral swap-ins* are initiated, Swap Analysis exits at this point.

- As its last priority, for the lowest-numbered domain with both an out-and-ready address space and a swapped-in address space with a lower composite RV, Swap Analysis performs an *exchange swap*, interchanging the highest-ranking "out" and lowest-ranking "in" address spaces.[8]

## Implications of Swap Analysis

The foregoing synopsis of swap analysis suggests some performance management implications:

- The primary attention given to swap-in fails may supply an explanation for swap-in delay, even in domains with generous minMPLs. If this condition is seen frequently, SRM's MPL controls in the OPT could be adjusted to reduce the system-wide MPL, thus increasing the supply of available frames.

- Unilateral swap-outs inhibit unilateral swap-ins in other domains until at least the next swap analysis cycle. If TMPLs change too frequently (causing a disruptively high level of unilateral swapping), perhaps overly sensitive controls, such as a DOBJ with too steep a slope, or incorrectly chosen service rates are to blame. Also, breaking a workload into several similar domains with small MPLs may lead to more frequent unilateral swap-outs. Consolidating domains with similar workloads could prove more stable.

---

8  The exchange swap is not done if the RV difference between the selected address spaces is less than 1.0 or if the swapped-in address space is within its Interval Service Value (ISV).

- Exchange swaps are low-probability events under the most favorable circumstances. To increase the likelihood of exchange swaps in a particular workload segment, ensure that a low-numbered domain is chosen.

## 6.1.5. Types of swapping

In discussing swap analysis, we touched on several types of swaps. We'll review those now and list other types as well.

### Unilateral Swapping

This is the type of swapping initiated at frequent intervals by SRM so as to move the MPL of each domain toward its target MPL. By controlling each domain's MPL, the overall MPL is controlled, and in turn the measurable factors (such as page fault rate) used to control MPL are themselves controlled. In this way, the SRM's MPL adjustment actions constitute a classical negative feedback control system, something like a thermostat controlling a heating or cooling system based on a temperature measurement, in turn controlling the temperature in the monitored space. When unilateral swapping of address spaces that are not performance-critical occurs, and when that swapping is controlled by the page fault rate, less page stealing and consequential page faulting is likely to occur in other workloads.

Response-oriented workloads such as short TSO transactions should not normally be unilaterally swapped out. On the other hand, a batch job may be unilaterally swapped many times before completion. As long as batch turnaround-time targets are safely met, unilateral batch swapping is a sign of sound installation control of SRM's workload management. The absence of such swapping (in a system with a sizable swappable workload and some degree of storage constraint) may indicate a system likely to incur a great deal of demand paging delay. Again, demand paging (page stealing followed by page faulting) is the less-efficient way to maintain the available frame queue when system MPL control through batch swapping is an available alternative.

## Exchange Swapping

The purpose of exchange swapping is to allow several batch jobs in a chronically "overloaded" domain to have nearly equal service rates on average over a reasonable time frame. Without exchange swapping, the elapsed time of a short-running batch job may be at the mercy of a longer-running job, in the same domain, that happened to have been initiated first.

An exchange swap will occur on an otherwise unproductive swap analysis cycle *only* if the following conditions are met:

- A domain is exactly at its (non-zero) target MPL

- At least one address space in the domain is "out and ready"

- At least one resident address space in the domain is "out of its ISV"—its service in the current resident interval exceeds its ISV for the current performance period

- The composite RV of an "out and ready" address space exceeds, by at least 1.0, the composite RV of a resident address space out of its ISV

Such a series of conditions is rarely met, yet exchange swapping was so feared in the early days of MVS that extraordinary measures were taken to prevent it. The default ISV of 100,000 service units was not enough to do the trick, so the WKL scale in the IPS as supplied with various preconfigured MVS offerings was changed from a range of 1 to 100 to a compressed range of 1 to 10, making it far more difficult to achieve an RV difference of 1.0 or more.

The factors making exchange swaps undesirable in the past no longer exist, and the original rationale for allowing them still holds. In installations with significant batch or long-running TSO workloads, encouraging exchange swapping can result in more uniform completion times for such transactions.

Often stringent service targets exist for unscheduled batch, yet resource constraints dictate a restricted MPL for all or part of the batch workload. The use of a low ISV (10,000 or 20,000 service units) can, by allowing exchange swaps, ensure a consistent degree of elongation for short-running jobs, regardless of the arrival order of large and small jobs in the restricted group.

## Swapping of Inactive Address Spaces

As we saw in Chapter 1, much of the evolution of MVS involved changes in the swapping of inactive address spaces, particularly TSO address spaces. Let's look at the progress and decision points of such a swap in today's MVS:

- The *inactive* condition is detected by SRM. The TERMINAL WAIT SYSEVENT (usually for input, sometimes for output) may have been issued by the TSO Terminal Monitor Program (TMP), a program may have issued the *WAIT* macro-instruction with the *LONG* operand, or an ordinary *WAIT* may have continued past the *detected wait* threshold currently in effect.[9] The distinction between terminal waits and other types of inactive address spaces will be important in the subsequent decision process.

- The address space is prepared for swap-out. First, it is *quiesced*, ensuring that all pending I/O is complete. Next, pages not in the working set are *trimmed*. (Swap trim is a special form of page stealing, from the address space to be swapped out.) A few trimmed pages may be *unchanged*[10] if they are backed by valid copies on auxiliary storage. The unchanged trimmed pages are added directly to the AFQ in systems without expanded storage.

  The *working set* includes pages with the hardware reference bit on, fixed pages, and the local system queue area (LSQA) of the address space. This "strict" working set is "enriched" for TSO address spaces by the addition of pages with UIC of zero, and of additional pages according to the value of the system-wide high UIC.

  For systems with expanded storage, the working set is bro-

---

9   The threshold in recent MVS releases is two seconds or eight SRM seconds, whichever is less. The latter limit is less in most systems.

10   In current levels of MVS, swapped-in pages are all marked "changed." If in the course of a transaction a page is stolen and written to auxiliary storage, page-faulted back in and then swapped out, it can be an unchanged trim page or working-set page. Such pages are rare.

ken into primary and secondary subsets. The primary working set includes LSQA, fixed pages, and one representative page from each segment in the address space. The secondary working set is all other working-set pages. Pages not in the working set will be trimmed.

With expanded storage, *unchanged* trimmed pages are evaluated against a criterion for movement to ES and are scheduled for movement if the test is successful. Unchanged pages are released to the available frame queue after the movement to expanded storage, if it was scheduled. If the test is unsuccessful, release to the AFQ is immediate, just as in systems without expanded storage.

With expanded storage, the *changed* trimmed pages normally will be placed on a queue for movement to expanded storage if and when the central storage frames are needed to prevent page stealing from other address spaces. Without expanded storage, the pages are scheduled for [blocked] page-out to auxiliary storage. Again, these frames are added to the AFQ once they are successfully backed up in expanded or auxiliary storage.

- The eligibility for logical swap is evaluated next. For TSO terminal waits, if the recent think time of the address space is less than the current system think time threshold,[11] the address space is eligible for a logical swap. For other inactive address spaces, they are eligible if the system think time is five seconds or more.

- If the address space is eligible for logical swap, the logical swap decision is then made, according to the system's ability to accept a logical swap at this time. If the system wide high UIC is not less than one-half the UIC lower limit for think time adjustment (LSCTUCTL), the logical swap will be done. The address space is then dropped from the dispatcher's true-ready queue, and other control block adjustments are made to indicate that the address space is "OUT—LOGICAL."

---

11 The logical swap think time is determined by SRM measurements against four value-pairs specified as OPT parameters. They are described in Chapter 7.

- If logical swap is not selected, and lacking expanded storage, a physical swap to auxiliary storage is scheduled.

- With expanded storage, address spaces that will not be logically swapped are evaluated for direct swap to expanded storage. The OPT parameter ESCTSWWS(2) specifies a *criterion age* for the working sets of TSO address spaces in terminal wait. ESCTSWWS(0) does the same for all swaps of privileged address spaces, and ESCTSWWS(1) determines the criterion for all other swaps. For other than terminal-wait swaps, the swap to expanded storage (known generically along with logical swaps in central storage as a processor storage swap) will be selected if the sum of the current expanded storage migration age (MA) and the system wide high UIC exceeds the criterion. For terminal-wait swaps, the address space's think time is added to the criterion age before the comparison is made.

The working-set pages of an address space selected for a processor storage swap to expanded storage are placed on the FIFO queue of pages (we'll call this the *pending-out queue*) to be moved out when real storage frames are needed. The entire trimmed working set will be moved out together.

- Lacking expanded storage, or if the test for processor storage swap eligibility fails, the trimmed working set is moved together to swap data sets if present, or to local page data sets, using the contiguous slot allocation algorithm, if possible.

At this point the address space is either logically swapped in central storage; physically swapped to auxiliary storage; or, either moved out to expanded storage, or awaiting such movement. Let us assume that the processor storage swap to expanded storage proceeds. We can now drop from consideration the direct swap to auxiliary storage. Nothing more happens in that case until the address space becomes ready for swap-in.

- A logical swap in central storage stays there until the expiration of the system think time. (In MVS releases prior to

SP 2.1.7, an arbitrary 15-second "grace period" was added on to this interval. The grace period in current releases is two seconds.) At this time the logical swap fails, and the address space now receives the same treatment that it would have if it had failed the test for logical swap at the outset.

- An address space swapped to expanded storage stays there until it is swapped back in unless migration reaches it. Migration takes place in stages, with the secondary working set being moved first, in groups of pages according to the device type of the local page data sets. Finally, the primary working set is moved to the swap data set(s), if present. With no swap data set, the primary working set goes to the local page data sets.

The impact on system and workload performance of expanded storage migration can be considerable; each migrated block of pages requires central storage to accomodate the move-in from expanded storage. The central storage frames are kept for the duration of the subsequent physical I/O to auxiliary storage as well. Since migration (a symptom of expanded storage constraint) may occur when central storage also is constrained, this added storage demand with migration can cause a sharp degradation in the performance of workloads sensitive to paging delay. A temporary cure for disruptive migration is to increase the OPT parameters (those named ESCTxxxx) that control expanded storage eligibility; the long-term cure is to increase installed expanded storage. In systems capable of logical partitioning, this increase may be accomplished by reapportioning expanded storage across partitions.

- Some time later, the address space becomes ready. (In the usual case of TSO, the terminal-user has pressed ENTER.) A logically swapped address space still in central storage is activated by queue manipulation which reverses the actions taken at the time of swap-out. A similar reinstatement takes place for an address space on the pending-out queue for expanded storage.

- An address space that has been physically swapped out may

be in expanded storage, in auxiliary storage, or in transition between the two owing to migration. In each case, the swap-in is *unilateral* according to the swap analysis procedure described previously. Until swap analysis permits the swap-in, the address space is counted as out-and-ready. Migration from expanded storage to auxiliary (through central storage) may still take place during the out-and-ready period.

The progress of a swap is complex. Obviously, the best case for performance is the successful logical swap in central storage, or the unfulfilled processor storage swap to expanded storage. When response-critical address spaces are physically swapped to auxiliary storage or (worse) migrated from expanded to auxiliary, they are subject to both I/O delays and possible delay for SRM MPL adjustment. Much tuning activity is devoted to overcoming both kinds of swap delay.

## Miscellaneous Swaps

Several other types of swaps can occur in MVS. Normally, they are all very infrequent and have no effect on performance. Two types triggered by storage shortages, however, may indicate serious resource imbalance problems. The types of miscellaneous swaps are:

- **Request Swap**—An authorized program has directed that an address space be swapped out or in. A common use for the requested swap-in is to bring in an address space to cancel the current job, session, or started task.

- **Transition Swap**—MVS requires that V=R job steps or nonswappable programs be allocated frames in preferred, nonreconfigurable storage. A transition swap causes such an address space to be swapped out just before the V=R or nonswappable status is fully established. When it is subsequently swapped into the appropriate kind of storage, the status is made effective.

- **Auxiliary Storage Shortage Swap**—Auxiliary storage must not be allowed to run out. When its usage exceeds a certain threshold, SRM directs that the address space acquiring frames at the highest rate be swapped out, and causes prominent operator messages to be displayed. At this time, address space creation is inhibited, and the system can rapidly "dry up." The condition is easily relieved by PAGEADDing an additional local page data set. When an installation experiences this condition, corrective action is easily implemented.

- **Real Storage Shortage Swap**—Much like the previous case, this kind of swap is triggered when thresholds for real storage use are exceeded. When a threshold is exceeded, address space creation and swap-ins are inhibited, and directed swap-outs of swappable address spaces holding the largest number of frames are initiated. This condition is not as easy to relieve as the auxiliary storage shortage. Frequent occurrence (more often than once a week) of a real storage shortage condition may indicate exhaustion of the central storage capacity. The thresholds are OPT parameters (MCCFXEPR and MCCFXTPR); in systems with a high but stable level of page-fixing, the thresholds may need to be adjusted.

Managing swapping in systems with significant batch and TSO workloads is challenging and often difficult. Chapter 11 covers the subject in detail.

## 6.1.6. Storage isolation

Storage isolation is a means of altering the sometimes inappropriately democratic process of page stealing, designating some frames of some address spaces as exempt from stealing. It came into existence in an informal way in the MVS/SE1 time frame with a popular system modification or ZAP known at the time as *fencing*. An address space's working set could be explicitly defined in this way, designating a number of frames that would be exempt from page stealing ("fenced off") under normal circumstances.

In MVS/SE2, fencing was formalized and externalized as storage isolation. Four new IPS parameters were introduced, providing several useful control options.

A further use for storage isolation was found when extended swap was introduced, first in an Installed User Program (IUP) and later in MVS/SP 1.3. Because the minimum protected working set is preserved across swaps, specifying storage isolation for TSO address spaces leads to enrichment of the swap-in working set (known as the *swap group.*) The balance between swap paging delay and demand paging delay may be adjusted by varying storage isolation until an optimum point is found. The tradeoff is not linear, because swap paging is more efficient than demand paging. Adding five or ten pages to the swap group might increase swap-in delay by less than 20 milliseconds but prevent three or four page faults, each taking 30 to 50 milliseconds to resolve.

In systems with expanded storage, storage isolation is applied to the sum of frames in central and expanded storage, and does not inhibit page stealing to expanded. Such page stealing and subsequent page fault page-in is normally fast enough (about 75 *micro*seconds each way) to disregard.

## Storage Isolation Parameters

Each storage isolation parameter is specified as a value-pair, with the first value less than or equal to the second. The upper value for frame counts may be specified as "*" to denote the maximum available value: 32767 in MVS/370 and MVS/XA, $2^{31}-1$ in MVS/ESA. The parameters are:

- CWSS=(low,high)—specifying the range of protected frame counts for the common area, including PLPA, EPLPA, CSA, and ECSA. CWSS is a global IPS parameter, preceding the first domain definition in the IPS.

- CPGRT=(low,high)—specifying the range of acceptable page-in rates for the common area, in pages per real-time second. CPGRT is a global IPS parameter, preceding the first domain definition in the IPS.

- PWSS=(low,high)—specifying the range of protected

frames for an address space. PWSS appears in the performance group period definition.

- PPGRTR=(low,high)—specifying the acceptable paging rate for an address space in page-ins per resident second. PPGRTR appears in the performance group period definition. An older PPGRT parameter (prior to MVS/SP 2.1.2) denoted page-ins per execution-time second for ordinary address spaces but was equivalent to PPGRTR for address spaces in cross-memory mode. PPGRT should not be used in systems supporting PPGRTR.

Each frame-count parameter interacts with its corresponding page-in rate parameter. The protected frame count at any time is called the *target*. The target starts at the low frame-count value and is increased when the page-in rate exceeds the upper page-in rate value until the upper frame-count value is reached. The reverse takes place when the page-in rate is less than the lower value.

Considerations relating to storage isolation include:

- Specifying a *maximum* frame-count value implies that any frames held by an address space (or the common area in the case of CWSS) in excess of that count are *preferred* for page stealing. Therefore, the maximum should usually be "*" unless every address space in the performance group is nonessential. In the case of an "unloved" address space, a restrictive maximum PWSS will guarantee preferred page stealing, possibly shielding preferred address spaces from stealing. (This technique is sometimes called *negative storage isolation*.) The maximum value for CWSS should always be "*".

- As in any regulated system, there should be enough of a neutral range between each set of upper and lower limits (as for page-in rates) to permit periods of stable operation without frequent adjustment. A series of measurement experiments is the best way to determine appropriate ranges. A suggested starting point is to estimate the maximum value and then make the minimum 80 percent of the **max-imum**.

- To use PPGRT in MVS/370, it is necessary to identify a typical page-in rate per execution second at a time when paging delay in each affected address space is acceptable. This value is available from most real-time performance monitors for MVS. Another way to get this number is to measure or assume an acceptable page-in rate per real-time second (this would be PPGRTR) and divide that by the fraction of a single CPU that the address space consumes. Thus, an address space that can safely sustain five page faults per second and uses 25 percent of a CPU needs a maximum PPGRT of 5/.25 or 20 page-ins per execution-second. Using the 80 percent relationship suggested above, the minimum should be 16:

$$PPGRT=(16,20)$$

- Storage isolation for first period TSO (and usually second period as well) is not subject to page-in-rate-based adjustment, since the time in short transactions is insufficient to allow a page-in rate to be calculated. The form of storage isolation for TSO initial performance periods is usually

$$PWSS=(120,*)$$

  where "120" is a typical value with IBM 3380 or equivalent paging devices, providing some enhancement of the swap group size if the observed frame count for first period transactions is about 100–110 frames. A short period of observation with a performance monitor can show the actual frame counts for TSO transactions at an installation.

TSO storage isolation is of limited value in systems with expanded storage unless expanded storage capacity is very limited. In that situation, and in systems without expanded storage at all, TSO storage isolation of response-critical performance periods is the closest thing to tuning magic available in MVS. A trivial increase in swap I/O time returns a many-fold reduction in page-in delay. Storage isolation for TSO is most critically needed when no swap data sets are in use (the preferred configuration) to ensure a minimum of single-page-movement I/O.

## 6.1.7. Dispatching priorities

We have looked at SRM's role in controlling swapping and page stealing. Its other major function is the control of dispatching priorities. In a default MVS system, SRM does not do this. Specific actions must be taken to wrest control of dispatching priorities from the users and place it firmly with SRM.

Dispatching priority in MVS exists as 256 distinct levels, ranging from hexadecimal 00 to FF. Address spaces are associated with dispatching priorities. Global SRBs are dispatched above priority X'FF'. Without SRM control, an address space can be assigned a dispatching priority directly through the DPRTY JCL parameter or through a corresponding TSO LOGON option. A JCL example that might be found in the default JCL for JES2 is DPRTY=(15,14), equal to X'FE', an unnecessarily high priority. Allowing such individual, uncoordinated control for each batch job, started task, and TSO session is likely to make the operating system's behavior inconsistent if not unpredictable.

As early as the time of MVS/SE1, it was recognized that central control of dispatching priority was essential if MVS was to be a trustworthy and consistent production operating system. The first such control in MVS was a rather tentative *automatic priority group* (APG) covering a narrow subset of dispatching priorities. In SE2 and since, APG has been superseded by the ability to give SRM control of all dispatching priorities, and to make 160 of the 256 possible priorities available to address spaces. Dispatching algorithms have evolved as well. To avoid confusion, we shall consider only the capabilities as of MVS/SP 2.1.7 and later.

### Translation

The system used to denote dispatching priorities under SRM control is different from the simple (0–15,0–15) scale used in the JCL DPRTY parameter. An IPS parameter called APGRNG denotes the range of priorities to be "owned" by SRM. Each value may be in the range 0–15; the lower may equal the upper. To prevent address spaces from claiming the top priorities, the upper value should be 15. To allow the full range of 160 priorities (organized as ten groups of 16) to be under SRM control, the lower value must be no greater than 6. Two views are common for APGRNG: Minimalists argue for APGRNG=(6–15); advocates of full control and ease of interpretation favor APGRNG=(0–15).

If APGRNG is specified in the IPS as APGRNG=(6–15), the "0" group of SRM dispatching priorities corresponds to X'60' to X'6F', and the "9" group to X'F0' to X'FF'. The lower dispatching priorities from X'00' to X'5F' (DPRTY 0,0 to 5,15) are available to anyone foolhardy enough to use them in JCL. Relating "real" dispatching priorities to "SRM" dispatching priorities requires constantly shifting origins from 0 to 6 and back.

If, on the other hand, APGRNG=(0–15) is specified, the "0" group of SRM dispatching priorities corresponds to X'00' to X'0F', and the "9" group to X'90' to X'9F'. No origin-shifting is necessary, but the dispatching priorities from X'A0' to X'FF' are barred to any address space. Most systems are set up with this choice for APGRNG. There is an additional benefit to this selection. System address spaces with dispatching priorities nominally set at X'FF' stand out in a monitor's display of address spaces and dispatching priorities. We shall assume this choice in subsequent discussion.

## SRM Dispatching Priority Groups

As specified in the IPS, dispatching priorities are organized in ten sets of 16 levels. Each set corresponds to the first hexadecimal digit of a priority designation. Within each set, there is a two-way division; the upper six levels of the set are individually specifiable as *fixed* priorities, while the lower ten levels in the set form a *mean-time-to-wait* group.

Dispatching priority is designated by the "DP" parameter or variations thereof. If a particular priority set is designated as "s," fixed priorities are specified as DP=Fs4 (highest) through

DP=$Fs0$ to DP=$Fs^{12}$ (the lowest fixed priority), and the mean-time-to-wait group of the set as DP=$Ms$. Assuming APGRNG=(0–15), the overall pattern looks like this:

| SRM Priority | "Real" Priority | Rank |
|---|---|---|
| F94 | X`9F' | Highest |
| F93 | X`9E' | ... |
| ... | ... | ... |
| F90 | X`9B' | ... |
| F9 | X`9A' | Lowest of the high |
| M9 | X`90'-X`99' | Highest MTTW |
| ... | ... | ... |
| F5 | X`5A' | About in the middle |
| ... | ... | ... |
| F04 | X`0F' | Highest of the low |
| ... | ... | ... |
| F00 | X`0B' | ... |
| F0 | X`0A' | Lowest fixed priority |
| M0 | X`00'-X`09' | Dead last |

## Algorithms

A fixed dispatching priority places an address space on the dispatching queue in a position relative to those of address spaces with higher or lower dispatching priorities. Within a given dispatching priority, address spaces are in a FIFO subqueue, ordered dynamically according to the sequence in which they most recently became dispatchable. (An inactive or nondispatchable address spaces is removed from this *true-ready* queue and added to the end of the subqueue for the specific priority when it again becomes dispatchable.)

The mean-time-to-wait (MTTW) algorithm divides each MTTW group into ten distinct fixed levels according to the average time between WAITs in each address space. Those with short inter-

12 This curious designation looks like an afterthought, and it is. An obsolete priority type called "rotate" occupied this slot previously. DP=$Rs$ was the old designation; it remains an acceptable alternative to DP=$Fs$.

vals between WAITs (usually for I/O completion) have higher priorities; those with long stretches of CPU use without intervening I/O activity have lower priorities. The priorities are reset frequently at the interval of an SRM second, so a program with a changing pattern of CPU-to-I/O activity balance is managed properly at each stage in its execution. MTTW faithfully performs the "I/O-bound high, CPU-bound low" allocation of dispatching priorities that was so hard to manage in MVT, and does it automatically according to the changing demands of each address space.

All of this benefit of MTTW can be lost, however, if multiple address spaces are not free to compete within a single MTTW group. Even so, MTTW may still fail if the wait time interval used by SRM to assign priorities is not well matched to the behavior of the address spaces. In Chapter 7, we'll see how to use a performance monitor to observe MTTW operation and correct it if necessary.

## Adjustment

SRM has several ways to adjust dispatching priority for an address space. For swappable address spaces, in which preference is to be given to short-running transactions, the progression through performance periods is the means of making significant changes in dispatching priority at each period change. A TSO performance group may start out with DP=F63 in first period, move to DP=F61 in second period, and then to DP=M5 in later periods.

For nonswappable workloads, there is no progression through performance periods, so adjustment is ordinarily limited to that available through MTTW or according to the first-come-first-served handling of fixed dispatching priorities or for each MTTW slot. If, for instance, there are several CICS application-owning address spaces at the same fixed priority, the most active one will have the highest average dispatching priority.

Suppose, however, that activity alone does not determine importance. In this case, the final SRM dispatching priority adjustment mechanism may be needed. That is *time slicing*, used to periodically alter the dispatching priorities of address spaces in one or more performance groups.

## Time Slicing

For systems with conflicting CPU-intensive workloads, time slicing may be used to apportion favored access to the CPU resource. Another common use of time slicing is to restrict the impact of address spaces with widely varying CPU demand on the rest of the system. Notorious examples include JES2 and DFHSM (HSM, IBM's Hierarchical Storage Manager).

Returning to our original view of time slicing, consider a system with two independent CICS subsystems, each serving a different group of users one time zone apart.[13] Each of them needs equal preference for the CPU for 40 percent of the time. Two performance groups of TSO users in first period need such preference ten percent of the time, and no workload is to be preferred the remaining ten percent of the time.

With time slicing, we can designate a normal DP for each of the three competing workloads and a higher TSDP for the favored period. We also need to specify a time-slicing pattern, TSPTRN, to select each time-slice group for the appropriate number of time slices, in order. The skeleton IPS entries might look like this:

```
TSPTRN=(1,2,1,2,3,1,2,1,2,*)

...

PGN=5, (TSGRP=1,DP=F62,TSDP=F63,.../*CICS1*/
PGN=6, (TSGRP=2,DP=F62,TSDP=F63,.../*CICS2*/
PGN=8, (TSGRP=3,DP=F62,TSDP=F63,.../*TSO1 */
PGN=10, (TSGRP=3,DP=F62,TSDP=F63,.../*TSO2*/
PGN=14, (DP=F62,... /* Other Workload */
```

The TSO address spaces will be preferred only once per ten SRM seconds and will compete equally for the CPU another SRM second in ten. On fast systems this is no problem, but on a relatively slow CPU, such as an IBM 4381, there may be a

13 The time zone misaligment invalidates any scheme for statically distributing the CPU resource.

perceptible irregularity in TSO response time. To avoid this problem, the parameter

`TUNIT=5`

might be placed ahead of the TSPTRN line in the IPS, thus performing the time slicing five times per SRM second.

## Layout

A sample layout of dispatching priorities is shown in Figure 6-1. Creating such a layout helps to ensure that SRM (and the person

| DP | Workload | Comment/Explanation |
|----|----------|---------------------|
| FF | *MASTER* | Predetermined priority |
| FF | RASP | Predetermined priority |
| FF | GRS | Predetermined priority |
| FF | DUMPSRV | Predetermined priority |
| FF | CONSOLE | Predetermined priority |
| FF | SMF | Predetermined priority |
| FF | CATALOG | Predetermined priority |
| F94 | | Reserved for emergencies |
| F93 | REALMON | Main real-time monitor |
| F92 | LATERMON | Historical monitor |
| F91 | VTAM | Network manager |
| F90 | VTAMMON | General-use VTAM-connected monitor |
| M9 | | System address spaces (SMS, LLA, VLF) |
| F83 | DB2MON | DB2 subsystem monitor |
| F82 | DB2SUBSY | DB2 address spaces |
| F81 | CICSMON | CICS subsystem monitor |
| F80 | CICSTOR | CICS terminal-owning region |
| F8 | | TSO first period |
| F73 | JES2 | JES2 TSDP |
| F72 | CICSAORx | CICS application regions |
| F71 | DFHSM | HSM TSDP |
| F70 | RMF | RMF writer address space |
| M7 | IMSMON | IMS monitors |
| F63 | IMSCTL | IMS control region |
| M6 | | TSO second period |
| M6 | IMSMPRx | IMS Message Processing Regions |
| F53 | JES2 | JES2 base DP |
| M5 | | TSO later periods |
| M5 | | Ordinary started tasks |
| M5 | | Batch first period |
| F4 | CICSTEST | Test subsystem monitor |
| M3 | | Batch later periods |
| M2 | HAPNMON | Change monitor |
| F13 | DFHSM | HSM base DP |
| M0 | "Sponge" | Measures CPU reserve |

Figure 6-1. Sample dispatching priority layout (ESA)

in charge of directing SRM) is in control of dispatching priorities and that the priorities in the IPS reflect the installation's work-load priorities.

In creating a dispatching priority layout, the suggestions made in Chapter 4 relating to the ideal of a "well-ordered CPU" should be reviewed. Remember that certain system address spaces have predetermined dispatching priorities, and that server address spaces usually need to be above their users in priority. Most monitors need to rank above the workloads they scrutinize to give accurate measurements of utilizations and delays.

In the sample, which assumes APGRNG=(0-15), the MVS/ESA address spaces whose priorities are predetermined are shown in order. We assume that the system supports production TSO, CICS (with DB2), and a somewhat less important IMS service. JES2 and HSM are time-sliced to ensure that response-critical address spaces may be dispatched with minimum delay.

## 6.2. Summary

We have introduced numerous SRM terms and, in passing, some representative parameters as well. With this preparation, we can move on to the next two chapters, presenting SRM parameters in a more structured manner.

# 7

# SRM Parameters I: OPT

Successful MVS performance management entails far more than merely selecting the right values for SRM controls. Numerous other PARMLIB parameters are important in determining how a system runs, and the physical configuration and its interaction with the workload is still the key fundamental factor influencing system performance and throughput. Finally, no matter how well the system is configured and set up, application programs designed without an appreciation of performance factors can undo it all.

On the other hand, the SRM parameters remain very accessible and can have a significant effect on system performance, workload performance, and throughput, even to the extent of compensating for configuration and application deficiencies. For that reason, but always with the awareness that we're looking at only part of the picture, we now look at the SRM controls in detail.

The IEAOPTxx (OPT) member of SYS1.PARMLIB defines global controls for SRM. In general, OPT parameters affect SRM algorithms directly, and workloads indirectly, through the operation of the algorithms. We'll consider these parameters in logical groupings, in approximate order of importance.

## 7.1. MPL Adjustment

*Initialization and Tuning* discusses at some length the operation of the algorithm controlling systemwide MPL. The basic process requires a unanimous vote of MPL adjustment controls to increase MPL, while a single vote can cause MPL decrease. One of the "voters" is a composite of three OPT parameters; all the others are based on single OPT parameters.

To set OPT parameters correctly is not merely a tuning action in response to some crisis. It is more like adjusting the driver's seat and the mirrors in one's car: the car will operate as it is received from the dealer, but it won't be as safe and effective as it can be, and it might be uncomfortable and dangerous.

The default values for many MPL adjustment parameters are inappropriate, tending to reduce MPL before the CPU is fully utilized, yet allowing paging delay to rise to harmful values on some systems without reducing MPL. In systems with expanded storage, MPL is not adjusted in response to page movement rates or migration activity.

Ideally, MPL should be controlled so as to keep demand page-in delay of key workloads, and CPU delay arising from expanded storage page movement, to acceptable values. Unfortunately, there is no MPL control parameter based on paging delay or CPU delay, none is workload-specific, nor is any MPL control based on expanded storage measurements. Lacking such ideal controls, less direct indicators of delay are used in the OPT. These include the page fault rate, the storage reference age (UIC), the demand paging rate, the size of the auxiliary storage manager's (ASM's) queue of pages to be moved, CPU utilization, real storage utilization, and average page delay time. These controls are of various degrees of usefulness, and all are somewhat flawed.

Most experts agree that the basic control of MPL should depend principally on the *page fault rate*, the rate of non-swap, non-VIO, page-ins from auxiliary storage, with other parameters either nullified or set to values well outside a normal controlling range and thus responsive only to extreme problems. In a system with a homogeneous paging configuration, with paging devices that all perform alike, page fault rate should be a good indicator of overall page-in delay.

The flaw in the original IBM definition of page fault rate is that it also included *reclaims*, stolen pages "rescued" from the page-out queue in response to subsequent page fault interrupts. Usually there are few reclaims in systems without expanded storage, but very high reclaim rates have been seen in systems with expanded storage. This flaw was eliminated in MVS/SP 3.1.3, the MVS/ESA version announced on October 24, 1989.

Each of the MPL adjustment parameters is discussed in the following paragraphs, followed by a summary table of default values and recommendations. They are presented in estimated order of importance.

## 7.1.1. RCCPTRT, page fault rate

In spite of the reclaim problem in earlier MVS releases, page fault rate remains the best available (to the SRM) indicator of storage constraint and thus the most appropriate control variable for MPL. As of SP 3.1.3, reclaims are no longer included in RCCPTRT. In a default MVS system, RCCPTRT is set to (1000,1000), normally nullifying it as a control.[1]

There is no way that a definitive recommendation for RCCPTRT can be given *a priori*. The IBM default can thus be understood. The best we can do is to suggest values based on the ability of the paging configuration to resolve page faults in some acceptable time frame.

Based on modeled results, device limits are suggested (in the table on the next page) for commonly used paging devices, based on minimum attainable device response times for several levels of underlying path busy $(B_p)$ and device busy $(B_d)$.

---

1   Note that (1000,1000) is not a distinguished value causing a parameter to be disregarded. Sometimes the numbers measured against those parameters do get into that range and cause MPL change. To cause a parameter to be disregarded as completely as possible, it should be set to the "unfavorable" extreme value of its range.

| Sustainable Paging Rates, Page-ins per Second | | | | | | | |
|---|---|---|---|---|---|---|---|
| Device | Response Time Target | $B_p$: | 0% | | 10% | | 20% | |
| | | $B_d$: | 0% | 10% | 0% | 10% | 0% | 10% |
| 3350 | 25 ms | | 10 | 7 | 6 | 4 | 2 | 0 |
| 3375 | 25 ms | | 12 | 9 | 7 | 5 | 2 | 0 |
| 3380/370 | 25 ms | | 20 | 16 | 14 | 12 | 9 | 7 |
| 3380/XA/ESA | 25 ms | | 20 | 17 | 19 | 16 | 17 | 14 |
| 3990 Cache | 5 ms | | 68 | 53 | 67 | 53 | 65 | 52 |
| SSD[1] 3.0MB | 4 ms | | 145 | 122 | 134 | 113 | 125 | 106 |
| SSD 4.5MB | 3 ms | | 176 | 147 | 163 | 136 | 153 | 128 |
| [1] Solid State Device, usually emulating an IBM 3380 | | | | | | | | |

Using these paging rates as guideline loading limits, one would choose the underlying device and path utilizations corresponding most closely to the actual paging configuration, read off the page-in rates, and multiply by the number of local page data sets, less one for each 100 logged-on TSO users in a system without swap data sets. The result will be a first approximation to the correct upper limit for RCCPTRT. Set the lower limit of RCCPTRT to 80 percent of that value.

**Example:** Suppose there are five local page data sets on dedicated (no underlying device busy) 3380s on lightly loaded paths (about 10% underlying path busy each) in an XA environment with 200 active TSO users. The suggested device limit is 19 page-ins per second. Discounting two devices for TSO swapping from the five locals, the upper value chosen for RCCPTRT should be 3 x 19 or 57. The lower limit should be 80 percent of that, or 46. In the OPT, specify:

### RCCPTRT=(46,57)

After a reasonable period of measurement, RCCPTRT should be adjusted upward if unilateral swaps are triggered by a high page fault rate when the system is not suffering excessive paging delay. It should be made lower if paging delay is excessive and MPL reduction is not taking place to compensate.

## 7.1.2. RCCUICT, UIC

Controlling MPL based on UIC depends on the assumption that UIC is an indicator of storage constraint. In systems without expanded storage, this is rarely so, hence the extreme default of (2,4) for this parameter. (UIC is the only MPL control for which *low* values indicate constraint.) Conceivably, low UIC can occur in a system with a stable and static workload and just enough real storage for it all to fit. In systems with more variable workloads and a high degree of real storage re-use, page stealing may commence before UICs get low enough to trigger MPL adjustment. Subsequent page faulting will cause MPL adjustment if RCCPTRT is set correctly. Again, the UIC control will not come into use.

With expanded storage, the picture changes. Page stealing is innocuous if there is sufficient available expanded storage. Delay due to page-in from auxiliary storage is handled well by RCCPTRT as usual, but other sources of delay are possible. If the page movement rate to and from expanded storage exceeds about 500 pages per second per CPU,[2] CPU delay will rise significantly. Such excessive page movement is a symptom of central storage exhaustion, and low UIC is a moderately correlated indicator of that constraint.

In systems with expanded storage, RCCUICT should thus be set initially to (10,15) and the page movement rate carefully monitored. The settings of RCCUICT may be reduced if peak page movement rates are significantly below 500, and made more stringent (increased) if page movement rates exceed the guideline.

## 7.1.3. PAGERT1 and PAGERT2, demand paging rate

The default values for PAGERT1 and PAGERT2 are based on processor model and may be found in Chapter 5 of *Initialization and Tuning*. The defaults are based on "unconstrained" paging configurations usually found only in laboratories. Under these conditions, the paging rate causing five percent incremental uniprocessor CPU utilization becomes the upper limit for PAGERT1,

---

2 This guideline applies to the IBM 3090-180S and its dyadic, triadic, and MP counterparts.

and the lower limit is about 80 percent of that. If PAGERT2 is not specified in the OPT, it is derived from PAGERT1 for the appropriate uniprocessor by the formula

$$\text{PAGERT2} = \text{PAGERT1} * \text{N(processors)} * .85$$

In most real systems, the paging configuration does have constraints. PAGERT1 (and PAGERT2) should be set according to the degree of constraint in the paging configuration. If RCCPTRT has been set according to device limits as discussed above, PAGERT1 and PAGERT2 should each be set to 1.8 times the respective RCCPTRT values, and adjustment of PAGERT1 and PAGERT2 should parallel that of RCCPTRT.

Why set PAGERT1 in a multiprocessor system, or PAGERT2 in a uniprocessor? On rare occasions, a dyadic may come up with a CPU disabled. In such a situation, reverting to a CPU-based MPL control default is doubly inappropriate. On the other hand, routinely setting both PAGERT1 and PAGERT2 removes one avoidable step from the plan for upgrading a uniprocessor CPU.

PAGERT$x$ is not a simple MPL control. It will allow MPL increase by itself but will only call for MPL decrease if CPU utilization exceeds the high threshold of RCCCPUP, or if the "average" page transfer time exceeds the high threshold of RCCMSPT. Under normal circumstances, neither of the additional parameters will call for MPL decrease.

The default values of PAGERT$x$, RCCCPUP, and RCCMSPT, with the turned-off default of RCCPTRT, together ensure that a default MVS system will tend to allow MPL increase until the CPU is saturated or the UIC approaches zero. RCCCPUP and RCCMSPT are discussed below in more detail.

## 7.1.4. RCCCPUT, CPU utilization

The idea of controlling the MPL based on CPU utilization seems to be consistent with the idea (a recurring theme in *Initialization and Tuning*) that the SRM controls "access to resources." However, access to the CPU is controlled effectively by adjusting relative dispatching priorities. Moving address spaces in and out of the multiprogramming set by means of swapping has two effects:

- Constraint on central (real) storage varies according to system MPL.

- Swapped-out address spaces receive no service.

Denying service may be necessary under some special circumstances. Usually, however, the denial of service associated with MPL adjustment is too transitory to deal with disruptive address spaces—those causing contention with other, more important address spaces. Such an address space, if swappable, needs to be RESET via operator command to a special performance group denoting a domain with (0,0) constraints, to be *kept* swapped out until the potential for contention is removed.[3] (It may be just as effective to put the offender in a more favorable performance group with higher dispatching priority and a domain with generous constraints *if* it is a batch job with a predictably short time to completion.)

Since MVS/SP 2.1.7, the maximum value for RCCCPUT has been 128 rather than 101, as it was in earlier MVS releases. With this limit, it is now possible to "dial in" an acceptable range of CPU overcommitment. With a range of (103,107), for instance, SRM will allow MPL increase even if the CPU had no wait time and an average of three address spaces received no service during an SRM summarization (RM2) interval. MPL reduction will be forced if seven or more address spaces received no service during the interval.

Why should such CPU overcommitment be desirable? With adequate real storage, it is harmless to leave inert address spaces in the multiprogramming set. Properly chosen dispatching priorities will control CPU access. Low priority address spaces will be in a position to take advantage of any momentary drop in higher-priority CPU demand and will receive service without the delay of even the most efficient swap-in. In an MVS system with a

---

3  Nonswappable "problem" address spaces can be even more disruptive. If contention is caused by mere ownership or allocation of resources rather than by usage, the address space may need to be shut down and restarted at some other time.

mixed workload and a well-balanced hardware configuration, a modest level of planned CPU overcommitment will get the most out of the hardware.

With a more stable and less varied workload, restricting CPU overcommitment will ensure that high-priority activity (such as I/O completion SRBs) triggered by low-priority address spaces will be less likely to tie up the CPU when "important" address spaces need it.

In systems running under IBM's PR/SM LPAR, NAS's MLPF, Amdahl's MDF, or VM, the SRM does not see a correct picture of WAIT time unless the WAIT COMPLETE option (of PR/SM) or another corresponding parameter is selected. Since this option can be harmful to interactive response time, it is usually not selected. Consequently, any MVS system running in a logically or virtually partitioned mode will be exposed to spurious MPL adjustment based on high CPU utilization, unless RCCCPUT (and RCCCPUP as well) is set to a range exceeding 100.

Summarizing the considerations for setting RCCCPUT:

- Basic recommendation: with adequate central storage and a TSO/batch workload, set RCCCPUT to (104,108) for a uniprocessor, to (108,112) for a dyadic or two-way, to (112,116) for a triadic, and so forth.

- With some degree of storage constraint, reduce the constraints by one or two units for each CPU.

- With high-priority workloads very sensitive to CPU delay, such as CICS, and very I/O-intensive low-priority workloads, cut back RCCCPUT one or two units in both the high and low values, per CPU.

- In a partitioned environment (other than physically partitioned), make sure that RCCCPUT is at least (101,101) regardless of any other factors.

- Adjust RCCCPUT upward if no significant CPU or storage delay is found in key workloads, and if address spaces are unilaterally swapped out, with RCCCPUT as a cause of MPL reduction.[4]

- Reduce RCCCPUT if this parameter rarely causes MPL reduction while workloads at relatively high dispatching priority experience significant CPU delay.

## 7.1.5. RCCCPUP, CPU utilization (combined algorithm)

The assumption of the combined algorithm is that an MVS system can accept an MPL increase if the demand paging rate is low, *or* if the CPU is not very busy while the page delay time is low. The combinatorial logic is complemented for the case of MPL decrease, as described above under the PAGERT*x* parameters.

The default range for RCCCPUP (95,98) will have virtually no effect on MPL increase and might lead to MPL decrease in rare circumstances. With correct settings for RCCPTRT and RCCCPUT, RCCCPUP becomes irrelevant. It should be set to high values (128,128) to nullify its occasional effect.

## 7.1.6. RCCMSPT, page delay (combined algorithm)

RCCMSPT is calculated according to Little's Formula, a standard statistical formula applying to a steady state queueing system. In its MVS application, Little's Formula takes the form

$$MSPP = ASMQ / PGRT$$

MSPP stands for "milliseconds per page," the measure of page delay time and the value compared with the constraints specified for RCCMSPT. MSPP is flawed in so many respects that it should be summarily ruled out as an MPL control. If we consider a system without swap data sets or expanded storage, the two quantities from which MSPP is derived are both nonuniform in character and far from steady-state. The ASM queue contains single pages and blocks of pages, private and common, page-ins and page-outs, page steals, page faults, swap trim, swap groups, VIO windows, and expanded storage pages to be migrated. Paging rate, however defined, is volatile over SRM samples as well as across summarization intervals.

---

4  Chapter 10 describes monitoring techniques to determine if such conditions exist.

Let us assume that our somewhat unrealistic system also has no swapping and no VIO. In this case, MSPP may be meaningful. If the system is busy, the total paging rate might be 100 pages per second and the ASM queue might average 10 pages. MSPP is thus

**10 pages / 100 pages per second =
.1 second = 100 milliseconds**

This value is the same as the low default threshold of RCCMSPT. (The high default is 130.)

Now suppose that our system is nearly dormant in the dead of night; batch is running, and a few system programmers are on TSO. With the available frame queue depleted by a full complement of production batch jobs, TSO swaps will be physical. The average demand paging rate is close to zero, say two pages per second, and the average ASM queue length is 3 pages, mostly due to occasional peaks of swap activity during an RM2 interval. MSPP will then be

**3 pages / 2 pages per second =
1.5 seconds = 1500 milliseconds.**

Note now that the CPU may be saturated with efficient batch, so RCCCPUP is above its default lower bound of 95 percent utilization. With MSPP above the RCCMSPT lower limit of 100 milliseconds, the MPL will be kept from increasing, and TSO users may encounter inconsistent response times due to MPL delay. Such caution does not seem to be justified.

## 7.1.7. RCCPDLT, page delay

The values specified for RCCPDLT are compared with the same MSPP value as those for RCCMSPT. The default for RCCPDLT, however, is (1000,1000), so this control is nominally disabled. As we saw in the discussion of RCCMSPT, MSPP can rise above 1000 when there is clearly no system problem. Unlike RCCMSPT, RCCPDLT can by itself cause MPL decrease. To avoid odd incidents of MPL decrease for no apparent reason, a better setting might be the permitted maximums, (32767,32767).

### 7.1.8. RCCASMT, ASM queue length

This parameter is defaulted at (1000,1000). The only recommendation that can be made for RCCASMT is to turn it off more firmly, setting the values to (32767,32767). ASM queue length is too volatile to serve as an MPL control, especially in systems with mixed workloads.

### 7.1.9. RCCFXTT, total fixed/allocated storage

The idea of controlling MPL based on the amount of real storage fixed or currently allocated for movement by the Auxiliary Storage Manager is appealing. Isn't a lack of available storage just what we're trying to prevent? A fallacy of this control is that the specification for RCCFXTT is not in frames but in percentage of frames. The default range of 66–72 percent, on a large system with 256 megabytes, would result in MPL reduction with 18,350 frames neither fixed nor allocated for page-in or page-out. If this control causes spurious MPL reduction or prevents MPL increase, its values should be raised closer to 100 percent.

### 7.1.10. RCCFXET, fixed below 16MB

This control, similar to RCCFXTT and similarly flawed, is designed to allow I/O with format-0 CCWs to proceed as it must, using only real storage below 16 megabytes. The need for this control will eventually fade as I/O routines are switched over to Format-1 CCWs.

### 7.1.11. Summary of MPL adjustment parameters

The table on the next page summarizes the preceding discussion of the SRM MPL adjustment parameters maintained in the OPT.

| Name | Default | Change to | Comment |
|------|---------|-----------|---------|
| RCCPTRT | 1000,1000 | Device-related | Most effective control |
| PAGERT1 | CPU-related | 1.8 X RCCPTRT | Must change default |
| PAGERT1 | CPU-related | 1.8 X RCCPTRT | Must change default |
| PAGERT2 | CPU-related | 1.8 X RCCPTRT | Must change default |
| RCCUICT | 2,4 | 10,15 | May help with E.S. |
| RCCCPUT | 98.0,100.9 | 104,108 & up | Allow full CPU loading |
| RCCCPUP | 95,98 | 128,128 | Disable! |
| RCCASMT | 1000,1000 | 32767,32767 | Ineffective control |
| RCCFXTT | 66,72 | higher if active | Ineffective control |
| RCCFXET | 82,88 | higher if active | Verify necessity |
| RCCMSPT | 100,130 | 32767,32767 | Disable! |
| RCCPDLT | 1000,1000 | 32767,32767 | Disable! |

# 7.2. Expanded Storage Selection Criteria

Pages are selected for move-out to expanded storage based on the interaction of the expanded storage migration age with a set of criteria in the *Criteria Age Table* (*CAT*). There are ten different categories of pages enumerated in the CAT, and most of them are further divided into three workload categories, specified with FORTRAN-style subscripts in the OPT.

Despite this complexity we will see that there may not yet be enough selectivity. The subscript values are:

> 0—for nonswappable, or privileged address spaces, or common-area pages, in paging decisions; for privileged address spaces only, in swapping decisions.

> 2—for all TSO address spaces in paging decisions; in swapping decisions, for TSO users in terminal wait only.

> 1—for address spaces neither in category 0 nor category 2—usually batch.

There is no selectivity within each of these broad classes as yet. We may in the future see these first-generation expanded storage controls brought into the existing MVS workload-oriented control structure—performance periods of performance groups. The only performance-period-related control pertaining to expanded storage is to specify storage isolation. Storage-isolated pages are protected only from LRU migration selection.

A page will be sent to expanded storage if the current migration age (for expanded storage as a whole) exceeds the address space's (or common area's) criterion[5] age for the class of page being considered. For swap trim and non-terminal-wait swap working-set pages, the migration age is augmented by the current system wide high UIC. For terminal-wait working-set pages, the UIC correction also applies, and the address space's think time is added to the criterion age as well.

The defaults for the initial set of expanded storage controls appear to have been selected before appreciable production experience had been acquired. When migration age gets down to the maximum criterion age in the default CAT, 100 seconds, migration may already have reached disruptively high levels. When the ESCTVIO and ESCTBDS controls were added in enhancements to MVS/SP 2.2.0 and MVS/SP 3.1.0, respectively, they were both set at a more aggressive default of 900 seconds.

The expanded storage controls are described in Chapter 5 of *Initialization and Tuning*. The default settings are appropriate for systems with adequate expanded storage. (In such a system, migration age is rarely less than 1000 seconds.) In systems with limited expanded storage, the criteria ages for less important workloads may be increased above observed migration ages to bar the pages of those workloads from expanded storage when it is fully utilized.

# 7.3. Logical Swap Controls

Logical swapping was an opportunistic enhancement to MVS at a time when "large" real storage first became available. A very large available frame count was perceived as an indicator of excess capacity. Using those frames for logical swap improved average TSO response time and contributed to the marketing

---

5    I cannot bring myself to use *criteria* as if it were singular.

momentum in support of the proposition that MVS could make good use of practically any amount of real storage.

Given the marketing climate of the time, it is easy to see why the original controls in MVS/SE1 for logical swap were firmly biased to encourage logical swaps over physical. When those controls were made visible in the OPT in SE2 and in later releases, the guideline of release-to-release compatibility dictated that the controls would not change.

Subsequent evolution has replaced the narrowly defined "logical swap" with "processor storage swap" in systems with expanded storage. The logical swap evaluation is made first, but if it fails, the trimmed working set of an address space may be retained in central storage on a pending-out queue for expanded storage, to be moved out only when the central storage frames are needed to fend off a cycle of page stealing. In such a system, "turning off" logical swapping may appear to be ineffective. It is effective in a strict and narrow sense; however, a pending processor storage swap to expanded storage looks just like a logical swap, hence the appearance that turning off logical swap is ignored.

Logical swapping is controlled by five OPT parameters. One (LSCTMTE) specifies the range of "think times" that the logical swap decision criterion may assume. The other four controls move the criterion up and down through the think time range. The two controls on fixed and allocated storage are absolute: Think time will be reduced if either control (LSCTFTT or LSCTFET) is above its maximum, and it will not be increased if either storage control exceeds its minimum.

The UIC (LSCTUCT) and AFQ (LSCTAFQ) controls are permissive. Assuming no effect due to the storage controls, think time will be increased if either unreferenced interval count or available frame count is over its maximum. Think time will be decreased if either is below its minimum. Conflict is resolved in favor of decrease. The UIC control serves another purpose: When the system UIC is less than half the lower limit, no new logical swaps will be allowed for the duration of the current RM2 interval.

Another use for the current think-time value is as an absolute control for making nonterminal-wait swaps logical. If the current think-time is at least five seconds, such logical swaps are allowed.

## 7.3.1. Logical swapping defaults

The following box summarizes the parameters governing logical swapping and their default values.

| Summary of Logical Swap Defaults | | | |
|---|---|---|---|
| Name | Default | Unit | Definition |
| LSCTMTE | 0,30 | seconds | Think time range |
| LSCTAFQ | 0,300 | frames | Available frame count |
| LSCTFET | 76,82 | percent | Fixed frames below 16 MB |
| LSCTFTT | 58,66 | percent | Fixed or ASM-allocated (all) |
| LSCTUCT | 20,00 | seconds | Unreferenced Interval Count |

## 7.3.2. Tuning with logical swapping

Because logical swapping is strongly preferred by the default controls, those with storage-constrained systems may wish to reduce the preference. Two approaches may be taken: either reduce the think time range or make the controls more disposed to reduce the think time. Both are usually done.

There is a caution that must be observed in this respect, as in all cases of tuning by means of adjusting the OPT controls. Any currently effective control will tend to place its controlling variable in its "happy"[6] range if the controlled variable is free to be adjusted. For example, suppose we set LSCTUCT to (40,50) and LSCTMTE to (1,10). If there is an abundant supply of logical swap candidates of varying think times, the system-wide high UIC will tend to settle somewhere between 40 and 50, with a

---

6   OPT controls were often called "happy values" in the past. "Happy" referred to the condition when the controlling variable was between the lower and upper limits, resulting in no change to the controlled variable. A more apocryphal origin goes back to the days when there were essentially no OPT parameters and SRM controls were adjusted by ZAPping values in MVS control blocks. To alter such a parameter successfully (without crashing the system) and effectively (producing the desired result) was a happy occasion.

think time criterion somewhere between one and ten seconds. If at the same time the UIC control of MPL (RCCUICT) is set to (20,30), the free adjustment of MPL will tend to keep UIC between 20 and 30. The UIC cannot be both between 20 and 30 and between 40 and 50. In this case, it will probably rise to the higher range and UIC will cease to be effective as an MPL control. If storage contention increases, UIC will fall to the lower range, leaving think time pinned at its lower limit but serving then as an effective MPL control.

This interaction between free and controlled variables, and the switching of control from one area to another, is not necessarily inappropriate; it just needs to be understood. If the ranges had been reversed, the SRM might have caused oscillation or other signs of instability as it tried to reconcile the conflicting demand to reduce MPL while increasing logical swapping, both based on UIC.

### 7.3.3. Typical logical swap adjustments

Following are a few examples of adjusting the logical swap controls from their default values:

- In systems without expanded storage and with some degree of real storage constraint, it is common to alter the logical swap controls to reduce the amount of logical swapping under normal conditions, and to cut it off before delay becomes unacceptable. The following are typical and usually produce the desired results:

$$\text{LSCTMTE}=(1,6)$$
$$\text{LSCTUCT}=(30,40)$$
$$\text{LSCTAFQ}=(250,350)$$

- With expanded storage and adequate central storage, logical swapping is sometimes encouraged more than by default:

$$\text{LSCTMTE}=(5,60)$$

- With expanded storage and with some degree of central storage constraint, severely reducing logical swap but still permitting processor storage swaps to expanded storage, will allow central storage to be fully utilized but will make the central storage frames available for prompt push-out when they are needed. The following OPT values have this effect, but must be adjusted based on measurement:

```
LSCTMTE=(0,6)
LSCTUCT=(40,50)
LSCTAFQ=(300,450)
```

## 7.4. Storage Load Balancing

Storage load balancing is an effective means of improving system throughput when there is some real storage constraint along with a supply of out-and-ready swappable address spaces of widely differing working-set sizes, all in the same domain. The load-balancing algorithm works by adjusting an address space's swap recommendation value (RV) if the address space meets the criteria for it to be regarded as a significant user of real storage. The RV is increased if storage is currently perceived by the SRM as unconstrained, and decreased if it is seen to be constrained.

Because storage load balancing was not included in the original definition of "response-throughput bias" (RTB) in MVS/SE1, it is inoperative by default. To activate storage load balancing and derive benefit from it, the following steps are needed:

- Activate the load balancer by specifying MSO=1.0 *in the OPT*. This MSO parameter has *nothing* to do with the MSO weighting factor for MSO service units in the IPS service definition coefficients. The value for MSO may range from 0 (turned off) to 9.9.

- Ensure that exchange swapping may take place by specifying relatively low ISVs in the last performance periods for batch and TSO. ISVs of 10,000 service units might be appropriate.

- Place all address spaces that will be candidates for load balancing in the smallest possible number of domains. A single domain would be ideal. All of the address spaces should be on the same objective (or very similar objectives) as well.

- To permit some discrimination in unilateral swapping, make sure that the selected domain has broad constraints.

- Ensure that RCCPTRT is properly set up.

- Examine the defaults in Chapter 5 of *Initialization and Tuning* for the MCCSBxxx OPT parameters (there are *eight* of them) and specify different values for those that appear wrong for the current workload. The default value for MCCSBSIG, 40 frames, for example, would generally be too low as a frame-count selector of significant real storage users.

- Finally, select address spaces for storage load balancing by specifying RTB=S or RTB=1 in each performance period of each performance group for which the load balancer is to be active.

## 7.5. CPU Mean-Time-to-Wait Adjustment

One OPT parameter used to control *CPU* load balancing (the use of which is *not* recommended) has another use—to set the interval of mean-time-to-wait associated with each dispatching priority step in the MTTW algorithm. The parameter is CCCSIGUR and has a default value of 45, in units of SRM milliseconds. If several dissimilar address spaces are in MTTW group $x$ and their actual dispatching priorities, as seen with a performance monitor, are not spread out in the range $x0$ through $x9$, an adjustment to CCCSIGUR could ensure that MTTW works properly.

If the priorities are clumped at $x9$, it appears that all address spaces have short MTTW. Thus CCCSIGUR is too large and should be decreased. If all address spaces have the lowest dispatching priority in the group, CCCSIGUR is too small and should be increased. Start by doubling or halving the value, then make smaller adjustments until the desired result is achieved.

## 7.6. Selective I/O Enablement Control

In systems with multiple CPUs, MVS/XA and MVS/ESA start normal processing after IPL with only one CPU enabled to handle I/O interrupts. An additional CPU is enabled when the percentage of I/O interrupts handled by the TEST PENDING IN-TERRUPT (TPI) instruction exceeds the upper threshold of the CPENABLE OPT parameter. A CPU will be disabled when the TPI percentage falls below the lower CPENABLE threshold. The CPENABLE defaults are (10,30).

If CPENABLE is to be changed from its default values, the following effects must be considered:

- If the CPENABLE range is increased, the CPU(s) not handling I/O interrupts will run more efficiently by avoiding status-switching overhead. There will be a small increase in I/O completion time owing to CPU queueing.

- Decreasing the CPENABLE range will minimize CPU queueing in handling I/O completions at the expense of increasing status-switching CPU overhead on all enabled CPUs.

- In a logically partitioned system, a decreased CPENABLE range might cause extra switching of processors between partitions or domains, with whatever overhead the hardware and microcode impose.

If the most important workload on the system is heavily dominated by I/O, reducing the CPENABLE range might improve I/O response times to a slight extent.

## 7.7. I/O Load Balancing

I/O load balancing is based on the proposition that I/O contention from some workloads can be disruptive and that the contention may be reduced if an offending address space is swapped out for a while. With today's devices taking full advantage of multiple paths, this kind of relief is rarely needed.

I/O load balancing acts similarly to storage load balancing, discussed above. In this case, however, an address space's RV is adjusted if it is considered by SRM to be a significant user of a logical path. If the path is "overutilized," the adjustment will be negative; it will be positive if the logical path is seen by the SRM to be underutilized.

The parameters controlling I/O load balancing are discussed in Chapter 5 of *Initialization and Tuning*. The defaults are usually satisfactory. In general, I/O load balancing should be specified only for *very* I/O-intensive batch jobs, such as DASD backups.

## 7.8. CPU Load Balancing

This final load balancer is of little benefit and its use is normally not recommended. Certain pathological workloads may have very large working sets and be very CPU-intensive as well. If sufficient central storage is not available to accommodate such an address space along with some more normal address spaces, CPU load balancing may be used to periodically cause the disruptive address space to be swapped out. Usually, a better policy is to combine time slicing with "negative storage isolation," leaving the CPU-and-storage hog in the multiprogramming set while stealing its least recently used frames.

## 7.9. Miscellaneous Controls

Certain additional and largely unrelated controls are in the OPT. We consider them briefly:

- **CNTCLIST**, a YES/NO variable with a default of NO. If YES is specified, the individual commands in a TSO CLIST or REXX EXEC are counted as individual SRM transactions. The default of NO counts the entire CLIST or EXEC as a single transaction.

  One application of CNTCLIST=YES is to ensure preferential treatment of large CLISTs that constitute end-user applications or that are invoked by LOGON procedures.

- **CNTNSW**, a YES/NO variable with a default of NO. If YES is specified, non-swappable address spaces will be counted in the current MPLs of their respective domains. If this choice is made, the minMPLs of the domains should reflect at least the current number of non-swappable address spaces.

  CNTNSW=YES might be chosen if a particular work-group moves between using TSO and testing nonswappable programs. The overall system impact from this group might be managed by placing both their TSO sessions and their test address spaces in the same domain and controlling that domain's contention index by means of a DOBJ.

- **DVIO**, a YES/NO variable with a default of YES. The default allows "directed VIO." VIO page-outs will go only to page data sets not designated as NONVIO in IEASYSxx or in a PAGEADD command. Specifying NO defeats directed VIO even if the NONVIO designation is used for one or more page data sets.

  Directed VIO can be beneficial in a mixed paging configuration if VIO is to be kept off relatively small high-speed paging devices. It should not be used with homogeneous paging configurations.

- **ERV** (enqueue residence value) specifies a number of CPU (TCB) service units an address space must accumulate before it may be considered for a unilateral or exchange swap-out if it holds an ENQ on a resource needed by another address space, or an exclusive ENQ leading to a device RESERVE. The default ERV is 500 CPU service units.

- **MCCFXEPR** and **MCCFXTPR**, percentage variables with defaults of 92 and 80, respectively. The first applies to fixed frames in central storage below 16 megabytes, the second to fixed pages, or those allocated for page-in or page-out, in all of central storage. If either threshold of real storage allocation is exceeded, SRM will signal a pageable storage shortage and begin a series of actions described in grisly detail in Chapter 5 of *Initialization and Tuning*. If the pageable storage shortage condition occurs with any regularity (i.e., more than once a week), the thresholds might be raised slightly and the cause investigated. If a pathological condition is responsible, raising the thresholds will have little effect.

* **RMPTTOM** specifies a scale factor for SRM invocation. The default is 1000, signifying a normal 1000 SRM milliseconds per SRM second. Reducing RMPTTOM will increase the frequency of SRM data-gathering; decision-making will receive some minimal benefit, but overhead will increase. RMPTTOM might be increased in an MVS test system running under VM, to reduce overhead somewhat. It should not be increased in a production MVS system running in a preferred, V=R, or V=F virtual machine.

* **SELTAPE** provides options for tape drive allocation selection in a list of eligible devices. NEXT, the default, designates selection in ascending device number order, returning to the lowest device number after the highest is allocated. Other options are RANDOM, FIRST, and LOWEST. FIRST differs from LOWEST in that the list is not necessarily in device-number order. Chapter 5 of *Initialization and Tuning* contains a description of how the eligible device list is generated.

## 7.10. Summary

OPT parameters can have a profound effect on MVS performance and the effective use of the hardware resource. Far too many MVS systems are operated with no OPT whatever, or an OPT laboriously constructed to duplicate the basic MVS defaults. The most dedicated IBM apologist cannot defend this choice. IBM's own frequent advice in publications and presentations is to establish a set of customized OPT controls, especially the all-important RCCPTRT.

As important as a correct OPT might be, it is not enough to do this job alone. The complementary task of controlling how the system allocates its resources to workloads must be done by creating an appropriate IPS. Making sure that workloads are properly assigned to performance groups is done by the ICS, another member of SYS1.PARMLIB.

The next chapter covers IPS and ICS parameters and choices.

# SRM Parameters II: IPS and ICS

## 8.1. Installation Performance Specification (IPS)

An IPS tells the SRM how to treat each address space in the system, and to some extent how to treat the common area as well. Within the overall bounds established by the OPT, IPS parameters specify how MPL is to be distributed, the ranking of address spaces in competing for CPU cycles, and the degree to which each address space and the common area is subject to page stealing.

The IPS contains several kinds of information in a particular order. Global definitions precede objectives, which are followed by domain and performance group definitions.

IPS concepts were discussed at length in Chapters 5 and 6. Here we'll concentrate on syntax, defaults, and recommended values. Note that there are two kinds of defaults in the IPS:

- basic default—the value assigned if the parameter is omitted in the IPS

- supplied default—the value specified in the default IPS supplied with current MVS releases

The basic defaults are unlikely to change; the supplied defaults have evolved to some extent over time.

## 8.1.1. Global definitions

Global definitions include service definition coefficients, which must come first, followed by specifications for APG range, privileged dispatching priority, time unit divisor, time-slice pattern, I/O queuing option, common-area storage isolation, and I/O service unit option.

All of these parameters are optional. Defaults exist for all but the APG range and time-slice pattern. A syntax error will exist if the obsolete APG parameter is used in any performance group definition in the same IPS with any of the parameters APGRNG, PVLDP, TUNIT, TSPTRN, or IOSRVC.

### Service Definition Coefficients (SDCs)

- **CPU** may range from 0 to 99.9. The "hard-wired" (basic) default is 1.0 if the coefficient is not specified, but a default of 10.0 is used in the supplied IEAIPS00 in an MVS/XA system as distributed.

  **Recommendation:** Use the supplied default value of 10.0. Maintain the CPU and SRB coefficients constant so that the MSO coefficient may be varied if need be to deal with storage constraints.

- **SRB** may range from 0 to 99.9. The basic default is 0.0 (because SRB service was not captured 'way back in MVS/SE1) if the coefficient is not specified, but a default of 10.0 is used in the supplied IEAIPS00 in an MVS/XA system as distributed. The value of the basic default makes it important that this parameter be specified in every IPS.

  For various reasons, those at some installations set the SRB coefficient to a different value than that of the CPU coefficient. This might be understandable if the SRB value were made greater than the CPU value, since SRBs have higher effective dispatching priority than TCBs, and thus a greater impact on workloads. Unfortunately, a faulty assessment of "importance" may be used, resulting in an SRB value lower than the CPU value.

**Recommendation:** Use the supplied default value of 10.0. Maintain the CPU and SRB coefficients constant so that the MSO coefficient may be varied if need be to deal with storage constraints.

- **MSO** may range from 0 to 99.9. The basic default is 1.0 if the coefficient is not specified, but a default of 3.0 is used in the supplied IEAIPS00 in an MVS/XA system as distributed.

**Recommendation:** Use the supplied default value of 3.0 for MSO, adjusting it upward in increments of one full unit if real storage constraint appears. The effect of such adjustment is to move heavy users of real storage through performance periods rapidly, making them subject to storage load balancing if that option is reserved for the latter batch performance periods.

- IOC may range from 0 to 99.9. The basic default is 1.0 if the coefficient is not specified, but a default of 5.0 is used in the supplied IEAIPS00 in an MVS/XA system as distributed.

**Recommendation:** Use the supplied default value of 5.0. It is unlikely that any alteration of IOC will be necessary.

## Other Global IPS Parameters

- APGRNG is the key parameter involved in controlling access to the CPU through a systematic dispatching priority scheme. It has no basic default, but the value in the supplied IEAIPS00 is APGRNG=(0-15).[1] To ensure full control of dispatching priorities, this choice is strongly recommended. An equally safe alternative is to specify APGRNG=(6-15). There is a Machiavellian flavor to this choice, however: "Any dispatching priority you specify with the DPRTY parameter in JCL will be ignored, unless it is lower than the lowest owned

---

1   Note the curious syntax—the only use of a hyphen to indicate a range in all of the SRM parameters.

by the SRM. You are free to rummage around for the CPU cycles that no one else wants."

Recommendation: Specify APGRNG=(0-15).

- **PVLDP** is the dispatching priority for privileged address spaces, including initiators at job and step transitions, TSO LOGONs, and other address spaces denoted as "privileged" in the *Program Properties Table* (*PPT*). Its basic default is PVLDP=M0 (the lowest SRM-owned dispatching priority), but it is specified in the default IPS as PVLDP=F54. As with any other dispatching priority, the value is meaningful only in context with other priorities. In the supplied default IPS, F54 ranks higher in dispatching priority than all workloads including first period TSO; initiators with this priority might cause TSO delays at job step transitions.

  **Recommendation:** Make PVLDP one step lower in priority than the lowest priority response-critical workload. For instance, if TSO first period is at F72 and production CICS address spaces are at F71 and F70, set PVLDP to F7 (or R7 in MVS/370 systems).

- **TUNIT** need be specified only if time slicing is to be used, and then only if the SRM second on the current CPU is not short enough to execute the time slice pattern without causing perceptible delays in some workload. The SRM time unit is also used in MVS/370 systems to adjust priorities when the *rotate* algorithm is used. TUNIT ranges from 1 to 10; the SRM second is divided by TUNIT to become the SRM time unit.

  **Recommendation:** Make TUNIT the smallest value needed to smooth out priority fluctuations if they are noticed.

- **TSPTRN** is required if time slicing is to be used. One such circumstance is the need to divide CPU preference among different subsystems or user subsets to satisfy the terms of a service level agreement.

  Assume, for example, that TSO users in performance period 1 of performance group 12 are to be preferred 30 percent of the time and those in period 1 of performance group 14 are to be preferred 50 percent of the time, regardless of the relative activity in the two performance groups. The time slice pattern should contain ten slices, five going to time slice group 1 (PG 14) and three to time slice group 2 (PG 12.) The remaining two are unassigned.

The simple assignment of
   **TSPTRN=(1,1,1,1,1,2,2,2,\*,\*)**

would cause each user-set to wait for five SRM time units before gaining preference, and other address spaces would need to wait for eight slices before no address space would be at its time slice priority. A simple re-arrangement minimizes such delay and makes a sub-divided (*via* TUNIT) SRM second unnecessary:
   **TSPTRN=(1,2,1,\*,1,2,1,\*,1,2)**

**Recommendation:** If time slicing is found to be necessary, try to minimize complexity by avoiding the need for the TUNIT parameter, as shown above.

- **IOQ** has two possible values, *FIFO* (the base default) or *PRTY*. IOQ=PRTY is specified in the IEAIPS00 shipped with MVS/XA or MVS/ESA.

  **Recommendation:** IOQ=PRTY is usually specified and can have a beneficial effect if there is a great deal of low-priority, I/O-intensive batch running along with other workloads and causing I/O contention with those other, more time-critical workloads. Since there seems little possible harm in making this choice, with some possibility of benefit, it is recommended.

- **CWSS** is used to specify storage isolation for the common area—SQA, PLPA, and CSA, as well as their "extended" counterparts above 16 megabytes. The base default is (0,\*), or no storage isolation. The lower value specifies a minimum number of frames never subject to ordinary page stealing; the upper sets a number of frames above which the common area is subject to preferred page stealing.

If CPGRT is not specified, the protected frame count remains at the lower value. With CPGRT, the number of protected frames (the *target)* is adjusted between the minimum and maximum according to the rate of page faults resolved from auxiliary storage.

**Recommendation:** *Always* set the maximum to "\*", denoting the largest possible value for the parameter and preventing preferred stealing from the common area. Set the minimum to the observed minimum sum of frame counts in the various common-area components at a relatively unbusy time of day. With expanded storage, the common-area paging rate from auxiliary storage is likely to be very low; CPGRT would have little effect and need not be used.

Without expanded storage, follow the recommendations of the next paragraph to set CPGRT.

- **CPGRT** sets a range of acceptable page-in rates for the common area. If the rate from auxiliary storage exceeds the maximum, the target is increased. When the page-in rate falls below the minimum, the target will be reduced, but not below the minimum CWSS value.

**Recommendation:** Without expanded storage, set CPGRT to a range that will lead to an acceptably low level of common page-in delay. Use the techniques described in Chapter 10 to make this determination. When starting with storage isolation, set CPGRT to high values, such as (10,15), and observe the target value of CWSS. If the target never rises above minimum, and unacceptable common page-in delay continues, reduce the range, maintaining the maximum at 1.5 times the minimum, until the CWSS target rises when storage constraint develops.

CPGRT may be omitted in systems with expanded storage unless the amount of expanded storage is very inadequate.

- **IOSRVC** may be specified as COUNT (the default) or TIME. The considerations for choosing are discussed in Chapter 5, in the section headed "I/O service units."

### "Workload" Specification (WKL)

There is no default for WKL. A typical WKL might be given as

**WKL=(1,50,98,99,100)**

reflecting the greater importance of high values on the scale compared to low. Deliberately specifying top values spanning two units allows explicit control of exchange swapping.

**Recommendation:** There is no particular purpose to a WKL specification other than to provide the mapping points for service rates in objectives and the RVs or contention indexes at those points. If the sample WKL given above is not suitable because some special need must be satisfied by an objective, adjust it appropriately.

## 8.1.2. Objectives

Objectives map service rates to recommendation values (RVs) or contention indexes (CIs), either of which is a value on the WKL scale. The considerations for creating objectives and their relationship with RV and CI values are spelled out in some detail in Chapter 5.

**Recommendation:** Use the smallest number of objectives needed to manage all required CIs and RVs, simply to avoid confusion and the agony of excessive choice. Remember that the same objective can serve multiple performance group periods as well as in the role of a DOBJ or AOBJ. It is rare that a system will require more than three or four different mappings of service rates to RVs or CIs.

## 8.1.3. Domains

Domains are defined with three parameters, only the first of which, denoting the domain number, is required. The other two parameters specify the MPL constraints on the domain and the algorithm used to determine the domain's contention index.

A domain defined without constraints has a default range of (1,999). If there is no algorithm specified, FWKL=1 is assumed.[2]

---

[2]  In the unlikely event that no domain in the IPS is defined with a target control keyword, a weight of 1 is assigned.

The default constraints allow wide SRM control of MPLs, in general a good strategy. A default lower constraint of 0 rather than 1 would be better; the extra increment of control is crucial in controlling storage-intensive workloads.

Two default domains are predefined:

**DMN=0,CNSTR=(999,999,1)** —or—

**CNSTR=(999,999),FWKL=1**

**DMN=1,CNSTR=(1,999,1)** —or—

**CNSTR=(1,999),FWKL=1**

Domain 0, for privileged address spaces, cannot be altered, nor can it be explicitly used for a performance group. Domain 1 is an ordinary domain; it may and should be redefined to suit the installation's needs.

**Recommendation:** Reread the discussion of domains in Chapter 6 and create the minimum number of domains needed to manage each distinct swappable workload component. Ensure that each domain's MPL is free to vary over as wide a range as possible. Set nonzero minMPLs only in domains supporting response-critical swappable address spaces, such as first- or second-period TSO.

## 8.1.4. Performance groups

All that has gone before in the IPS and in our consideration of its parameters is mere prelude to its real business—the definition of performance groups for the purpose of managing workloads. In the performance management model we wish to encourage, each address space is assigned to a performance group through the ICS, described at the end of this chapter. The ICS is the bridge between the outside world of job names, job classes, and user-ids, and the SRM's view of address spaces, each assigned a performance group number.

The definition of a performance group is simplicity itself:

**PGN=**_number_

defining a number in the range 1-999 as an acceptable performance group number to be a target of assignment in an ICS, a PERFORM specification in JCL or a TSO LOGON command, or in a operator RESET command.

Each IPS must include definitions of performance groups 1 and 2; all others are optional.

If only the minimal definition is provided, default assignments are made for domain (domain 1), objective (1), dispatching priority (M0), ISV (100K), I/O priority (M0), storage isolation (none), time slicing (none), RTO (none), and load balancing (none). If the default parameters are not acceptable (as of course they will not be for most performance groups), additional specifications are needed.

## Performance Periods

Alterations to the default address space management parameters are added to the basic performance group definition as separate groups of value assignments enclosed in parentheses. The first of these *performance period* definitions is set off from the performance group name by a comma. Additional period definitions are delimited by enclosing parentheses with no intervening comma. As many as eight periods are allowed in a performance group.

Each SRM transaction starts execution in the first period of its performance group. As service or time accumulates, SRM advances the transaction to the next period after a sufficient accumulation is noted. This process occurs only for swappable address spaces; nonswappables are not moved through periods, and remain in the first period of a multiperiod performance group. If a swappable address space is made non-swappable after progressing past the first period, it retains the attributes of the period in which the change took place. The following sections describe the set of parameters that may be defined for each performance period.

## Performance Period Parameters

- **APG=** is an obsolete parameter designating a position in the original MVS Automatic Priority Group. Its use in an IPS invalidates the use of several other important parameters. Do not use APG in any IPS.

- **DP=** is the correct way to specify the dispatching priority of each address space in a performance period. The details of specifying DP are covered in Chapter 6. If the DP parameter is omitted in a performance period definition, a priority of M0 is assigned.

- **DMN=** designates the domain in which address spaces in this performance period will be managed. If the parameter is omitted, domain 1 is assigned by default unless there is a prior period in the performance group. In that case, the domain of the prior period is selected. If CNTNSW=YES has not been selected in the OPT, there is no need to specify a domain for a performance group serving only nonswappable address spaces. Whatever the definition of domain 1 (assigned by default if no DMN= appears), it has no effect on a non-swappable address space.

- **DUR=** specifies the minimum duration of the performance period. DUR *must* be specified in each period of a multiperiod performance group, except the last period. Its value may range from 0 to 999,999,999 or 999,999K. The unit of the value is SRM service units, unless UNT=R has been specified in the period definition as well. In that event, the unit is in real-time seconds and is limited to a maximum value of 1,000,000. No error is indicated if the limit is exceeded.

  The actual duration may exceed the number of service units specified; the SRM determines when to switch periods through sampling of address spaces and performs the switch only after the required service has been accumulated.

- **UNT=** can alter the unit of DUR from service units (UNT=S, the default) to seconds in real-time (UNT=R).

UNT=R can be used for such clever tricks as ensuring that a transaction that exceeds a certain number of service units is subjected to a punitive delay:

```
DMN=86,CNSTR=(0,0)
...    ...
PGN=2, (..., DUR=400,...)
       (..., DUR=4000,...)
       (DMN=86,DP=M0,..., UNT=R,DUR=60,...)
       (..., ISV=10000,...)
```

Transactions ending in period 1 or period 2 will end normally; those going over 4400 service units will be subjected to a minute in the "penalty box," swapped-out. After the one-minute delay, a transaction is allowed to proceed. At some MVS installations, this technique is used to "discourage" TSO users from executing long-running transactions (such as program compiles) from the terminal.

Imposing such a procrustean judgment on the behavior of on-line users is most emphatically *not* recommended. Many TSO transactions other than compiles can often consume a large number of service units.[3] A well-meaning attempt to discourage apparently wasteful behavior can result in "innocent" users being subjected to unacceptably poor response time.

Another issue arises here: What might happen if the Data Center Manager said to the Manager of Financial Applications Development, "I think all of *your* programmers should submit all of their compiles as batch jobs. It makes *my* system management job easier." The M.F.A.D. might reflect on relative priorities, and their next meeting might take place in someone else's office—say, that of the Vice President of Corporate Services.

The action of imposing an arbitrary delay on inconveniently lengthy transactions is entirely equivalent to such arrogant

---

3   A given transaction may vary in size. When storage demand is low, the count of MSO service units will be higher than when demand is high. The punishment is more likely when the behavior is less likely to do harm.

words. It is all too easy to conceal an unacceptable policy
position if it is embodied within the mystery of an IPS.

- **IOP**= is in the same form as the DP parameter. Normally
(by default), the I/O priority of an address space is equal to
its dispatching priority. A different I/O priority may be
selected with the IOP parameter. Address spaces in a
mean-time-to-wait group have unchanging I/O priorities. As of MVS/SP 3.1.0e, IOP=F$n$ is not yet allowed.

**Recommendation:** Always specify IOQ=PRTY to gain the
benefits of priority I/O queuing. Accept the IOP default unless and until analysis of workload problems indicates that
a key workload is suffering excessive I/O queueing delay
that cannot be relieved by normal responses such as removing contending I/O from a device. As a last resort, a
higher I/O priority may help. On the other hand, if a
workload causing I/O interference with another is safely
meeting its service target, giving it a lower I/O priority
might help both workloads to succeed.

The possibility of improvement is small, and more direct
methods are usually more effective.

- **ISV**= specifies a number of SRM service units each address
space in a performance period must receive before its serv-
ice-derived recommendation value is allowed to drop down
from the high value corresponding to zero service rate.
This high RV, called its *cutoff value*, prevents other
address spaces from competing for MPL within a domain
with a newly swapped-in address space. ISV has a default
of 100,000 service units.

The default ISV of 100K was instituted early in MVS's history as a reaction (perhaps an overreaction) to dismal early
experience with unrestricted exchange swapping. Because
the early MVS auxiliary storage manager was not easily
able to deal with swapping, exchange swapping became
regarded as a dispensable luxury. It was inhibited both by
the new ISV default and by encouraging (through the

choices made in preconfigured MVS offerings) a compressed WKL scale running from 1 to 10, rather than 1 to 100.

Because the ISV is cumulative through each resident interval, many IPSs are seen with an ISV specified in each performance period, carefully calculated to reflect the sum of the current DUR plus all preceding DURs. Such painstaking effort is usually unnecessary. Unless exchange swapping is desired before a transaction (for instance a batch job) enters the last period of a performance group, or if the cumulative service before the last period is more than 100,000 SUs, ISV need *not* be specified in other than the last period.

**Recommendation:** Determine the amount of service that represents a nominal batch job or long-running TSO transaction. Add a reasonable tolerance factor, say 50 percent. The resulting value is a good initial ISV for that performance group. Specify the ISV in the last performance period to allow each long-running transaction in the last period's domain an equal opportunity to run to completion without other transactions seizing and holding the domain's MPL slots.

For example, suppose that the average long-running batch job finishes with 35,000 service units. 150 percent of that is 52,500 SUs. An ISV of 50K or 55K in the last period of the performance group would allow a job 50 percent "bigger" than average to finish without an exchange swap; jobs consuming more service would be subject to exchange swap.

- **RTO=** may be specified only in the first period and applies only to TSO performance groups. Its purpose is to ensure uniformity of TSO response time for short-running transactions. If the average response time in the first period is faster than desired, an RTO may be specified, denoting a somewhat higher target. The greater the gap between the native response time and the specified RTO, the more uniform will be the resulting response time—in theory.

Unfortunately, it's not that easy. The idea of RTO is flawed in the first place if current evidence linking minimum (subsecond) response time to enhanced TSO-user productivity is to be believed and applied. Because RTO is applied only to physical swap-ins, the performance difference between physical and logical swaps is likely to increase.

**Recommendation:** The only plausible reason for using RTO in a production TSO system is if a system's workload is expected to increase in the future and to then impose enough constraint to result in increased TSO response time. In that case, specify an RTO close to the expected ultimate trivial TSO response time, so that response-time expectations may be properly conditioned.

In a system with a clearly subordinate TSO workload, an RTO of 1.5 to 2.0 seconds might discourage the TSO users enough to abandon TSO in favor of another subsystem or to use personal computers instead.

- **RTB=** is the means of specifying load balancers. Its name comes from the early notion of "response-throughput bias," the idea that maximum delivered service is at odds with best interactive response time. In its early form, RTB ignored storage use and biased swap recommendation values according to the relationship between CPU or I/O resource constraint and the degree to which each designated address space uses that resource.

In its current form, RTB can assume any of five different values, as well as various combinations. They are:

  - RTB=0, denoting no load balancers

  - RTB=1, denoting all load balancers

  - RTB=C, denoting only CPU load balancing

  - RTB=I, denoting only I/O load balancing

  - RTB=S, denoting only storage load balancing

  - RTB=(list), the list specifying any combination of C, I, and S

We examined the load balancers in Chapter 7, in considering OPT parameters. The only consistently effective load balancer is storage load balancing. Dispatching priority control (including effective use of mean-time-to-wait) manages the CPU well. I/O load balancing is marginally useful in the event that a disruptively I/O-intensive job (such as a DASD management utility) must be run occasionally along with other workloads.

**Recommendation:** Activate storage load balancing by setting a non-zero MSO value in the OPT. Select storage load balancing in the last period of ordinary batch and TSO, and in any special one-period performance group established to serve known resource-intensive batch jobs. If I/O load balancing is desired, establish a separate reserved performance group for jobs known to perform destructively intense I/O. Do not use CPU load balancing.

- **PWSS**= is used to specify storage isolation for each address space in a performance period. Along with dispatching priority, it is one of the few IPS controls applicable to nonswappable address spaces. PWSS is specified as two values defining a range for a target protected working set in frames. Both values are in the range 0 to 32767 (in MVS/370 and MVS/XA), and 0 to 2,147,483,647 in MVS/ESA. The maximum value in either case may be denoted by "*".

Storage isolation may be static or dynamic. If neither PPGRTR nor PPGRT is specified along with PWSS, the target is always the minimum value specified. If either of the paging-rate controls is added, the target varies between the minimum and the maximum according to the page-in rate of the address space.

The target applies to the sum of frames in central and expanded storage. An address space at or below its target working set is protected from ordinary page stealing. If its frame count exceeds the target, stealing is done down to the target at the time the address space is reached in the normal ASID-ordered scan of address spaces. If an address space's frame count exceeds the maximum, it is targeted for preferred page stealing in a preliminary address-space scan of the page stealing algorithm. All frames above the maximum are vulnerable, up to the currently required number of frames.

One further aspect of storage isolation is noteworthy: when a storage-isolated address space is swapped out, swap trim does not go below the minimum PWSS-value. In other words, the minimum target working set is preserved across swap-in and swap-out. This property defines the *swap group* size and is of crucial importance in managing TSO paging delay in systems with some degree of storage constraint.

Most page faults in TSO transactions (60 percent or more) are re-reference page faults, bringing in pages formerly used in the session. If storage isolation is specified for response-critical TSO performance periods (usually first and second) at a value somewhat above the mean frame count for active transactions, re-reference page faults will be reduced drastically, at the expense of a few extra frames being tacked on to the last swap set.

For example, if an all-locals paging configuration on 3380s is used, the effective swap set size is 30 slots. If the mean frame count is 103 (by "eyeball averaging" on a performance monitor's display), four swap sets will be needed for the average swap-out. Specifying PWSS=(120,*) does not increase swap I/O, except to increase the average number of pages transferred in the last swap set, at a cost of 1.34 milliseconds per page. Page faults might be reduced by 3 to 6 per transaction, at about 50 milliseconds per page fault.

**Recommendations:** Storage isolation has numerous benefits and almost as many pitfalls. Several recommendations are in order:

° For nonswappable subsystem "loved ones" such as CICS, specify storage isolation to control paging delay. A minimum PWSS may be used to ensure minimal delay following a period of inactivity. A limiting maximum PWSS *should not be used* for a preferred workload, and dynamic adjustment of the target according to page-in rate should be used. For a CICS address space,

**PGN=14,(PWSS=(200,*),PPGRTR=(1,3),...**

is a typical specification.

° For TSO performance groups, use PWSS to define the swap group size. A paging-rate control is not appropriate, nor is a restrictive maximum. PWSS=(120,*) is a typical starting point. If frame counts frequently exceed the target (or if unacceptably high levels of page-in delay are observed), raise the PWSS minimum to the next multiple of the swap set size.

° One of the many performance management aphorisms attributed to those in the IBM Washington Systems Center is, "Know who your loved ones are—and always have someone else to kick around!" For address spaces to be fitted with *KICK ME* signs, a special form of storage isolation ensures that their frames are the first ones stolen, thus protecting respectable workloads from such treatment.

Specify *negative* storage isolation by specifying PWSS with a zero lower limit and an upper limit less than the normal working set of the address spaces in the performance period. For batch jobs normally needing about 100 frames, PWSS=(0,60) will make about 40 frames of each address space in the performance period available whenever page stealing is needed. Page-in delay in the system will move toward these address spaces and away from other workloads.

• **PPGRT[R]**= is the other part of specifying storage isolation. It is used to adjust the target working set according to page-in rate. When the page-in rate exceeds the upper limit of PPGRT or PPGRTR, the target is raised. A page-in rate below the lower limit causes the target to be reduced. With a page-in rate between the limits, the target is not adjusted.

PPGRT was the first form of this parameter available; it is still accepted in MVS/XA and MVS/ESA and is the only form available in MVS/370. PPGRTR was added early in MVS/XA. The paging rate specified in PPGRTR has a uniform meaning for all kinds of address space: page-ins per resident second of real-time. Such paging rates are easy to read directly from most performance monitors.

If PPGRT must be specified (in an MVS/370 system), it is measured in page-ins per *execution-second* for ordinary address spaces. For address spaces in cross-memory mode, the unit is the same as for PPGRTR.

Only one form of page-rate parameter is allowed in any performance period definition. If either is specified without PWSS, a PWSS of (0,*) is assumed.

**Recommendation:** Use PPGRTR if page-in rate control is to be used. In an MVS/370 system in which only PPGRT is available, make sure to correct the specified page-in rate to page-ins per execution-second. If this value is not readily available, use page-ins per resident second divided by the fraction of CPU time used by each address space of the workload. For example, if a CICS address space can tolerate four page-ins per second and uses 40 percent of the CPU, the upper limit for PPGRT should be 4/.4, or 10. The lower limit is usually 50 to 80 percent of the upper limit. For our CICS address space, either

$$PPGRTR=(3,4)$$

or

$$PPGRT=(7,10)$$

are roughly equivalent as long as the CPU demand of the address space stays near 40 percent.

As with all controls of this nature, PPGRTR should be adjusted so that in normal operation the target protected working set is not at either extreme of the range.

- **TSDP=** is the alternate, higher dispatching priority when time-slicing is used. The form of the time-slice priority must be the same as the form of the base priority: if DP=F52 is specified, TSDP=F71 or TSDP=F9 are acceptable, but TSDP=M7 is not.

- **TSGRP=** designates the time-slice group for the performance period.

## 8.2. Installation Control Specification (ICS)

The ICS is not strictly an SRM control; it serves simply to assign performance groups to address spaces. Since there is no ICS by default,[4] it is essential to create and use an ICS so that entry to each performance group is controlled as desired. The ICS is organized in a two-level hierarchy. A SUBSYS statement introduces each section for batch (normally the primary subsystem), for TSO, or for started tasks, as well as for secondary subsystems that create address spaces. A default PGN (performance group, called in this context a *control* performance group) is usually specified on the SUBSYS statement. Also allowed are definitions for a default report performance group (RPGN) and for one or more optional control performance groups (OPGN) applying to each address space in the performance group.

Following each SUBSYS statement may appear additional statements defining exceptions to the SUBSYS defaults, defined on the basis of user-ID, job class, address space name, or (in XA and ESA only) accounting data. For each such subset of address spaces, PGN, RPGN, and OPGN may be specified in any combination. In current XA and ESA releases of MVS, name specifications may include a "wildcard" or "mask" character, specified as a single character in a MASK statement that must come first in the ICS if it is used.

The ICS is well documented in *Initialization and Tuning*, so its parameters will not be discussed in detail here.

---

4   There is, sort of. Without an ICS, TSO sessions are assigned by default to performance group 2 and other (nonprivileged) address spaces to performance group 1. Privileged address spaces go to the mysterious performance group 0.

## Recommendations:

- Above all, make sure that there *is* an ICS. Without one, a carefully constructed scheme for controlling dispatching priority and other execution attributes is at the mercy of every batch job and the distributed JCL for every started task, unless well-designed exits screen JCL and enforce correct performance group assignments.

- The OPGN parameter is often ignored. Its use suggests an uncertainty about which address spaces should be in which performance group. If the OPGN is perceived to be more favorable than the base PGN, it will be selected with little consideration. With a less favorable OPGN, it is unlikely to be used at all. To the extent that a choice is allowed, it should be one with clearly defined benefits to all possible choices under different conditions known only to the person responsible for the address space.

  For instance, if there are at least two different TSO performance groups, PGN might denote a performance group with steeply declining MPL and dispatching priority in later periods but a high MPL in the first and second periods. OPGN would designate a performance group with more gradual decline in favor and more generous storage isolation, but a lower MPL for first-period transactions. Users planning to do only editing of programs or text might receive better service in the default performance group, while those intending to use a fourth-generation or query language, or to initiate frequent online compiles or text processing runs with SCRIPT/VS, might choose to use the OPGN. In each case, the wrong choice means poorer service.

- Use the ICS to assign each started task to an appropriate performance group. The default assignment should have relatively low dispatching priority, similar to that of ordinary batch. Be aware of installation naming conventions and conform the STC TRXNAME entries to them, using the MASK capability if available.

Some started tasks, even if assigned to particular performance groups, will not pick up all of their characteristics. The GRS address space, for instance, operates at a predetermined dispatching priority. The benefit of assigning GRS to a performance group is that its default storage isolation can be changed. GRS appears to have a default storage isolation something like PPGRT=(0,0); its target working set is increased by any page fault and is (almost) never decreased.

## 8.3. Other SRM controls

In each edition of *Initialization and Tuning*, there is a page at the end of Chapter 5 labeled "SRM Constants," describing values for some thresholds not found in the OPT. In the rare event of a problem in such an area, it might be appropriate to use the SUPERZAP service program to alter these values. Most of the frequently altered SRM controls have been added to the OPT over time. In other cases, there is no control available, as for MPL according to expanded storage page movement rate.

One exception is the two-level threshold against which the number of in-use auxiliary storage slots is measured. The less disruptive threshold, MCCASMT1, has a default value of 70 percent. When more than this number of slots is allocated, the SRM bars new work (such as TSO LOGONs) from entering the system. At the second threshold, MCCASMT2, 85 percent by default, address spaces acquiring auxiliary storage are swapped out. The system may eventually become paralyzed.

In today's systems with very large page data sets, especially when expanded storage carries the bulk of the paging burden, these thresholds are far too restrictive and, if exceeded, can cause periods of great disruption. Adjusting these thresholds so that a reserve of, say, 20,000 slots is maintained should be safe in most systems.

## 8.4. Other Controls

*Initialization and Tuning* in its first four chapters describes many members of SYS1.PARMLIB other than those controlling the SRM. Many of them can have a profound effect on MVS performance. It is beyond our intended scope to make recommendations for each of these parameter sets. We leave these as an exercise for the reader, with the plea that an analysis of potential performance impact be added to the planning cycle.

This principle must be extended to subsystem and application planning as well. Choices such as buffering options, residency and page-fixing options, the use of STEPLIBs, and many others need to be put in context with priority, resource availability, cost, and service level agreements. While it is true that most performance problems are responsive to analysis of workload delays and tuning to minimize delays, planning and impact evaluation can shorten the time needed for workloads to stabilize with acceptable performance.

## 8.5. Summary

The set of SRM parameters in the OPT and IPS members of SYS1.PARMLIB, and the workload assignment information in the ICS member, are the means of controlling how MVS deals with its resources and workloads. The history of MVS, embedded in the defaults of OPT and IPS, can cause inconsistent and often counterproductive system operation. An essential step in performance management is to take control of the system away from the software vendor and place it firmly with the installation that paid for it.

The information provided by IBM about these parameter sets and their individual elements is factual and nonjudgmental. In this chapter and the three preceding chapters, we have developed a more evaluative view of how the SRM can and should be controlled. When advice is offered, justification and explanation accompanies it. Readers may draw their own conclusions about the worth of the advice, but they are urged to try it before rejecting it.

# Introduction to Performance Problems

## 9.1. Initial Example

Suppose that you are running a program to calculate *pi* to 50,000 decimal places, and you need the results in one hour to gain an entry in Grumbick's Book of World Computer Records. On your fastest uniprocessor that can run MVS, the program requires 43 minutes of CPU time and will complete in 49 minutes if it is the only nonsystem workload. However, under normal system loading conditions, the elapsed execution time is no better than 72 minutes.

The mission fails: There is an unacceptable mismatch among objectives, program, and the computational problem. In such a case, "the problem" may be viewed in various ways:

- First, and most simple, the constraints may be too stringent. Often a rough estimate becomes a firm requirement simply because no refinement to the estimate had been available before the project gained momentum. There might have been an excessive safety factor in this part of a problem definition—perhaps the record to be broken is only 40,000 decimal places in an hour and a half.

- Scheduling may be inappropriate. The job may be too CPU-intensive to be suitable to run on prime shift. At 3 a.m., the job may complete well within the target.

- Contention may be responsible. The elongation of elapsed time might be due to contention with other work, even off-shift. If the job is given a more favorable dispatching priority, other work in the system will suffer, but there is some chance that the target elapsed time will be achieved.

- The program may be poorly designed or implemented. If the numerical approach embodied in the program is amenable to multitasking or to vectorization, adding to the CPU resource (with a multi-engine CEC or a vector processor, or both) may be effective. Some of today's FORTRAN compilers can generate programs that take advantage of multi-processors or vector processing features. By exploiting multitasking or vectorizable content, the impossible might become easy.

- The fundamental algorithm or design embodied in the program may be flawed. The greatest improvement in execution time is often associated with rethinking the fundamental design of an application program. In the case of a compute-intensive problem like the one we're considering, even a small change in the numerical algorithm can have a profound effect on requirements for computing resources.

## 9.2. Types of Performance Problems

Even though the foregoing has been an oversimplified and contrived example, note one key element: The way we recognized a performance problem was to note that **a workload failed to achieve its service goal.** Without that distinguishing factor, we tend to fall into a vague search for improvement, without knowing when to stop. Such a lack of focus makes for frustrated performance analysts and a system unresponsive to legitimate performance problems. Establishing performance targets and assessing actual performance against those targets provides a rational basis for performance management activities. Assessing measurements can take place in real-time, for interactive workloads and key unattended workloads, or after the fact for ordinary batch workloads. Performance monitors capable of making such measurements and more will be discussed in Chapter 10.

We now examine, in a more abstract way, the kinds of problems we've touched on so far:

- **Unrealistically ambitious service expectations.** To give another example, attempting to achieve 1.5-second CICS mean response time may be unreasonable if most transactions are more than ordinarily complex. A typical user of the application's transactions may require 30 or 40 seconds of think-time and data-entry time to fill a complex screen. Response time is thus a minor component of task service time. Sizing a system to provide requested but unjustified performance at initial activation of an application system may be a waste of money if the response time turns out to be 50 percent better than what is needed.

  Attainment against properly planned and structured service targets may be measured, and exceptions may be made visible in real-time or after the fact. What is to be done with such information? One approach is to simply report the results, taking action to correct "anomalies" only when the delivered service in a reporting period has become overtly unacceptable.

  The approach we characterize in these pages as **performance management** is more activist. If those in charge of providing the service have a level of self-measurement more stringent than the commitment to the end-users of the service, response time anomalies can be detected before the customers notice them. If, in addition, the service providers have diagnostic and repair tools to allow corrections to be made in real-time, there need be very few reportable service deviations.

- **Poor scheduling.** Often an installation has no service target for unscheduled batch and no incentives (or disincentives) to condition the expectations or behavior of the users bringing batch jobs into the system. Consequently, batch jobs varying wildly in resource requirement, setup need, contention potential, and business value compete freely. If some scheduling rules or preferences (including incentives to avoid contention and substantial financial or budget incentives to wait longer for results) were to be made known to the submitters of the jobs, enough people may alter their behavior so as to result in a substantial reduction of resource utilization on prime shift. Moving "heavy" batch off-shift can help to hold off a planned upgrade in capacity.

- **Avoidable contention.** Although end-users or application owners can rearrange work to avoid contention that they are warned of in advance, most resource contention is not visible until an unanticipated service level problem appears. Resolving such problems involves many paths and is often the principal activity of those responsible for performance management.

- **Poor implementation or installation choices.** An application program may have an inspired design and be written flawlessly. It may then be installed for production by someone who is careless or uninformed about the capabilities and services to be found in an MVS environment. As simple a mistake as placing a large card-image file in an unblocked sequential data set may create avoidable stress on a device, a string of devices, a storage director, a channel, and one or more CPUs. Because program residency takes longer than it should, real storage may be excessively utilized as well.

  In the MVS/ESA environment, failure to understand and make effective use of data spaces, hiperspaces, and data-in-virtual, as well as the more prosaic VIO and buffering options available since the beginning of MVS, can result in inefficient and wasteful use of system resources.

- **Flawed basic design or application architecture.** Even though poor follow-through in installation can lead to inefficiency, it takes an inherently flawed design to make a program spectacularly deficient. Stories abound of inept program designs. A typical pattern is that an application program survives long beyond its originally expected life span, and that the conditions of its execution change enough to make it run poorly.

Sometimes an increase in volume alone is enough. Sorting algorithms, in particular, are very sensitive to volume. A correct choice for sorting 100 items may be hopelessly inefficient for 100,000. However, the high-volume sorting algorithm may require the execution of so much setup code that its overhead is unacceptable for a frequently invoked in-line sort of a few hundred items. A "one size fits all" optimal sort is very unlikely.

A scale-up problem should be suspected when a previously acceptable application program starts missing its service targets chronically, especially when a gradual increase in its input volume has occurred. Confirmation may be gained by doing a "reasonableness check" on the gross activity of the suspect program. Is the increase in run time proportionally greater than the increase in input volume and output volume? Is much more intermediate I/O done with only a small increase in volume? Does CPU consumption or real storage requirement jump, again more than proportionally to the volume increase?

In such cases, time devoted to digging up long forgotten source code and re-analyzing the fit of the application to today's hardware may be well spent.

## 9.2.1. Capacity planning and performance management

When workloads and consequent hardware resource use grow over time, the management of such concerns is usually considered to be purely a matter for capacity planners. However, if the design of a principal application is of the kind just described, the hardware may be slated for an expensive upgrade before it is really necessary. More-than-proportional increases in run times of key applications should cause those applications to be re-examined as part of the upgrade justification process.

## 9.3. Resource Contention

To a great extent, performance problems originating in a lack of capacity are simple to solve. Add more capacity, or improve the underlying program to relieve the lack of capacity, and the problem is gone, or at least postponed.

Much more challenging problems are possible. They occur when multiple workloads need concurrent access to specific system resources. The delay in transaction completion caused by resource shortage might be a form of simple elongation: If 40 minutes of CPU time is required to complete a job that required 20 minutes before a volume increase, the job's run time will extend by little more than 20 minutes.

If, however, there is contention with other workloads for the CPU resource, the additional queueing delay may be many times the elongation due to additional resource use. If the resource in contention is DASD, an even greater delay may be introduced in all contending workloads, depending on the amount of seeking added to the I/O time of each.

If a resource contention problem is known to exist, the measures needed to deal with it are different from those used to diagnose and solve resource exhaustion problems.

### 9.3.1. Workload assignment

In a multisystem environment, inappropriate workload assignment choices may lead to avoidable contention. For example, in systems with shared DASD, in which GRS or an equivalent is not handling cross-system ENQeues, an exclusive ENQ request causes a RESERVE to be placed on the volume containing the data set. If other data sets on the volume are required by a system other than the one from which the RESERVE was issued, access is blocked for the duration of the RESERVE.

Such denial of access can cause long delays if an interactive subsystem or set of users need an affected data set. The original reason for creating the potential contention might have been an attempt to separate TSO users maintaining an IMS subsystem from the production system providing the IMS service. If any data set used by a TSO user is on a volume needed for production, delays caused by RESERVEs are possible.

Even if GRS or an equivalent facility is used to eliminate most RESERVEs, activity on the "off-side" system can cause delays on the production system. To get a complete picture of shared DASD contention requires a merging of usage data from all sharing systems. Predictive modeling is badly flawed if such a complete picture is not input to the model.

## 9.3.2. Workload scheduling

Sometimes workloads damage each other so much through contention that they cannot coexist. A daily transaction analysis and validation batch job operating on an online system's data base might cause the devices serving the application to become so busy that acceptable response times are not possible. Daily backups of critical disk volumes are in the same category. An efficient utility program performing data backups will drive its devices at nearly 100 percent utilization. Something must be done to keep these necessary batch jobs from destroying the performance of the interactive application. What alternatives are available?

- If there is a daily, naturally inactive period of sufficient duration to accommodate the daily jobs with enough time to handle at least one rerun of the longest-running job, a simple scheduling approach may do. Such an interval is usually known as the "batch window." Performance management action, including real-time monitoring of production batch completion times, and close capacity-planning tracking are needed to ensure that the time constraints are *always* safely met.

- Many online applications must be available virtually all the time. Less antagonistic and less resource-intensive approaches to backup and auxiliary batch operations are necessary. Volume backups might be done on a weekly basis instead of daily, supplemented by incremental daily backups of only changed data sets. Validation and adjustment might be done against transaction logs, with an exception set of amending transactions being generated for entry through a less intensive path than batch.

- Eventually, applications might well need to be designed for continuous operation, generating parallel data streams for backup, and performing validation and amendment in concurrent processes. Today's large multiprocessing systems are capable of dealing with such applications easily.

### 9.3.3. Accommodating contention

One of the problems pointed out earlier is that without service targets, performance management has no endpoint. Approaches that focus on data about resources and infer the possibility of contention for those resources might lead to numerous "corrective" actions to reduce service time, utilization, queue length, or the appearance of contention. Without input from a workload-oriented point of view, such adjustments may be unnecessary at best. A balanced viewpoint is essential. Starting with the workload view, the prime justification for a "tuning" or "resource-balancing" action would be a failure to meet a service target, or a clear trend indicating that such a failure is imminent.

Based on such evidence, an investigation of specific resources tied to the threatened service level can lead to the solution of a real problem.

## 9.4. Summary

In this chapter, we have attempted to identify several typical ways in which workloads can fail to meet their service targets. We've also suggested ways to monitor the workloads and measure their performance, as well as performance factors related to system resources. The discussion is by no means complete, and the "war stories" of how performance problems manifest themselves have no limit. In the next chapter, we'll examine measurement and monitoring methods and tools.

# 10

# Measurement and Prediction

Performance management depends on decisions driven by information:

- Has any condition occurred in the last 24 hours that requires corrective action?

- CICS response time is not acceptable for users in Accounts Receivable. How extensive is the problem and what is the appropriate action to take?

- Has short-term tuning introduced a new problem?

- Can this system accommodate 50 more TSO users?

- What is the most effective way to spend my hardware upgrade budget this year?

All of these determinations require information in order to be made effectively and efficiently. There are two basic sources of such information: measurement and modeling.

*Measurement* takes place at many levels within MVS and is concerned with a wide variety of data. *Resource* data may be collected to learn the extent of CPU, channel, and device utilization over various time intervals. *Activity* rates in the system are gathered, analyzed, and displayed or stored. *Workload* data of many varieties may be measured in various ways.

Measurement data will suffice to answer most questions and provide support for most day-to-day decisions in performance management. When the question concerns future expectations or seeks to understand processes for which measurement data is impossible to obtain (or just not available with the current set of tools), *modeling* may be the appropriate discipline to use.

Modeling falls into two major categories, similar in spirit to the principal schools of stock market analysis. *Analytic modeling*, through an understanding of the way in which a system works, seeks to create a mathematical model whose behavior mimics that of the system. Analytic modeling resembles the "fundamentals" approach to market analysis. *Stochastic modeling*, like "technical" stock market analysis, looks at behavior patterns and examines and projects those patterns, largely independent of internal considerations.

We now examine various approaches to performance management and to measurement, summarize the kinds of decisions aided by each kind of measurement, and then illustrate one aspect of analytic modeling technique by developing a piecewise analytic model of DASD I/O. A full discussion of analytic modeling, as well as any consideration of stochastic modeling, is beyond the intended scope of this book.

## 10.1. Approaches to Performance Management

Differences of approach are common in performance management. They derive from differences among tools and the vendors who supply most of the tools, as well as the background and experience of individual practitioners.

The way in which data processing relates to the overall business has an effect as well. Data processing might be relatively new in an establishment and its advocates untrusted by senior managers. In such an environment, capacity planners must constantly struggle to justify both today's DP budget and the essential relationship between business growth and DP capacity growth. They must also work to persuade a skeptical or hostile audience that growing dependency on DP leads to ever more stringent expectations for performance and availability, and a corresponding growth in the need for performance management tools.

In such an environment, tracking and accounting for resource usage is a daily concern, so it is natural that performance management is approached from the perspective of resource use and distribution. The early history of performance management took place in a time when the cost of hardware per transaction was much greater than it is today, so the resource-oriented point of view is well entrenched.

## 10.1.1. Resource-oriented performance management

When looking at resources, how is a performance problem identified? When a pattern of satisfactory operation has been established and key measurements taken, *any* deviation from history is suspect and might signify an abnormal condition. For example, if the CPU is usually about 75 percent busy at 2:00 p.m., for utilization to drop suddenly to 50 percent might mean almost anything—but not that the CPU has instantly become more powerful! If such a deviation from normal operation is detected in real-time, further data may be gathered and possible causes and consequences might be determined, depending on the tools available.

The implicit assumption of resource-oriented methods is, "If the numbers look good, the system looks good." Which numbers? Ideally, the critical numbers should be determined by each installation according to its own measurements. What often happens, however, is that less experienced system programmers and performance analysts seek out help from others, requesting advice in the form of questions like:

- How busy should the CPU be?

- What's a good paging rate for a 3090-300E?

- How high can device and path utilization go on a DB2 data base on 3380?

As the numbers become detached from the experience and expectations for which they were appropriate, they degenerate into mere "rules of thumb." At this point, a system might well be measured against someone else's operating limits, and for a different kind of workload. Depending on such methodology often produces results that reinforce the atmosphere of distrust touched on above.

The resource-oriented approach is inadequate because it promotes a focus on measures of resource activity rather than on the service achieved on behalf of key workloads.

## 10.1.2. Workload-oriented performance management

Even though inferences can be drawn about workload performance factors from resource measurements, it is difficult. A performance management methodology built on resource measurements is uncertain and often too dependent on archived resource usage data to be useful in solving an acute problem. A more direct approach is necessary and is made possible by performance monitors that view the resources of the system from the perspective of its workloads, or of the workloads from each other's viewpoint.

Such measurement tools operate by sampling the execution-states of the workload(s) of interest. The accumulation of sampled data provides a pattern describing how often the workload is found in each state. We look now at how such information can help to solve problems.

### Execution-state Analysis

To determine how to deal with a missed service target, a straightforward problem-solving approach will attempt first to identify the problem's cause. Typical causes include:

- A hardware component may be degraded or operating poorly. A performance-enhancing feature such as a high-speed buffer might be disabled, a CPU or some storage could be offline, or a path to a high-use I/O device might be inoperative.

- Available resources are insufficient to permit the service level to be met. Application data volume might have increased suddenly or over time, causing greater resource need.

- Changes in the application program, the system environment, or the amount or distribution of stored data might have introduced inefficiency in the way the application executes. The introduction of extra SEEKs into frequently executed I/O operations (as in the case of a randomly accessed data set that grows into widely separated multiple extents) might cause unacceptable increases in run times or transaction response times.

- Growing demand for nonspecific system resources such as storage or CPU cycles could cause delays while waiting to gain access to sufficient resources to complete a work unit.

- Another workload might be using a specific resource (usually an I/O device) needed by the workload failing to meet its service target. Contention for an I/O device will elongate the elapsed time for all competing address spaces. If a data set is needed by both the "loved one" and the source of contention, and the contention source has EXCLUSIVE access, the affected workload will receive no service until the EN-Queue bottleneck is broken.

The first of these possible causes might be diagnosed by a very complete resource availability monitor. The second might be spotted after the fact by analysis of SMF or RMF resource data. The others are virtually impossible to diagnose without execution-state analysis or direct contention analysis, or both.

In a workload-oriented methodology, focus is first on creating service targets, and then measuring their attainment. The process of doing this contributes to communication and trust between the data processing center staff and the managers of various groups using DP service. Credibility thus attained can lead to credibility and trust at higher levels of management, and turn the users' management into allies in the DP forecasting and capital budgeting process.

The key emphasis in a workload-oriented methodology is on *service* measurement. Once a deviation from a service target is identified, investigation can proceed with resource-based tools, or with more modern tools based on the decomposition of transaction times into their execution-state components.

Using resource-oriented methods to diagnose problems is indirect and uncertain, but a product opportunity has materialized to take advantage of these very characteristics. "Expert systems" are offered by several vendors to evaluate resource data and "diagnose" whatever problems might be represented in the data.

If resource data were all that was available, this approach might be the best possible. Consider the massive investment in early supercomputers used for weather forecasting, particularly for predicting storm tracks. A mass of temperature, pressure, and wind velocity readings rimming the Gulf of Mexico and the Carribean might have been combined to give an imprecise prediction of a hurricane's time and location of landfall. The programming of such computers represented the "expert systems" of their day.

Of course, all we need to do today is use the detailed observations from weather satellites to extrapolate the directly observed storm track. The availability of direct observation makes the tedious "expert" analysis of indirect data unnecessary. Likewise, workload-oriented performance measurement tools make it possible to diagnose workload problems directly and rapidly.

## 10.2. Classifying measurement tools

There are several ways to classify performance measurement products. One frequently used division is between *monitors*, which present data as they collect it, and *data collectors*, which store data for future use. In some measurement products, both approaches are taken; some data is immediately available while data representing past conditions is stored.

### 10.2.1. Real-time monitors vs. data collectors

How does one choose? While it is certainly true that a creeping increase in response time may be diagnosed by a series of real-time measurements, why bother? A data collector with a well-conceived reporter program can present the history of the problem in summary or graphical form and guide the analyst to a solution that is not unduly influenced by instantaneous events.

On the other hand, a problem such as a sudden increase in allocation of the Common Service Area (CSA) must be revealed and understood promptly. Action must be taken to find the cause and stabilize CSA use before the system "crashes" when a crucial function cannot obtain needed CSA. A real-time monitor with a constantly active "alert" capability provides the best way to become aware of such a problem. Because simple awareness is not enough, a more complete real-time monitor would provide additional functions to identify the holder of CSA accounting for the most allocation or for the most rapid rate of allocation growth,[1] as well as some means of freeing a CSA block in an emergency.

A real-time monitor tends to be primarily oriented to basic concerns affecting the availability of the hardware and software configuration. It is not *per se* a performance monitor. The exhaustion of CSA is an availability problem, not a performance problem. Typically, a real-time *performance* monitor will also evaluate service data and emit an alert if a critical response-time or elapsed-time service level is in jeopardy. It may also include a facility to decompose those times into their component parts, so that the most likely cause of a service anomaly may be quickly identified.

As capable as real-time monitors may be, they are not the best choice for the more deliberative job of correcting subsystem or application performance problems. Such service anomalies tend to be chronic or cyclical. They do not arrive on the scene as full-fledged crises one fine day, and they do not politely wait until someone is looking at the display of a real-time monitor.

A data collector has advantages as a measurement tool for performance management. Only the collector portion need run at high dispatching priority, to ensure accurate CPU-delay measurements. The data analysis and display portion can run as a

---

1   Even in a "real-time" monitor, the data to support these functions must be gathered before it is needed for display. The essence of the real-time monitor is in the immediacy and current relevance of data presentation, not in the manner or timing of its collection.

batch job or as a TSO command or CALLed program. If the data is stored online in a form the reporter can query directly, the reporter's immediacy can be close to that of a real-time product.

If instead the standard MVS System Management Facility (SMF) is used as the data repository, there can be less overhead attributable to the collector.[2] Reporting must be deferred until the SMF data is dumped and processed.

However, there are other benefits of routing performance measurement data through SMF. Writing the data out is automatic, through facilities provided with the operating system and designed for continous operation. There are also several complementary products available for data analysis and presentation. These include IBM's Service Level Reporter and SAS Institute's Statistical Analysis System (SAS®), as well as higher-level data-base and reporting packages built on SAS. (These include Legent's MICS® and Merrill Consultants' MXG®.)

## 10.2.2. Measurement techniques

Another basis for classifying measurement products is according to whether data is obtained by sampling, by direct access to existing summary information, or by intercepting events. All of these methods are commonly used. IBM's Resource Measurement Facility (RMF) is primarily a sampling system. In MVS/370, RMF obtained data about I/O devices by sampling the states of devices as shown in control blocks of the operating system. In MVS/XA, however, the XA channel subsystem includes architecturally defined measurement interfaces, so what once had to be sampled could now be "harvested" using supported interfaces. In Candle Corporation's DEXAN and EPILOG for MVS, execution state data for address spaces is sampled, but CPU usage data is based on the accumulators updated by MVS at every dispatcher transition.

Transaction-oriented measurement systems attempt to capture data relating to each transaction of interest. To do this, they are event-driven, capturing and buffering the key data for each

---

2  The data is placed in the SMF buffers and system routines write it out. The resources used for this purpose may or may not be "captured," but they will certainly not be associated with the data collector.

transaction and moving it to a logging facility as quickly as possible. Data composition, reduction, and analysis are done at a later time.

MVS includes a "hidden" set of data collection facilities most commonly used by the Generalized Trace Facility (GTF). Distributed thoughout MVS system code are numerous implanted MONITOR CALL (MC) instructions. Each such instruction has within it a four-bit monitor class field. Normally, the MC is a no-op. When appropriate control register settings are made to activate the MONITOR EVENT facility and to select the active monitor classes, an MC, when executed, causes a program check. Control is then routed through a specialized second-level interrupt handler to code that will eventually log some data associated with the monitored event.

MONITOR CALL is a disruptive instruction to use. Each time the program check occurs, the system undergoes the flow-of-control disruption of a status switch and spends a portion of the subsequent processing time disabled for all interrupts on all processors of the complex. The processing time for the interrupt is tacked on to the TCB or SRB time of the program incurring the interrupt.

Consequently, the use of GTF is considered abnormal; most installations require special authorization to allow its use, and then only for limited time intervals. Granted, GTF is very accurate and can collect data available no other way; it is simply incompatible with production operation of an MVS system, and its high overhead causes inflation of reported CPU times throughout the system. A performance monitoring program gathering data by means of MONITOR CALL obviously should not operate continuously in a production system. Selective and limited use of MONITOR CALL can be effective if the event-related data it gathers is useful and available no other way.

Depending on what information is required, composites of these basic techniques are common. For instance, RMF accumulates TSO response time data through each collection interval by event-driven capture of transaction completions. In RMF, the individual transaction data is lost by the accumulation process. Candle

Corporation's OMEGAMON for MVS can "reach over" into RMF's accumulators and display quasi-current values for TSO response time. Legent's TSOMON starts with the same basic transaction completion data as RMF, but by capturing it without aggregation, TSOMON can later display much more detailed information about TSO response time by user subset or by transaction identity.

## 10.2.3. Resource measurement

### IBM offerings

*System Management Facility (SMF).* The most basic measurements are those gathered by built-in data collection routines in the operating system and reported through SMF. A diligent analysis of SMF data makes it possible to determine how much of each system resource was used for each work unit (TSO session, batch JOB, or terminated started task). SMF interval records (Type 30) make it possible to do resource usage tracking and accounting for unending subsystems as well.

*Resource Measurement Facility (RMF).* Although basic measurement data at the workload level is available from SMF, it is usually necessary to have an overview of how the system is performing as well. Understanding the relationship between system capacity and workload is made possible using data collected by RMF and written to SMF data sets in the form of records in the type range of 70 through 79. RMF evolved from a no-charge facility, MF/1, that was part of SVS and early MVS. RMF reports on CPU, channel, and device utilizations, system activity rates, and the distribution of service by performance group or domain.

Using RMF data, estimates of workload delay factors may be inferred as well. Delays for swapping, IOS queuing, paging, and CPU queuing may be calculated from RMF data. Information to quantify these delays is not provided directly in RMF reports, but rather derived through mathematical and statistical manipulation according to implicit or explicit models of system and workload behavior.

### Independent Vendor Offerings

A number of independent software vendors produce resource-oriented performance monitors. They include Candle's OMEGAMON for MVS, Boole & Babbage's Resolve Plus, Computer Associates' CA-LOOK, and Landmark's The Monitor (TMON) for MVS. These products also include features to monitor hardware availability and configuration elements, as well as some measures of service, delay, and contention. Candle's EPILOG for MVS draws on both resource data (in turn "harvesting" data from RMF) and execution-state data as described below.

## 10.2.4. Workload-oriented measurement

Workload performance problems are most effectively diagnosed using tools that examine the workloads and expose contention, bottlenecks, and tuning opportunities.

### Execution-state analysis

The basic technique of workload-oriented measurement is execution-state analysis. By examining the state of each address space of interest at regular intervals (sampling), a frequency distribution of execution states may be constructed, as shown in simplified form in Figure 10-1.

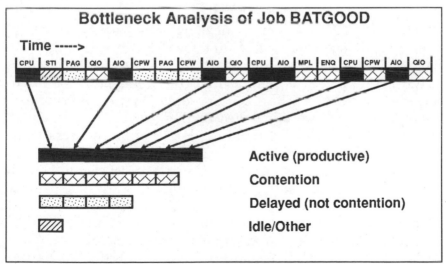

Figure 10-1. Basics of execution-state analysis.

The ranking of execution states can be used to characterize the problems (if any) associated with the workload. If the address space of interest is not meeting its service target and "using CPU" is the dominant state, the appropriate "cure" might be a more powerful CPU or a more efficient program.

Dominant states like "waiting for CPU," "swapped out for MPL," or "waiting for paging" represent resource shortages as seen by the address space. Such delays might be viewed as contention, but the workload in contention would be identified as "anything else." In such a case, the classical tuning tradeoffs are exercised: If other, less important work is meeting its service goals (or has none), system parameter changes can adjust dispatching priority, domain constraints or contention index, or quantity of storage isolation, thus redistributing resources. If such tradeoffs are not available, a hardware upgrade might be needed.

If the "loved one" spends much of its time waiting for an I/O device or for an enqueue resource, a contention problem with a specific workload exists. More investigation is needed to see if the contention arises from within the critical workload, or if it is caused by another address space or the aggregate of many address spaces, such as TSO users.

*IBM offerings.* IBM's Resource Measurement Facility (RMF) includes an independent set of functions known as Monitor III, part of the RMF program products for MVS/XA and MVS/ESA only. Another name for Monitor III is the *Workload Delay Monitor*, the name of an earlier IBM Research Division internal tool, ideas from which were included in the design for Monitor III. Monitor III depends on a separate data collector address space called RMFGAT. A reporter called RMFWDM is invoked as a TSO command and is used to display the data collected by RMFGAT, both in real-time and with some capability to study past periods.

Monitor III supports a concept called *workflow,* defined as "using" (a resource or set of resources) divided by the sum of "using" and "delayed" (for the same resource or aggregate). If a TSO workload is idle 80 percent of the time, absorbing CPU cycles 5 percent and waiting for some resource 15 percent of the time, the work-flow of that workload is $\frac{5}{5 + 15}$ or 25 percent.

Workflow is applied to both workload and resources in Monitor III, and the methodology suggested by the product documentation favors high workflow.

In addition to workflow, Monitor III shows how a workload's time is spent. Time is broken into processor use, processor delay, storage delay, and I/O delay. Other states are lumped as "other" or "unknown." Finer breakdowns are available for I/O delay, identifying the devices causing the most delay to a workload.

This brief description of Monitor III is necessarily incomplete. The appropriate IBM publications provide full information.

*Independent Vendor Offerings.* Candle Corporation offers a technology called variously *degradation analysis, bottleneck analysis,* and *execution-state analysis* in two system-level products—DEXAN for MVS and EPILOG for MVS. The same techniques are used in other products supporting the IMS and CICS subsystems. Data is collected by sampling the states of address spaces and supplemented by the CPU time accumulation kept in MVS control blocks. In DEXAN, operating along with Candle's OMEGAMON for MVS, the accumulated data is presented in real-time. EPILOG stores its data in a data set called the EPILOG Data Store. A reporter program, invoked as a TSO command or in batch, interrogates the data store and displays its data. EPILOG can also write its data to SMF, either alone or in parallel with writing to the data store.

Candle's analysis is somewhat more complete than that of RMF Monitor III, reporting on time spent using or waiting for each I/O device, on each specific enqueue delay, and on numerous other execution states.

## Direct contention analysis

When a favored workload is delayed because another workload is using a needed resource, knowing the details of execution states is not enough to open the bottleneck. Using resource data to supplement execution-state data helps a bit but can be misleading. For instance, if CICSA has spent 35 percent of its active time in the past 15 minutes waiting for volume DATA77 on device 03B7, it is naive and ineffective to simply consult an RMF Monitor III report to see who the other users of the device are. The users accounting for the most time may not be causing the interference; it may come from CICSA itself, or from another address space using the device synchronously with CICSA. A very small percentage of device utilization may account for a large measure of contention. While it is almost certainly true that one of the listed users of the device is the culprit, the ranked list does not always guide the analyst to the true source of contention.

What is needed in this case is a different kind of tool. A sampling execution-state monitor can be extended to perform a deeper kind of analysis when delay states are found. If such a monitor finds queued I/O delay for CICSA, the monitor goes beyond simply identifying and counting the delay state. A contention analyzer will examine other information available in the system to determine which address space is using the device in contention *at the time the delayed address space needs it*. By accumulating counts for each such occurrence, the monitor can produce a ranked listing of contending address spaces. A simplified view of direct contention analysis is presented in Figure 10-2 on the next page.

*IBM offerings.* RMF Monitor III appears to collect true contention information for CPU contention only. For other resources in contention, Monitor III shows what might be termed *coincident usage* data. In the case of DASD contention, Monitor III shows a ranking of the address spaces using a device in contention without determining whether their use was in fact in contention with the workload of interest.

*Independent Vendor Offerings.* Candle Corporation's DEXAN for MVS includes a true contention analysis capability known as Impact Analysis. Impact Analysis, first made available in Candle's OMEGA-MON for CICS, can produce ranked reports of contention against single address spaces, performance groups, or arbitrary work-

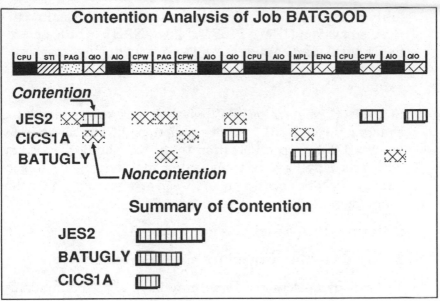

Figure 10-2. Direct Contention Analysis

loads. The contention is attributed to address spaces or performance groups. The latter can be broken down to address spaces within performance groups. The resources in contention can be displayed as well, with optional detail down to device numbers (with volume serial numbers) or individual enqueue-names.

## 10.2.5. Change monitoring

Large computer systems are inherently stable and reproducible. Unless something breaks or changes, a given workload will run today as it did yesterday. Some vendors offer tools that capture change activity in the system. Two such tools are Computer Associates' CA-EXAMINE and Candle Corporation's DELTA-MON for MVS.

If a sudden change in performance of a key workload is observed from day to day or (typically) between a Friday and the following Monday, it is very likely that something has changed in its environment. Possibilities include:

- Hardware—a CPU or channel path may be offline or storage, (central or expanded) may be different than it was at the previous IPL. While this might have been a far-fetched possibility in the past, a production partition in a logically partitioned system (IBM's PR/SM LPAR, NAS's MLPF, or Amdahl's MDF) can be changed all too easily during "test time" and not necessarily restored to normal before production resumes.

- Software Configuration—MVS system parameters may have changed through IPL or operator action, JES initiators may be in a different configuration than they should be, or key data sets may have been moved or may have gone to secondary allocation with a gap between extents causing longer-than-usual SEEKs.

- Software—the possibilities are widespread.

- Application—the possibilities are even greater.

- Volume—transaction volume may have changed suddenly due to business changes not communicated to the data center staff.

Not all of these changes are detected by commercial change monitors. The available queries and reports should be examined, and the possibility of other changes should be examined as well.

## 10.2.6. A balanced methodology

A performance analyst can find value in any of the tools described above. A common pitfall to avoid is the Carpenter's Fallacy: If the only tool at hand is a hammer, every problem looks like a nail. For a performance management methodology to be complete, it must include a variety of tools to address each kind of problem typically encountered:

- **Undocumented or unexpected change:** Before wasting time going through a laborious process to determine the cause of a sudden change in performance, first use any means available to rule out a change in some factor that could affect the workload's computing environment.

- **Resource exhaustion:** Detecting resource exhaustion is an essential complement to capacity management. This condition is revealed by resource monitoring tools in conjunction with statistical analysis and graphical trending packages. Execution-state analysis tools can improve the accuracy of capacity projections by breaking down into resource usage and delay components the response time (or elapsed time) trend for the workloads of concern.

- **Mismanaged workloads:** A workload performing poorly is identified first by monitoring some measure of its service, such as response time. When a service exception is detected, execution-state data can then be used to determine the nature of the delay. Dominant states like "Waiting for CPU" or "Swapped by SRM—MPL" indicate that the workload might be mistuned in the system, and that a tuning opportunity exists. Such a determination is best done using smoothed historical data rather than real-time data.

- **Chronic contention:** Continuing the methodology above, if the dominant state of the workload is one indicating contention, such as "Queued I/O" or "Waiting for ENQueue," tuning may be of little benefit. Instead, the workload should be monitored by a direct contention analyzer at previously characterized times of vulnerability. Once the contending workload is identified, it should be easy to decide how to eliminate or minimize the contention.

- **Acute contention:** Service analysis in real-time can also be used to trigger the investigation of contention. It is less likely that system parameter errors will lead to a sudden erosion of performance than that some other workload is causing acute contention. For this reason, contention analysis is the technique of choice in the event of acute performance degradation, with execution-state analysis a secondary tool.

Practical examples of problem-solving based on the use of these techniques and tools will be found in the last two chapters of this volume.

## 10.3. One Kind of Modeling

Modeling is a key tool of capacity planning. It is not widely used in diagnosing or resolving system or workload performance problems. Accordingly, a full discussion of modeling techniques and tools is not included in this chapter. However, we will consider an *ad hoc* approach to modeling DASD I/O, since it is very simple to implement with a calculator or a spreadsheet program.

An analytic model of a typical DASD I/O operation is relatively easy to construct, given the published facts about devices and their connections to systems, and measured data from performance monitors. The first step in constructing such a model is to decompose the time span of the I/O operation into its component steps and to assert or derive a formula describing each component. Such a breakdown for an IBM 3380 READ or WRITE is shown in Figure 10-3.

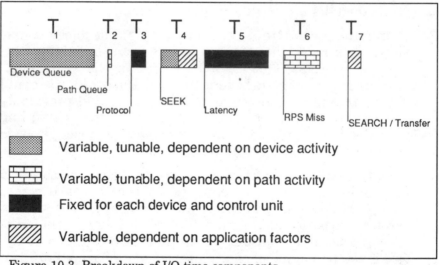

Figure 10-3. Breakdown of I/O time components

When the formulæ include quasi-independent variables such as path busy or device busy, or assumptions such as the choice of a queueing model, the model should be evaluated for each meaningful value of such parameters. Predictions of overall service times or response times should then be checked or *calibrated* against actual experience and the model refined until it is valid for significant cases.

A significant pitfall in DASD modeling is to assume that the numbers reported for device and path utilization for a single system characterize the device or path, even though it is shared between multiple physical, logical, or virtual systems. Especially when device queueing is to be calculated, only overall device utilization (from all sharing systems) is an accurate input.

Let us assume that we will find a block size of 4096 bytes useful for further analysis. We analyze a READ operation as follows:

## 10.3.1. $T_1$, UCBBSY delay

MVS will not attempt an I/O operation if the device is already known to be busy executing an I/O operation initiated by the current system. This condition is indicated by the "on" condition of a bit symbolically named UCBBSY in the device's *Unit Control Block (UCB:* a logical resource that MVS uses to represent the device). The operation is placed on a queue associated with the UCB until the previous I/O is completed.

UCBBSY delay cannot be represented by a simple formula. It is entirely dependent on the type and duration of the competing I/O activity on the device. Most authors assume that the competing I/O is independent of the operation being analyzed, and that the device has an exponential distribution of service times. These assumptions define an M/M/1 queueing model. Using that model, the expected value of the queueing delay is

$$T_1 = \frac{S_d \cdot B_d}{1 - B_d}$$

Where

$T_1$ is the name we assign to this component.

$S_d$ is the expected value of device service time.

$B_d$ is the mean device busy fraction of time.

The M/M/1 assumptions do not hold up if competing activity is not independent, or if the service time distribution is more deterministic than an exponential distribution. Consider, for instance, a case in which a data set is being copied, block by block, to another extent on the same device. M/M/1 can be thrown out because its assumption of independence does not apply. The delay can be calculated without resort to queueing theory and represents a worst-case example of *synchronous delay*.

As another exception to M/M/1, consider a dedicated paging volume responding only to single page faults. In this case, the M/M/1 model is too pessimistic, since the device service times are likely to be very consistent or *deterministic*, rather than exponentially distributed. In this case, M/D/1 is a more appropriate model, and yields half the queueing delay of M/M/1.

## 10.3.2. T$_2$, Initial path delay

We continue to assume that the CPU time component of I/O service time is negligible. The next opportunity for delay, after the device itself is found not to be busy from the current system, comes about when the selected path is busy due to another I/O operation. In MVS/370 when both channel paths are busy, queueing takes place at a symbolic entity known as a *logical channel*, and the START I/O FAST instruction has not yet succeeded. In MVS/XA (or MVS/ESA), the START SUBCHANNEL instruction always succeeds and the dynamic channel subsystem hardware tries and retries all defined and available paths until the I/O actually begins. When the path-busy condition can be attributed to busy control units, the queuing in XA takes place at the level of a *logical control unit* or *logical path*, a symbolic entity managed by the channel subsystem. This delay is known as *pending* (PEND) time in XA and ESA I/O reports.

Initial delay due to device controller (head of string) contention appears at this stage of the I/O operation, as does device delay due to use by another system (shared DASD contention). Estimating shared DASD delay requires knowledge of device activity due to all connected systems, and follows the same models as T$_1$ above.

Initial path delay, other than for shared DASD, is estimated according to a simple formula for single-path devices:

$$T_2 = \frac{B_p \cdot S_p}{2}$$

Where

T$_2$ is the name we assign to this component.

B$_p$ is the fraction of time that the path is busy, interpreted as a probability.

S$_p$ is the expected value of a burst of path service time.

The probability-weighted service time burst is halved because the current demand for service is random with respect to the previous path activity. For a typical 3380 case, $T_2$ is about half a millisecond.

With multiple paths, we have no simple estimator of the path-busy probability like the single path-busy fraction. If we regard $B_p$ as a probability and the activity of multiple paths as independent, we can raise $B_p$ in the formula above to a power representing the number of paths available for the I/O operation. It may be seen that $T_2$ is negligible for an I/O device using two or more paths.

## 10.3.3. $T_3$, Initial CONNECT period (protocol)

Once the path is secured, CCWs specifying positioning actions are transferred to the control unit and then to the device controller for execution. During this time, path selection microcode in the storage director and device controller is executed, and dynamic allegiances are created between the channel and the storage director. The time used for all this intercommunication is known as *protocol* time and varies from device to device, from connection option to connection option, and even from microcode level to microcode level, but is typically one to three milliseconds. Protocol time for some control units is divided into two subcomponents, *overlapped* and *unoverlapped*. Unoverlapped protocol requires connect time; overlapped protocol can be executed during disconnect time but does contribute to the path busy component.

Typical protocol values for various devices include:

| Device | Overlapped | Unoverlapped |
|---|---|---|
| 3350 | 0.8 ms | 1.0 ms |
| 3375 | 0.8 | 1.0 |
| 3380-A04 | 0.48 | 1.0 |
| 3380 (DPS) | 1.6 | 1.0 |
| 3380 J/K (3990) | 0.5 | 1.0 |
| 8380-RQ* | 0.5 | 1.0 |
| * The 8380-RQ device is described at the end of section 10.3.6. | | |

Protocol times have not been published for solid-state devices. The manufacturers typically state an "access time" of about .3 millisecond. We will assume an unoverlapped protocol time of .5 millisecond for solid state devices, an access time of .1 millisecond for a miss, and .5 millisecond for a hit in cache devices, the latter in addition to the base control unit protocol. The 3990 protocol time is a very preliminary estimate from an unofficial IBM source. The 8380-RQ time is estimated based on comparable technology.

### 10.3.4. T4, Disconnect for SEEK

When actuator motion is required, a SEEK CYLINDER device order is executed. During the time of motion, only the device is active, and the rest of the path is disconnected. (The allegiances established at path selection are retained, so that protocol time is not needed for the subsequent reconnect.) SEEK times are published for each device, but again, they must be interpreted according to the pattern of I/O activity in progress. For example, reading a half-track-blocked sequential data set will require a repeated pattern of 30 no-movement SEEKs followed by a one-cylinder seek. If another data set is active on the device, however, this pattern will be broken up by SEEKs between the active data areas.

Published "average SEEK" times represent seeking across one-third of the cylinders on the device. However, measured results for typical application mixes have shown that a 25 percent incidence of "average SEEKs" is a good approximation to the mixture of no-movement SEEKs, minimum SEEKs, and average SEEKs experienced in those workloads. The following table shows minimum, maximum, average, and typical SEEK times for a selection of devices.

| Device | Minimum | Average | Maximum | Typical |
|---|---|---|---|---|
| 3350 | 10 ms | 25 ms | 30 ms | 6.25 ms |
| 3375 | 4 | 19 | 34 | 4.75 |
| 3380x04 | 3 | 16 | 30 | 4.0 |
| 3380AA4 | 3 | 16 | 30 | 4.0 |
| 3380xD4 | 3 | 15 | 28 | 3.75 |
| 3380xE4 | 3 | 17 | 31 | 4.25 |
| 3380xJ2/4 | 2 | 12 | 21 | 3.0 |
| 8380-RQ | 2 | 12 | 21 | 3.0 |
| 3380xK4 | 2 | 16 | 29 | 4.0 |

SEEK time is not present for fixed-head devices such as the IBM 2305, for solid-state devices, and for READ-hits on cache devices. For READ-misses, the operation proceeds as for uncached DASD, with the details of particular hardware determining whether data transfer to the channel is in parallel with cache staging, or done as a subsequent operation.

Performance characteristics of WRITEs to cached devices are more highly dependent on hardware variations. If the cache is managed in the "store-in" manner, or if a separate integrity-write area of storage is provided, WRITE hits are performed without a disconnect, followed by later asynchronous updating of the backing store device. With "store-through" cache management, the WRITE is not completed (the device remains busy) until the DASD is updated. In most cache designs, WRITE misses are equivalent to uncached WRITEs, but more responsive options are possible with nonvolatile buffering storage.

SEEK delay on DASD can be minimized with planning, and with subsequent tuning actions when justified because of delay to a key workload. For instance, several data sets required at the same time should not be on the same device if good response time is required. In more complex data structures, multiple areas of a direct-access data set or data base might be separated across volumes. Allocations of space on DASD should be compact; routine maintenance using defragmentation utilities can hold down seeking due to the use of multiple extents when data sets grow.

When numerous small, active data sets fill a high-capacity device, great benefit comes from attaching that device to a cached control unit. SEEK and latency delay is cut dramatically, and RPS miss is virtually eliminated.

## 10.3.5. T5, Latency

Disk storage devices are not truly direct access or random access. There is an element of sequential delay while waiting for data on a track. The time spent waiting for the first byte of desired data to appear under the read head is called *latency*. Finding the correct record is done with a combination of SEEK and SET SECTOR, device orders established by separate CCWs. In most current device and control unit combinations, both of these commands are fetched together and communicated to the device as a combined device order. With newer control units, a combined operation called LO-CATE RECORD may be used with the same effect.

With SEEK completed, latency begins. Plainly, the latency delay ranges from zero to the time taken for a full rotation of the disk. After the specified sector (circumferential or rotational position) is at the heads, the path must be reestablished so that the record may be located and the data transfer initiated. (The possible additional delays of the reconnect, also dependent on device rotation time as one factor, are covered under $T_6$ below.)

| Device | Rotation Time | Nominal Latency |
|--------|---------------|-----------------|
| 3350 | 16.67 ms | 8.33 ms |
| 3375 | 20.20 | 10.10 |
| 2305-2 | 10.00 | 5.00 |
| 3380 | 16.56 | 8.28 |

An early engineering triumph over latency delay was achieved at high cost on the now-obsolete IBM 2305-2. Latency was reduced by use of a multiple requesting feature included with the device and its IBM 2835 control unit. The device appeared to MVS as a cluster of eight devices with successive addresses, and each such address or *exposure* could be driven independently. If requests are independent of each other (as for page-ins),[3] I/O delay may be reduced because the order of reconnect, and hence of I/O completion, is determined by the circumferential order of the desired data on the disk surface. The same multiple exposure approach was used with the IBM 3880 Model 11 cached paging subsystem, permitting multiple requests to be sent to the subsystem and letting hits be completed while misses were being serviced from the backing DASD.

Solid-state and cache devices eliminate or reduce latency much the same as they cut down SEEK delay: No motion means no delay.

---

3  A page-in to resolve a page fault has no related successors, since the address space incurring the page fault cannot proceed.

## 10.3.6. T$_6$, RPS miss (reconnect) delay

The saga of Rotational Position Sensing (RPS) and RPS miss began when Disconnected Command Chaining (DCC), introduced along with block multiplexor channels and the IBM 2314 two decades ago, was extended to include not only SEEK, but latency as well. DCC was introduced to increase the beneficial utilization of scarce and expensive channels and control units by allowing the active path elements to be freed while slow, device-specific operations could proceed on their own. DCC for SEEK was unconditionally helpful. When the SEEK was completed and the device was ready for reconnect, no further delay was possible; the device waited patiently for the path, and the subsequent SEARCH and data transfer were then executed.

The latency period, half a rotation on average, was a connected operation; SEARCH requires the entire path from channel to device. When the SEARCH was satisfied, data transfer proceeded with no further delay. Why, then, was RPS needed? Remember that channels were expensive and that SEARCH required the channel. Suppose that the disconnect continued after the SEEK was completed, extending into a device-specific simple operation to detect a particular angular position. Reconnect could then take place, followed by a much-reduced SEARCH and then the data transfer operation. Thus RPS was introduced, along with an unwanted new phenomenon.

RPS succeeded in improving the effective data transfer rates of channels and storage directors. Beneficial utilization went up; overall usage went down. The price for the improvement, however, was the creation of a new kind of performance degradation. If the path was busy when reconnect was attempted after the SET SECTOR operation was satisfied, the device could not wait for the path as it could after SEEK. Instead, a full rotation was wasted before the reconnect could be attempted again. If we make the queueing-theory leap of faith, that the average path utilization ($U_p$) over some interval is a good approximation to the probability that the path will be busy at some time of interest, we see that the probability of an RPS miss is equal to that utilization, and that the magnitude of the miss is exactly one rotation period. Subsequent misses are possible, with probabilities given by successive powers of $U_p$. This seems simple enough.

But it isn't. The path utilization of interest is not the entire utilization, but rather what Tom Beretvas of IBM calls *residual path busy* (RPB)—path busy with the activity of the device being analyzed removed. In the formulæ for RPS miss, $U_p$ is in all cases RPB, given by

$$RPB = \frac{U_p - U_d}{1 - u_d}$$

where $U_p$ is the path utilization, and $U_d$ is that part of the path utilization due to the current device. It may be seen that RPB is zero for a device on a dedicated path, reminding us that devices on dedicated paths cannot experience RPS miss.

The formula for the simple case of RPS miss on a single path is thus

$$M_e = R_d \cdot (U_p + U_p^2 + ...)$$

where $M_e$ is the expected value of RPS miss, $R_d$ is the device rotation period, and $U_p$ is residual path busy. In closed form, the formula is precisely the M/M/1 queueing formula for delay in a queue to a single server with exponentially distributed service time $R_d$ and utilization $U_p$:

$$M_e = \frac{R_d \cdot U_p}{1 - U_p}$$

In MVS/370, path elements can appear to be busier with respect to a given device than indicated by overall utilizations; multiple paths in MVS/370 improved availability at a cost in performance. An *effective path busy* correction (for the performance loss caused by multiple paths) is needed in addition to the residual path busy correction. The net effect in MVS/370 was that RPS miss (a function of effective path utilization) became a source of significant I/O performance degradation, and a prime problem to be solved in the process of I/O performance analysis and tuning.

With Extended Architecture, the beginning of a solution was at hand. First, the 3380, with Dynamic Pathing, was announced, before the XA announcement. The 3380-AA4 was initially announced as a device that offered only Dynamic Path Selection. This feature seemed at first (before XA) indistinguishable in practice from String Switching, available on the IBM 3350 and a source of performance degradation as the price of an improvement in availability.

When XA was announced, the full Dynamic Pathing capability was revealed, and the shrewd analysts who recommended 3380-A04s (without dynamic pathing) were considerably embarrassed. Dynamic Path Reconnect (the other part of Dynamic Pathing) exploited two paths at first, cutting RPS miss drastically. (The probability of the first miss was now roughly comparable to that of the second miss in MVS/370.) With the 3990 control units and 3380 J and K models, four paths are supported, nearly eliminating RPS miss at moderate path utilizations.

Contemporaneous developments also reduced the magnitude of the RPS miss problem. Devices that do not disconnect from the path have no reconnect problems; solid-state devices, and cache devices encountering hits, do not disconnect. Channels are now relatively cheap and fast, so there is less need to multiplex on individual channels. With the 3990, individual control units are less expensive as well.

As we view the rise and fall of RPS miss, we might wonder: Is RPS needed any more? Are average channel utilizations low enough now to render connected SEARCHes a nonproblem? Can further improvements in outboard intelligence render connected SEARCHes unnecessary? Can a device (and possibly its head-of-string) handle a new kind of SEARCH and data transfer without rotational delay beyond nominal latency? Can read-head buffering eliminate some part of latency as well? The answers to these questions may establish a new base of efficiency for DASD I/O in the future, without the compromises inherent in old solutions like RPS.

The initial device in the new generation is Storage Technology Corporation's 8380RQ, a 3380-class device with *actuator-level buffering* (ALB™). (An 8380R model offers ALB as an optional feature.) The device features a single track-size buffer which starts to fill as soon as SEEK is complete. Latency is the only rotational delay. SET SECTOR takes on the character of SEEK: the device waits for the first time the path is available, then data transfer proceeds without need for synchronization. Because the buffer is limited to a single track, multitrack operations (as for block paging) may suffer a second latency delay, or the microcode might suppress buffering for multitrack operations. A second track buffer could make sequential exchange buffering possible.

## 10.3.7. T7, SEARCH and data transfer

Once reconnect is achieved, the remainder of the I/O operation is dependent only on the physical characteristics of the device. For solid-state devices and for cache READ hits, a minimal access delay is followed by data transfer at the rated device speed. Thus our 4096-byte transfer will take 1.37 milliseconds at 3 megabytes per second or .91 millisecond at 4.5 megabytes per second. Access delay adds about one-half millisecond, so the times become 1.87 and 1.41 milliseconds, respectively.

On "real" DASD, SEARCH time must be added. If we note that ten 4096-byte records can be contained on a 3380 track, it seems right simply to assume that finding and transferring one of them takes no more than one-tenth of a device rotation period, or 1.66 milliseconds. The SEARCH time is absorbed in this approximation.

## 10.3.8. Summary of modeling results

To make use of such modeled results, it is necessary to assume an underlying level of device and path utilization, and an incremental I/O rate to be analyzed. (If the model is being used to analyze a real system, measurement data can supply precise starting values.) The modeled quantities $T_2$ through $T_7$, and finally $T_1$, are then calculated and accumulated to arrive at estimated response times.

Several cases of single-page (4096 bytes) READs on various devices, in 370 and XA environments, are examined below. (ESA environments are equivalent to XA in this context.) The first case represents best-case performance. No competing device activity is assumed, and the entire path to the device is assumed to be only 10 percent busy from other devices. (No I/O rate appears in Case 1; these are response times for isolated I/Os on idle devices.)

| Case 1—Unconstrained Device Performance | | | | |
|---|---|---|---|---|
| **Device** | **Director** | **System** | **Response Time** | **Notes** |
| 3350-A2 | 3880-1 | MVS/370 | 21.3 ms | |
| 3350-DP | 3880-1 | MVS/370 | 21.3 | (Dual Port) |
| 3375-A2 | 3880-1 | MVS/370 | 20.8 | |
| 3375-ABBD | 3880-1 | MVS/370 | 20.7 | (Dual Port) |
| 3380-A04 | 3880-3 | MVS/370 | 16.9 | |
| 3380-AA4 | 3880-3 | MVS/370 | 16.8 | |
| 3380-AA4 | 3880-3 | MVS/XA | 16.8 | |
| 3380-AD4 | 3880-3 | MVS/XA | 14.9 | |
| 3380-AE4 | 3880-3 | MVS/XA | 15.4 | |
| 3380-AE4 | 3880-23 | MVS/XA | 4.4 | (cache) |
| 3380-AJ4 | 3880-3 | MVS/XA | 14.1 | |
| 8380-RQ | STC | N/A | 14.0 | (ALB) |
| 3380-AK4 | 3880-3 | MVS/XA | 15.1 | (cache) |
| 3380-AK4 | 3990-3 | MVS/XA | 3.1 | (+ 4.5 MB) |
| SSD | N/A | N/A | 2.2 | |
| SSD | N/A | N/A | 1.8 | (4.5 MB) |

The second case represents "normal" device and path loading according to commonly accepted rules of thumb. Because we are assuming uniform block size and minimal seeking, it is appropriate to use the M/D/1 queueing formula to estimate device queueing delay. Device utilization is held to the rule-of-thumb limit of 33 percent. Total path utilization is held to the common System/370 guideline of 30 percent; in XA (and ESA) configurations, DASD path utilization goes to 40 percent. Path utilization for cache and solid-state devices is 75 percent. The 3990-2 cases assume four-path operation.

| Case 2—Devices Loaded to Guidelines | | | | | |
|---|---|---|---|---|---|
| Device | Director | System | I/O Rate | Response Time | Notes |
| 3350-A2 | 3880-1 | MVS/370 | 13.1/sec | 31.5 ms | |
| 3350-DP | 3880-1 | MVS/370 | 13.2 | 31.2 | (Dual Port) |
| 3375-A2 | 3880-1 | MVS/370 | 12.9 | 32.0 | |
| 3375-ABBD | 3880-1 | MVS/370 | 13.0 | 31.7 | (Dual Port) |
| 3380-A04 | 3880-3 | MVS/370 | 15.7 | 26.2 | |
| 3380-AA4 | 3880-3 | MVS/370 | 16.2 | 25.4 | |
| 3380-AA4 | 3880-3 | MVS/XA | 18.2 | 22.5 | |
| 3380-AD4 | 3880-3 | MVS/XA | 18.5 | 22.2 | |
| 3380-AE4 | 3880-3 | MVS/XA | 18.0 | 22.9 | |
| 3380-AE4 | 3880-23 | MVS/XA | 46.6 | 8.8 | (cache) |
| 3380-AJ4 | 3880-3 | MVS/XA | 20.5 | 20.1 | |
| 3380-AK4 | 3990-2 | MVS/XA | 20.0 | 20.6 | |
| 8380-RQ | STC | N/A | 23.7 | 17.3 | (ALB) |
| 3380-AK4 | 3990-3 | MVS/XA | 80.1 | 5.1 | (cache) |
| 3380-AK4 | 3990-3 | MVS/XA | 81.3 | 5.1 | (+ 4.5 MB) |
| SSD | N/A | N/A | 133.3 | 3.1 | |
| SSD | N/A | N/A | 169.5 | 2.4 | (4.5 MB) |

The last case represents heavily loaded devices and paths. We assume the device to be 50 percent utilized, but with exponentially distributed arrival rates and service times. M/M/1 queueing is thus assumed. Total path utilization is assumed to be 40 percent for 370 DASD, 50 percent for XA or ESA DASD, and 80 percent for cache and solid state devices. Again, the 3990-2 cases assume four-path operation.

| Case 3—Heavily Loaded Devices | | | | | |
|---|---|---|---|---|---|
| Device | Director | System | I/O Rate | Response Time | Notes |
| 3350-A2 | 3880-1 | MVS/370 | 17.5/sec | 57.1 ms | |
| 3350-DP | 3880-1 | MVS/370 | 17.7 | 56.5 | (Dual Port) |
| 3375-A2 | 3880-1 | MVS/370 | 16.8 | 59.5 | |
| 3375-ABBD | 3880-1 | MVS/370 | 17.0 | 58.9 | (Dual Port) |
| 3380-A04 | 3880-3 | MVS/370 | 20.5 | 48.9 | |
| 3380-AA4 | 3880-3 | MVS/370 | 21.2 | 47.1 | |
| 3380-AA4 | 3880-3 | MVS/XA | 23.9 | 41.9 | |
| 3380-AD4 | 3880-3 | MVS/XA | 24.2 | 41.3 | |
| 3380-AE4 | 3880-3 | MVS/XA | 23.6 | 42.4 | |
| 3380-AE4 | 3880-23 | MVS/XA | 64.8 | 15.4 | (cache) |
| 3380-AJ4 | 3990-2 | MVS/XA | 34.7 | 28.7 | |
| 3380-AK4 | 3990-2 | MVS/XA | 32.5 | 30.8 | |
| 8380-RQ | STC | N/A | 35.9 | 27.8 | (ALB) |
| 3380-AK4 | 3990-3 | MVS/XA | 95.7 | 10.4 | (cache) |
| 3380-AK4 | 3990-3 | MVS/XA | 96.2 | 10.4 | (+ 4.5 MB) |
| SSD | N/A | N/A | 201.4 | 5.0 | |
| SSD | N/A | N/A | 256.1 | 3.9 | (4.5 MB) |

## 10.3.9. Conclusions from modeling

A few observations can be made from these modeled results:

- For 3380s without track buffering, XA or ESA provide a significant improvement in response time over that of MVS/370, as well as higher I/O rates.

- There are small differences among 3380 models, smaller than between 370 and XA.

- Cache and solid state devices suffer far less response time degradation with increasing load than do pure DASD, even with much higher I/O loads.

- The new ALB technology appears to erase the XA advantages in throughput and response time.

## 10.4. Review of Measurement and Modeling

A key need in understanding and implementing MVS performance management is to be familiar with readily available tools for measuring all aspects of system and workload performance. Whichever tools are at hand are often used only occasionally, when acute problems occur. In the confrontational environment often encountered by performance analysts, learning a tool "under the gun" is not a good career choice.

If service level targets are agreed upon by data center and user management, measurement to those targets is the first necessary step. (The importance of service targets cannot be overemphasized. If you're aiming at nothing, that's what you'll hit.) While the targets are being met, using an historical execution-state analysis tool can help the analyst understand impending constraints and assist in refining capacity projections to the extent of determining when CPU or storage upgrades are needed.

When targets cease to be met consistently, the type of incident determines the time span of the tool to be used. A gradual and consistent erosion is usually best analyzed with an historical tool. Sudden loss of a target, on the other hand, should be diagnosed with a real-time monitor. (Such a sudden change in performance should be examined with a change monitor as well. A system or application does not wake up and call in sick. If performance changes, something has changed in some other factor: hardware, system software, application software, volume, system parameters, etc.)

Modeling is usually used to aid in capacity planning. An *ad hoc* form of analytic modeling can be used to make performance predictions or choices, or to analyze DASD performance when DASD represents a significant bottleneck.

# 11

# Solving Performance Problems

So far, we have examined MVS's resources and the factors that affect the performance of workloads. In the previous chapter we looked at ways to monitor resources and workloads and to model the behavior of DASD I/O. We thus have the means to identify service problems. In this chapter we will consider ways to anticipate and prevent performance problems, and define further the steps that may be taken to solve problems found by monitoring.

## 11.1. Lost Opportunities

At many installations, MVS is received and installed in preconfigured offerings known by such names as IPO, MVS Express, CBDPO, and CBIPO. While these offerings simplify greatly the process of installing MVS and keeping it current, they necessarily bring with them a highly constrained hardware environment. Getting MVS "up and running" is reduced to restoring two or three DASD volumes and then IPLing from one of them. Those volumes include all of the MVS parameter, procedure, and load libraries, JES SPOOL space and the JES2 CHKPT data set, page data sets, SYS1.LOGREC, and SMF data sets. Again, in the case of a new MVS system, proving the viability and basic functionality of the system, and merging applications with it, are activities that correctly receive higher priority than adjusting the system for best performance. It is easy to take the position that adjustments can wait until the workload has built up and the first problems appear.

IBM recognizes that this is not a productive approach. Spelled out in the online and printed documentation for IPO and its successors are explicit and frequent admonitions to distribute the key system and subsystem data sets across multiple paths and volumes. The harried system programmer, however, remains too busy with functional issues to be concerned with reading such publications, let alone responding to their prescriptions. In practice, therefore, performance problems tend to appear as the production workload is applied.

### 11.1.1. A typical scenario

Consider the appearance and evolution of "paging problems" in a typical mixed-workload new MVS system without expanded storage. There is a gradual buildup of TSO users and the batch jobs that they submit. At the same time, more and more users log on to CICS and soon produce a significant transaction rate. What happens all too frequently is that some time during the buildup, CICS response time starts suffering and TSO users begin to experience intermittent long delays.

What's happening is that MVS's default real storage management strategy is being allowed to run without installation-specific control. That strategy has these elements:

- As the multiprogramming level (MPL) increases, the working set of active address spaces (initially just the aggregate of allocated frames) increases, depleting the available frame queue (AFQ). When AFQ goes below its low threshold (MCCAFCLO), page stealing commences.

- Another influence leading to depletion of the AFQ is MVS's default bias in favor of logical swapping. Even though the AFQ may be empty, logically swapped address spaces will not be converted to physical swaps until a logical swap duration exceeds the system think time, plus a release-dependent "grace period."[1]

- MPL will not be reduced until the defaults enumerated in Chapter 7 are crossed: Demand paging rate exceeds the value that would account for five percent of CPU utilization, the system wide high UIC is less than 2, or the CPU is fully utilized and at least one address space has not been dispatched during an SRM RM2 interval.

- Address spaces (other than TSO users in a rapid succession of trivial transactions) will be subject to substantial delay from page fault processing, caused by subsequent reference to pages previously stolen.

What's wrong here? Nothing! MVS is doing exactly what its default parameters tell it to do. There are two complementary mechanisms to control the available frame queue. The micro-level control, page stealing, operates without the need for direction and is always active. Macro-level control is done by MPL adjustment. However, the MPL adjustment mechanism is to all intents and purposes crippled by default. More precisely, it is not responsive to any control variable related directly to real storage constraint. Compounding the potential for problems, the default control of logical swap eligibility is strongly influenced only by UIC (if less than 30) and only weakly controlled by AFQ and the amount of storage already allocated.

As pointed out in Chapter 7, RCCPTRT is the OPT parameter most appropriate for MPL adjustment, but it is shipped disabled. Simply beginning to use this parameter can overcome most initial "paging problems." In this chapter we'll describe setup activities that should prevent these kinds of avoidable performance problems.

Note that with expanded storage, the effect of central storage depletion is an increased page movement rate to and from expanded storage. If the page movement rate goes above about 500

---

1  System think time by default ranges from zero to 30 seconds, starting at the high value and not moving down until the UIC goes below 10. The grace period was 15 seconds for MVS/370 and XA releases prior to SP2.1.7. In later releases it has been two seconds.

pages per second per 3090-180S (or equivalent) processor, "MVS overhead" (specifically SRB time in the MASTER address space) will appear to increase significantly, leading to "waiting for CPU" delay in all address spaces when central storage is fully utilized.[2] Observable "waiting for page-in" delay will appear only when the amount of expanded storage is inadequate and stolen pages are being migrated from expanded storage to auxiliary storage, or inhibited from going to expanded storage because of low migration age.

## 11.1.2. Consequences of neglect

While it is possible to recover after the fact from most performance problems, being constantly in "react mode" takes its toll. For most performance anomalies, the threshold of notice is much lower for the direct users of the system than it is for those managing it. As response time of a key workload becomes occasionally unacceptable and then consistently substandard, there will already have been a flow of complaints from the most aware (and probably the best informed) of the users. If the data center staff is doing nothing to monitor the quality and consistency of delivered service, the complaints come as a surprise, and the credibility of both those reporting the problem and those accused of causing it come into question.

As the complaints mount, they will tend to be escalated to higher levels of management. In many cases, the ego-involvement and *ad hominem* character of the dialogue worsens until issues reach executive levels. Only then might a decision be made to conduct an objective investigation and create a plan to solve the current problem. The task force (the formation of which is a very likely development) may call in a consultant or rely on the hardware vendor's marketing support staff for advice. There is little doubt that money will be spent, and that the data center staff will have a solution imposed on them that further attacks their credibility.

---

2   The delay will be there, but it cannot be measured by any monitor because the page-fault handling code operates at the top priority in the system. A sampling monitor will never see an address space waiting for expanded storage page movement.

It doesn't have to be this way. The critical failing that led to the sorry sequence of events was failure to monitor delivered service for quality and consistency. In many installations, more is spent on resource usage accounting systems that capture usage data and apportion costs to the users than on performance monitors and staff to ensure consistent user satisfaction.

In an installation where customer[3] satisfaction is a genuine goal, the cost of tools to measure, track, and report on service and to help solve problems rapidly is paid willingly. In turn, the cost of such tools is more than paid back by eliminating the *ad hoc* emergency measures put together for dealing with problems that are ignored until they have been escalated.

### 11.1.3. A better way

With a proactive attitude regarding performance management, a data center staff can expect a cooperative relationship with its customers, rather than the all-too-frequent adversarial one. When the data center and those it serves agree on the volume of demand, on performance targets, on the methods of measurement and reporting, and on the quality of service shown by those measurements, the benefits can be considerable. The data center staff gains a reserve of credibility and can use that credibility to obtain well-thought-out business volume planning information. The resulting data center capacity plans and their embodiment in hardware come far closer to what is optimal for the business than plans developed in a grudging atmosphere of mutual distrust.

### 11.1.4. Picking up the pieces

Although it is more difficult to repair a reputation than to build one in the first place, such a step is essential when organizing the performance management function in an installation that has not had one in the past. Where there is not sufficient mutual trust to elicit agreement on service targets, the repair process may take even longer. A strategy that has worked is for the data center staff to begin publishing (to management in general)

---

3  Substituting the word "customers" for "users" is an important consciousness-raising device for the data center staff in pursuit of quality service.

frank reports of the data center's own targets and attainment of those targets. After a few months of such unilateral performance reporting, the results take on the character of *de facto* service targets. When the customers begin holding the data center to its own published targets rather than to some vague and subjective measure of acceptable service, the barriers begin to come down.

The fragile measure of trust built in this remedial mode must be reinforced by a consistent orientation to providing acceptable service and accepting, and being responsive to, every complaint from a customer. By now it should be obvious that monitoring and measuring with the appropriate tools is an indispensable part of such a program.

## 11.1.5. How problems arise

Computing systems, especially MVS systems, are generally stable and determinate. Hardware components rarely fail, and the system's hardware behavior is unlikely to change without apparent cause. Somewhat more often, an MVS system software component goes wrong, based on an exceptional input or a rare combination of values. Operating system defects usually lead to ABENDs rather than to performance anomalies. Similarly, subsystem and application program defects usually lead to functional failures.

How, then, do performance problems arise? If not caused by random factors or out-of-the-way program bugs, what will cause a production job to complete within 25 minutes on Tuesday just as it did the thirty previous runs, and then take two hours to complete on Wednesday? Why should TSO trivial response time, previously stable at half a second, increase to two seconds some Monday morning?

The answer is usually unremarkable: Something has changed. Perhaps it was the workload. However, the operations production control staff will know if there is an exceptional increase in volume for a key application, and an unplanned sudden increase in the number of logged-on TSO users is hardly likely.

## What changed?

If we can rule out workload change or random influence as the likely cause for a performance problem, we must conclude that something changed in hardware, software, operating system parameters, or the operating environment of the affected workload.

Most installations have more or less structured change management systems. Such systems tend to concentrate on keeping track of change plans based on what people say, and do not include a means of verifying that an asserted change really occurred.

Access control systems such as IBM's RACF and Computer Associates' Top Secret and ACF2, with logging options active, can keep track of access for update to key data sets. However, they do not intervene in hardware changes, nor can most systems bear the overhead of their logging accesses to all potentially troublesome data sets.

A different kind of program, exemplified by Candle Corporation's DELTAMON for MVS and Computer Associates' CA-EXAMINE, is a change monitor. These programs record and detect status and change information about various hardware, operating system, and data set elements, enabling them to subsequently report on what changed within a time frame.

The combination of change management systems, access control systems, and change monitors can provide the information needed to identify the factors that cause performance changes.

# 11.2. Configuring for Performance

The proactive approach to performance management begins with configuring the hardware and its workloads. Stability depends on being sure that unplanned changes or unforeseen consequences of planned changes can be identified rapidly using the approaches suggested above. The following topics spell out other actions to be taken in advance of problems appearing.

## 11.2.1. Complementary workloads

One of the common mistakes made in setting up MVS systems is to assume that different kinds of workloads together on one system will inevitably interfere with each other. In the interest of preventing such interference, some choose to set up one-dimensional systems with, for instance, one or more systems running only a CICS workload and all-TSO on another system.

If the CICS-only system is production-only, it is difficult to derive full benefit from the CPU resource, because CICS internal queueing will cause considerable delay to transactions ranking low on CICS's internal dispatching queue, at the level of about 70 percent uniprocessor utilization. If the system is a multiprocessor, a highly divided CICS MRO system is needed in order to take full advantage of all processors.

Suppose, however, that we had loaded the system with CICS to a level of 60 percent CPU utilization (representing CICS and MVS overhead, monitors, and necessary supporting subsystems), then added batch to fully load the CPU. If the batch is well behaved, (that is, if it does not make unusual demands for real storage, perform inefficient I/O, or interfere with CICS's I/O devices or ENQueue names), CICS performance should be close to what it could be in a one-dimensional system loaded to about 70 percent CPU utilization.

If there is a clear hierarchy of importance and time urgency in the overall array of MVS work in a data center, it should be possible to load each system to a level just short of that at which internal queueing causes perceptible delay in the highest urgency workload, then to bring the system up to nearly 100 percent utilization with low urgency work. When doing this, it is important to recognize contention possibilities, taking steps to avoid inherent contention in advance, and monitoring key workloads' performance to detect operational contention.

A contention pitfall, related to the idea of setting up one-dimensional systems, is the belief that a development subsystem should be isolated from its corresponding production subsystem, to the extent of placing each on a separate system. While there can be justification for such separation based on integrity considerations, there is often a severe performance penalty. If the entire environment were duplicated on the second system, there would be little potential for interference.

In practice, however, some libraries are left on the production system, with shared access from the development system. Since the purpose of the development system is to bring about change in the production environment, it is almost inevitable that library updates can tie up production libraries. If, on the other hand, production and development run on the same system, member-level updates are much less disruptive, and the impact of development I/O activity is much easier to measure and deal with.

Once again, if workloads are split across systems, make sure the split is as complete as possible.

## 11.2.2. How much real storage?

With Gary King's *Workload Characterization* and *Processor Storage Estimation* methodology available in various forms from IBM, SHARE, GUIDE, and CMG[4], it cannot be said that there is no guidance on establishing a correct real storage configuration. King's methodology is clear and simple, and should be used routinely to check and track workloads against configurations.

One way of looking at real storage is simple: There should be enough real storage to allow the CPU to become fully utilized with acceptably low paging delay in all key workloads. When expanded storage is available, the criteria are a bit more complex:

- The total amount of central and expanded storage should be sufficient to allow all processors to become fully utilized with the desired workload distribution, with little or no page migration to auxiliary storage. Sufficient central storage should be installed (or configured, in a logically partitioned system) to keep the bidirectional expanded storage page

---

4  King's papers may be found in the 1987 and 1988 *Proceedings* of SHARE, GUIDE, and CMG. His IBM *Technical Bulletins* may be obtained through local IBM offices.

movement rate below about 500 pages per second per processor. For an MVS/ESA system, expanded storage should be sufficient to accommodate all current and projected needs for ESO (expanded-storage-only) hiperspaces, in addition to the amount needed as above to prevent unacceptably high page migration.

- For TSO and batch workloads, in which many or most address spaces are swapped out at any given time, relatively less central storage and more expanded storage are needed. Nonswappable subsystem workloads such as CICS derive little direct benefit from expanded storage other than the reduction of paging delay. (In MVS/ESA, VSAM buffers and data tables in hiperspace, and use of LLA and other VLF data spaces provide substantial indirect benefits from expanded storage. CICS/ESA [Version 3 of CICS] will further exploit the ESA environment.)

When PR/SM, MLPF, or MDF is installed, each logical partition or MDF domain must have adequate real storage. Even if storage could be reallocated dynamically down to the level of a single megabyte (as it can be on the latest 3090s with PR/SM), there must be enough to satisfy the peak demand with some reserve available to support reconfiguration. One benefit of multiple-image options is that any system image may have precisely the amount of storage it needs at the moment. A corollary is that the overall system should always be somewhat over-configured for storage in order to be responsive to increases in workload needs.

There is no damage done if real storage is excess to these needs, and there is a loss of apparent CPU capacity if there is insufficient real storage. It would be prudent always to round both central and expanded storage estimates to the next *higher* optional increment size.

Yet another view of storage need is based on "megabytes to MIPS" ratios. In past days, having three megabytes of real storage per MIPS was a common guideline. When the IBM 3084-QX with 128 megabytes became available, the ratio could go up as high as seven to one. A 3090-200 was about as powerful as a 3084-QX, so 128 megabytes would seem to be a normal real storage configuration for a Model 200. The only problem was that the original

3090-200 came with only 64 megabytes of central storage, so expanded storage had to be added to get maximum benefit. Storage-intensive workloads such as CICS caused high page movement rates on such systems. That problem was not solved until central storage sizes were increased on the 3090 E-models.

## 11.2.3. Paging subsystem without expanded storage

In an MVS system without expanded storage, the paging subsystem must have sufficient capacity and responsiveness to avoid becoming a system bottleneck and thus keep workloads from meeting their service targets. Capacity and responsiveness are interrelated. Depending on loading and with model-to-model variations, 3380 paging devices can deliver single page response times of from 20 to 40 milliseconds. When used in a locals-only configuration (without swap data sets), occasional delays waiting for swap I/O (at 50 milliseconds of data transfer time per burst) are traded off for improved average responsiveness based on a large number of local page data sets.

Estimating system paging rates is covered in King's *Workload Characterization*, cited earlier. Setting up an initial paging configuration based on estimated paging rates is derived from Tom Beretvas's modeling (also presented frequently at conferences and described in IBM Technical Bulletins), supported by extensive measurement data. A basic guideline is that a 3380 can sustain between 16 and 24 page-ins per second. For simplicity (and because precision is not very necessary), we assume a capacity of 18 page-ins per second per 3380 page data set.[5] We also assume that a 3380 can handle the swap requirements of about 100 TSO users, thus discounting the number of page data sets by one per hundred TSO users when calculating paging capacity.

The page-in rates are precisely the values to be set as upper limits in the OPT parameter RCCPTRT. The lower limit should be 80 percent of the upper limit, the RCCPTRT values should each be multiplied by 1.8 to arrive at PAGERT1 and PAGERT2, and both PAGERTx parameters should be specified.

---

5  Only one page data set should be defined per 3380 actuator.

**Example:** A large MVS system has 300 TSO users at four page faults per transaction, entering 15 transactions per second. There are five CICS address spaces, each with an acceptable page-in rate of three per second, and one batch swap per second with 15 page faults per batch swap. Miscellaneous paging is five VIO page faults per second and ten page faults per second from other sources. Total page-in rate is accumulated from these elements:

$$
\begin{aligned}
15 \ \text{x} \ 4 &= 60 \quad \text{(TSO)} \\
5 \ \text{x} \ 3 &= 15 \quad \text{(CICS)} \\
&\phantom{=} \ 15 \quad \text{(Batch)} \\
&\phantom{=} \ \ 5 \quad \text{(VIO)} \\
&\phantom{=} \ \underline{10} \quad \text{(Other)} \\
&\phantom{=} 105 \quad \text{(Total)}
\end{aligned}
$$

At 18 page-ins per second per 3380 local page data set, we need six locals for paging and three more to cover the swap activity of 300 TSO users. The batch swapping is absorbed by this configuration without a need for more data sets. RCCPTRT should be set at (86,108); PAGERT1 and PAGERT2 should be set to (156,194).

Caution: The story is not yet complete. TSO and production CICS address spaces *require* storage isolation to function properly in this environment. Not more than one page data set should be on a path. PLPA and CSA page data sets are needed as well, and a duplex page data set should be used to back up the common-area page data sets to ensure maximum availability. The duplex should be separated from PLPA and CSA by unit, string, storage director, channel group, and MP side to the greatest extent possible.

Page data set size is important too. Assume that swapping requires 120 frames per TSO user, and that 1500–2000 frames are needed per production CICS, 200 frames per concurrent batch job, and about 200 frames per system address space. (More precise estimates appear in King's *Workload Characterization*.) The whole requirement should then be quadrupled, since the benefits of contiguous slot allocation begin to disappear at about

25 percent slot utilization per data set and are severely curtailed at 35 percent.

In systems prior to MVS/ESA, a page data set was limited to 65,400 slots, so a number of data sets can be estimated from slot requirements. (MVS/ESA permits full-volume page data sets on any supported device; the benefit is more in enabling a device to be easily reserved for paging than in creating one huge page data set. The latter benefit is of some use with expanded storage.) The number of required page data sets based on assumed paging rates and that based on slot requirements should be compared and the larger number selected.[6]

## Swap Data Sets

Swap data sets were a useful footnote in MVS history. They are obsolete and their use is counterproductive in the vast majority of today's MVS systems. A system with no TSO workload and insignificant batch has no need for swap data sets. A system with nothing but TSO and batch also has no need for swap data sets. The only potential candidates for swap data sets are systems with a mixed workload and a significant level of real storage constraint.

Although swap data sets are never truly required, in some unusual configurations they might be of some benefit. Two such far-fetched exceptions are:

- The system is very constrained for real storage, and solid-state devices (SSDs) are being used for paging. Since there is no block paging benefit with solid-state devices, swap data sets on DASD can divert a load that may otherwise cause the solid-state device to overflow paging to DASD. With an adequate solid-state configuration, swap data sets are not necessary. Using the quantities assumed in the example given above, 144 additional megabytes of SSD would be needed to support 300 swapped-out users.

- A key workload has such a pathologically random storage reference pattern that storage isolation is of no help. Fast

6   See section 11.2.4 for another factor affecting page data set size.

and consistent paging response time requires the use of swap data sets, as well as an isolated cluster of paging volumes or enough solid-state paging capacity to avoid spill.

When swap data sets are used, TSO storage isolation is a must to complete the job of unloading the local page data sets. Enough swap data sets to accommodate the approximate 90th percentile swap-group size, on separate paths to ensure full I/O concurrency, minimize the time spent waiting for a subsequent swap-in I/O while holding a partial working set.

## Related Considerations

*Storage Isolation.* As indicated above, storage isolation is an integral part of real storage management, especially without expanded storage, with or without swap data sets. There are several ways to use this powerful tool:

- **TSO first and second period:** Specify PWSS=($sgs$,*), where $sgs$ is the desired swap group size. The purpose of this specification is to eliminate up to 60 percent of TSO page faults by including recently referenced pages in the swap-in group. In turn, page data set I/Os are reduced, thus improving demand page response times. The cost (in added data transfer time for swapping) is negligible.

  To estimate the proper value for $sgs$, observe the real storage frame counts for TSO address spaces in first and second period at a time of peak usage,[7] using a tool like OMEGAMON for MVS or RMF Monitor II. Estimate the smallest value exceeding about 90 percent of the address spaces' frame counts. Round this count up to the next higher multiple of the swap set size for your system. (Local page data sets on 3380s have a swap set size of 30 slots; swap data sets use a 12-slot swap set.)

  Tune $sgs$ (and verify that storage isolation is beneficial) by observing execution states for the workload. (EPILOG for MVS is an appropriate tool.) If PRIVATE PAGE-IN WAIT is

---

7  The frame count at peak activity times is likely to be close to the minimum working set due to page stealing.

significantly greater than SWAP PAGE-IN WAIT, increase *sgs*. If SWAP PAGE-IN WAIT is significantly greater than PRIVATE PAGE-IN WAIT, decrease *sgs*.

- Production Subsystems: In the single performance period definition for a subsystem, specify PWSS=(*min*,*) and PPGRTR=(*ok,high*), where *min* is your estimate of the minimum frame count needed in the address space to provide basic functions without incurring a page fault, *ok* is a tolerable page fault rate, and *high* is the maximum acceptable page fault rate for the address space. The purpose of this specification is to eliminate a large number of page faults by retaining recently referenced pages in the address space. The cost (of limiting page stealing in these address spaces) is seen as added page stealing and consequent page faulting in unprotected address spaces.

- **Unfavored Address Spaces:** Specify PWSS=(0,*max*), where *max* is the frame count above which you want preferred page stealing to take place. This "negative storage isolation" may be helpful if the preferred workload on the system has an erratic storage reference pattern such that normal storage isolation is ineffective, or if the less preferred workload has an unusually large virtual storage requirement but a much smaller working set over some interval like one to two seconds.

*Logical Swap Controls.* The default controls favor logical swapping unless the UIC is consistently less than 20. There is a full discussion of various strategies for changing the logical swap controls in Chapter 8.

## 11.2.4. Paging configurations with expanded storage

Expanded storage changes MVS systems significantly. Assuming a sufficient amount of expanded storage, its principal effect is to eliminate direct dependency on page data sets. Enough auxiliary storage slots must still be available to avoid running afoul of auxiliary storage shortage thresholds[8], but performance becomes a secondary consideration in establishing the paging set-up. In an MVS/ESA system, one full-volume local page data set may be sufficient.

**Caution:** Make sure that RCCPTRT, PAGERT1, and PAGERT2 reflect the capabilities of the actual paging subsystem, with possible derating to reflect some level of page migration. The only time the paging subsystem will be called upon to any great degree is when expanded storage is fully utilized. It is important, therefore, to track expanded storage occupancy and migration rate over time to guard against unwelcome surprises.

The balance of central to expanded storage is reflected in the page movement rate. When this value exceeds 500 pages per second (in and out) per processor, central storage has become constrained. Other than a central storage capacity upgrade, two moves that can help are to reduce the number of fixed pages and to cut back on logical swapping.

The migration of pages from expanded storage to auxiliary storage is disruptive (requiring use of CPU and central storage at a time of system stress). Migration that brings the CPU to saturation is a sign of desperately overloaded expanded storage. This condition is very likely to appear in MVS/ESA systems as ESO hiperspaces and high-performance (I/O avoidance) options of DFSMS and of the base control program come into wide use. As ESA use grows and matures, a capacity planner would do well to track migration age over time and yell loudly for help when the highest criteria-age threshold (900 by default for ESCTVIO and ESCTBDS) is crossed consistently.

## 11.2.5. Shared DASD considerations

A given amount of DASD contention has a greater impact in a shared DASD environment than on a single system. Channels, control units, and device controllers have more work to do and are therefore busy longer. GRS or equivalent facilities also work harder with an increased level of cross-system ENQueues. As-

---

8   These values, MCCASMT1 and MCCASMT2, are *not* OPT parameters. They remain as ZAPpable constants and are documented on the last page of Chapter 5 in each edition of *Initialization and Tuning*.

sessing DASD delay in a shared environment is considerably more difficult than on a single-image system.

When there is a choice of keeping related workloads together or splitting them across systems, the effects of coupling through shared DASD should be a key factor in making the decision. Two developing trends complicate the picture. The ease of creating multiple system images with PR/SM-LPAR, MLPF, or MDF may increase the incidence of shared DASD problems. On the other hand, as System-Managed Storage in MVS/ESA unfolds, a solution to data sharing may be part of the picture.

Until there is a no-penalty way of sharing DASD, placing applications on systems so as to maximize data clustering on individual systems and minimize active sharing can help reduce the impact of shared DASD contention.

## 11.2.6. Use of PLPA and LLA to reduce I/O

The pageable link pack area (PLPA) is a classical MVS tradeoff. Placing modules in PLPA eliminates I/O and program fetch processing by allowing only a single copy of a sharable module to serve all users. The price of this convenience is use of virtual storage in commonly addressed storage. As virtual storage constraint below 16 MB increased, taking modules out of PLPA became a necessary activity, especially in MVS/370. In MVS/XA and MVS/ESA, the Extended PLPA (above 16 MB) can regain the PLPA benefit while easing the virtual storage constraint in the lower addressing range. As more modules become capable of running in EPLPA, XA and ESA systems will again realize the full benefit of sharing reenterable modules.

When the major benefit of placing a module in PLPA is I/O avoidance rather than module sharing, MVS/ESA makes another option available. The ESA Library Lookaside Area places modules in a data space, making functions provided by such modules available without I/O, and without compromising the size of the common area below 16 MB. LLA is slightly slower than PLPA (because Program Fetch is involved), but non-reenterable executable modules are also eligible for inclusion in LLA ; they can not be in PLPA.

Modules that are heavily used by multiple swappable address spaces such as TSO are good PLPA candidates. Those loaded infrequently by nonswappable address spaces could better be placed in LLA. The reduction made possible in PLPA size can then be added to the private area for all address spaces.

## 11.2.7. XA and ESA options to avoid I/O

### Library Lookaside

The Library Lookaside Area in ESA provides a way to trade virtual storage in a data space (and its backing expanded or auxiliary storage) for the I/O of program fetch. In MVS/XA, "LLA" stands for *Linklist* Lookaside Area, a more limited function that eliminates only directory I/O.

### VLF

The ESA LLA function is built on a lower-level function, the Virtual Lookaside Facility (VLF), that can use data spaces to contain whole, or parts of, selected libraries not restricted to load module libraries. In TSO, for instance, ISPF panel libraries and command procedure (CLIST) and REXX (EXEC) libraries can be managed by VLF to trade virtual storage in a data space for I/O.

### Data-in-Virtual

MVS/XA and MVS/ESA both support Data-in-Virtual, a set of primitive functions enabling an application program to manage a large random-access data aggregate as an object embodied in a VSAM Linear Data Set. Only the required pages of such an object are brought into virtual storage. Bytes of the mapped pages can be accessed and changed in normal program execution without regard to the need for updating. At the time the connection to the DIV object is terminated, only the changed pages are written back to the linear data set.

DIV is somewhat difficult to use because the assembly language primitive functions are not readily available in high-level languages. The potential benefits may be realized eventually as DIV merges with hiperspaces (a related concept) and as subsystems, languages, and application packages exploit the DIV benefits.

## Hiperspaces

The DIV experience will not be repeated with hiperspaces. IBM has provided a broad spectrum of initial support for hiperspaces in critical subsystems, ranging from direct use for VSAM buffers and CICS data tables to accessible high-level language primitives called *data windowing services*. The lower-level representation of hiperspaces as objects akin to data spaces will encourage system programmers and those constructing major application packages to experiment with hiperspaces much more readily than they did with DIV. It is also reasonable to expect that hiperspaces will eventually come into use as part of the storage hierarchy of system-managed storage. The Hiperbatch facility announced with MVS/SP 3.1.3 is just such a use of hiperspaces.

The backlog of new application programs waiting to be designed and written is enormous, and development cycles are long. Perhaps by 1992 or 1993, major applications designed *ab initio* to make effective use of hiperspaces will realize the full data addressing and performance potential of MVS/ESA.

## 11.2.8. Avoidable I/O contention

While many instances of I/O contention are found and corrected in the process of resolving service anomalies in workloads, many, especially those within an application family, can and should be anticipated and prevented before the fact. In designing applications and planning their installation for production, a simple time-line plot can show the planned pattern of use for each data set or data base. In this way, possible sources of conflict can be flagged, leading to an optimal data set placement pattern for the application.

Data set growth and volume fragmentation should be tracked for key applications, particularly those with critical timing windows or real-time response targets and heavy I/O content. Again, while it is possible to detect and correct sudden increases in SEEK delay after overt service problems appear, routine storage management actions should reveal the impending problem before service is affected.

The promise of system-managed storage is that many of these considerations will eventually be handled automatically—if DFSMS is properly instructed with a well-designed class structure. Data placement decisions, made in the initial implementation of DFSMS only at allocation time, might eventually be affected by feedback from performance monitoring during the entire life of data objects. To the extent that DFSMS does not support such feedback, the storage management task for the installation must continue to include performance assessment of key workloads. Some DASD management tools are available, including Legent's DASDMON and Boole & Babbage's DASD Advisor, but their main orientation is to the resource view rather than the workload view.

It is important for the users of such systems to realize that the object of "DASD tuning" is not merely to create "homogenized" RMF device reports. If every I/O request is processed with the same response time, workloads with modest DASD performance requirements will be too well served, and those that are response-time sensitive will do badly. The perspective is key: DASD tuning (beyond cleaning up fragmentation and contention) is justified only on behalf of workloads.

## 11.2.9. Path contention

As the number of channels available and installed on systems increases, and as four-path DASD subsystems become commonplace, path-loading considerations fade in significance. Again, system-managed storage could eventually take note of path response times in placing data sets with a fast response time requirement.

## 11.2.10. Using cache control units

Cache controllers are of significant value in systems that are heavily dependent on random-access I/O with a significant re-reference pattern. More than likely, the applications are relatively old and transaction volumes have increased to the point that using cache controllers is the only readily available means of meeting response-time requirements.

The current generation of cache controllers, typified by the IBM 3990 Model 3, have features that reduce the need for laborious planning and validation to decide which data should be cached. However, overt planning is still needed. Yet again, system-managed storage will ultimately allow a "management by objectives" approach to classifying data according to its performance requirements. With the full power of SMS, cache will be used to its potential with minimal day-to-day human involvement.

More advanced features of new cache controllers provide specific targeted benefits for sorting programs and for designated critical data base elements. Little experience with such facilities has been published to date.

As more applications are re-implemented to exploit data spaces and hiperspaces, the need in such applications for cache devices is likely to be reduced, in exchange for greater dependency on expanded storage.

## 11.3. Resource Exhaustion

There comes a time in most systems' lives when upgrades appear to be inevitable. Storage or CPU might be fully utilized, or queueing for CPU or I/O devices has put service targets in jeopardy. To go ahead and order more hardware at this point seems natural. However, the system may not be out of capacity at this time. Reprioritizing the workload may buy valuable time.

### 11.3.1. Forestalling the inevitable

The CPU is running at close to 100 percent utilization through first shift; is the system out of capacity? If there is excess capacity at off-prime times, and if a portion of the workload has a service requirement that can stand delay, more high-priority work can be added to the system until CPU queueing compromises service targets. Only when that occurs is more capacity needed.

How much planning is needed to keep up with workload growth? If an installation's processors are not at the growth limit for a vendor's product family, most upgrades take less than a day to install and little lead time. When a new physical "box" is needed, floor space considerations can intrude. When a single-sided processor becomes physically partitionable (two-sided) in an upgrade, a large increment of floor space, as well as more installation time, is necessary. Of the 20 possible upgrades shown in Figure 11-1, 11 retain approximately the same physical configuration before and after the upgrade. The decision to upgrade to a two-sided configuration need be made only once in the life of a system. Physical partitionability enables further non-disruptive

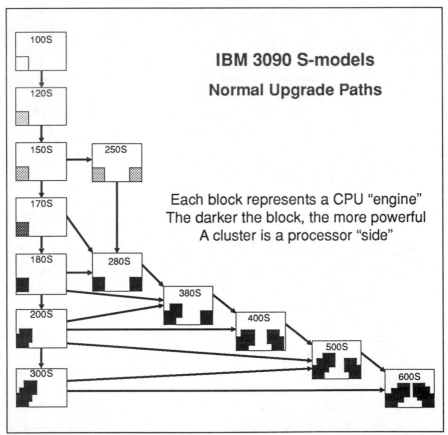

Figure 11-1. Typical processor family upgrade paths

upgrades in large systems, once the initial disruption of installing a two-sided configuration has been endured.

In a large installation with many processor complexes, backup systems can often absorb the workload of a system being upgraded. Shops that haven't yet grown to that level require more care to avoid outages associated with upgrades. Sometimes it is possible to schedule preparatory activity on several successive weekends; more aggregate time is needed for the upgrade, but with less disruption.

## 11.3.2. Tuning for efficiency

As processor complex capacity becomes exhausted, it is more important than ever to ensure efficiency. Although the constant emphasis in this book is on workload-oriented performance management, at this point our attention switches from tuning workloads to tuning the system. Success based on either approach is usually beneficial at both levels.

Measures that generally help the system and all workloads without negative consequences include:

- Making sure that block sizes for sequential and partitioned data sets are as large as the maximums supported on the devices

- Using storage isolation for first and second period TSO to minimize avoidable page faulting

- Making maximum effective use of PLPA to eliminate redundant program loading and to reduce the working set sizes of address spaces, especially TSO

- Making maximum effective use of LLA in MVS/XA and MVS/ESA to minimize directory searching. In ESA only, realize greater benefits by reducing program loading times and eliminating the need for STEPLIBs in production applications

- Making sure that heavily used or shared data sets are monitored to prevent wasteful seeking across multiple extents. In ESA beginning with SP 3.1.3, use facilities such as Hiperbatch and batch local shared resources to avoid I/O when possible

- Acting to prevent logical swapping from dominating real storage when it is constrained, forcing unnecessary page stealing

- Adjusting the OPT MPL controls controls to ensure maximum resource utilization without wasteful swap-in delay (when real storage is sufficient) and without requiring manual intervention to control the size of the multiprogramming set.

# 11.4. Resource Contention

When contention analysis is an available tool for diagnosing performance problems, it is easy to fall victim to the Carpenter's Fallacy.[9] However, not all performance problems are contention problems. There are some genuine instances of resource exhaustion, and there are all too many examples of poorly designed or implemented applications that create their own problems. We'll limit our discussion of contention to instances of contention for a named, specific resource such as a data set, volume, or ENQueue resource name.

In this section, we'll identify some key contention scenarios and suggest ways to avoid them, or to deal with them when they do come up.

## 11.4.1. Prevention

Suppose three CICS address spaces (order entry, order fulfillment, accounts receivable) in an MRO subsystem are set up so that all are in use at the same time, and that they each use the same VSAM customer information file (CIF) for query, verification, and occasional update. Each address space processes a different set of transactions, with different dependent files on the same volume as the CIF being updated, as well as on other volumes. Suppose further that all CICSs have been just barely meeting their response time targets.

With strong forebodings of impending disaster, we now plan to expand the geographical service area of this system such that

---

9 "When the only tool is a hammer, every problem looks like a nail."

the transaction rate can be expected to double. It seems prudent to act now to avoid the problems which seem certain to come. Using or collecting execution-state analysis data for each of the address spaces, we could determine if there is already a concentration of contention-delay states such as "waiting for queued I/O" or "waiting for ENQ." If such states show up, it is almost certain that they will increase dramatically with volume growth.

If I/O contention already exists, it is most likely to appear on the central data volume containing the CIF. Contention within the CICS subsystem may be relieved by splitting the subsidiary files to other volumes; however, the possibility of causing contention with another workload should be a consideration in selecting the target volume. Exercising advanced options such as shared buffering, or placing the buffers in a hiperspace in an MVS/ESA environment, especially for the CIF, can help to avoid the I/O that is the source of contention.

## 11.4.2. Avoidance

How can we avoid creating new contention while not leaving resources idle? What we need to find are complementary or compatible workloads. If two workloads need access to the same resources but at different times of the day, there is no harm in allowing the sharing. If they both need the same resources at the same time, they will be in harmful contention unless the sharing can be promoted to a hardware resource level that has acceptably low impact on performance. From best to worst, the levels would include:

- data in DIV or hiperspace, as in Hiperbatch

- data replicated for each using subsystem

- shared buffering (global or local shared resources)

- cached, same system

- shared DASD, cached, different systems

- uncached, same system

- shared DASD, uncached, different systems

- shared DASD, uncached, different systems, with global EN-Queue management

- shared DASD, uncached, different systems, no global EN-Queue management

### 11.4.3. Detection in real-time

As with any approach to diagnosing a problem, contention analysis starts with identifying a condition that requires investigation or possible action. A real-time monitor such as Candle's OMEGAMON for MVS can issue a warning message when there is an ENQueue lock-out or a device not responding, or with abnormally high service time. As we've already noted, such warnings are little more than false alarms if the workloads affected by such conditions are not sufficiently important to merit operator attention. A real-time monitor with workload awareness can issue exception messages against the response time or elapsed time of specified critical workloads, most effectively using the history of the particular workload as the basis for the threshold.

When a workload exception appears, the person investigating the problem can use the probing features of the monitoring program to display the execution-state profile of the workload and its direct contention sources. If the monitor does not collect contention data, it may maintain a history of workload activities and resource use that might provide less direct evidence of contention.

Knowing (or strongly suspecting) the identity of the delaying resource and the workload causing the contention, if there is one, the analyst can now decide whether to take action, and if so, which actions could eliminate or minimize the contention.

### 11.4.4. Solutions

Let's review what can be done about a contention problem:

- **Tolerate It**—If service is acceptable for the moment, track the execution states of the workload over time, looking for a sudden rise in a contention-delay state, at which time action will be necessary.

- **Accommodate It**—With data set contention, take action to promote the data in contention to a faster device, or to exercise buffering options that can reduce the contention impact. For CPU or storage contention, a short-running program causing degradation to a subsystem might be "accelerated" by placing it in a more favorable performance group. Ultimately, application rework may be necessary to cut contention impact to the minimum. Batch jobs that cause CPU contention usually do so by causing a high rate of SRB activity to service I/O completion. The appropriate solution in such a case is to eliminate or minimize the disruptive I/O, usually by increasing block sizes.

- **Avoid by Workload Scheduling**—If the service schedule for one of the workloads in contention can be changed to eliminate the contention, take the opportunity. This approach may be useful if a production batch job interferes with an online service. As the "batch window" shrinks with the growth of extended online service hours, this option becomes difficult to implement.

- **Avoid by Replication**—If data sets in contention are read-only, making multiple copies can eliminate contention. The price paid is a new need to synchronize the copies.

- **Avoid by Sharing**—Options such as shared buffering and caching serve the same purpose without the administrative burden of replication. If load module libraries are the objects subject to contention, the use of PLPA or the MVS/ESA LLA can eliminate most contention. Early objection to placing unauthorized application modules in the LINKLIST was overcome early in MVS/XA when APF authorization of LINKLIST libraries could be made selective rather than universal.

- **Avoid by Movement**—If device contention (queued I/O) is the main problem, move data sets to decouple the workloads in contention. This action is effective even if the device contention is self-contention between different processes within the same workload.

- **Avoid by Rearrangement**—A CICS workload may have been split across address spaces in MVS/370 because of virtual storage constraint. Now, in MVS/XA and MVS/ESA, the same configuration is used because of habit or inertia, even though the constraint is no longer a problem. Reconsolidating an unnecessary MRO or resplitting according to a minimum contention pattern may cut out enough contention to maintain consistent service.

- **Avoid by Rewriting**—The last remedy considered in most installations is to re-implement the application to eliminate sources of contention. A new data base design using options available in relational systems may completely bypass the source of contention.

## 11.5. Summary

Solving performance problems is often difficult and time-consuming. It is also intellectually challenging and very satisfying when successful. Doing the job well is aided greatly with proper preparation and placement in a supportive environment containing these elements:

- suitable tools, especially execution-state and contention monitors

- well-defined service targets

- freedom to make changes in system control parameters

- a performance management job description, evaluation policy, and management structure that recognizes cumulative success and supports the risk-taking necessary to solve problems caused by the actions or inactions of others

- a capacity-planning and hardware acquisition function in the installation that strikes an optimum balance among projection of past experience, forecasting of future loading, timely acquisition of new technology, serving the performance expectations of customers, and deriving full economic benefit from capital assets

Even though every practitioner develops an individual approach, each such person should take pains to remain open-minded about different approaches. He or she *must* keep current with developments in operating systems and subsystems, hardware, monitoring software, and behavioral studies about human interactions with computer systems. Today's systems do not respond well to yesterday's management techniques.

And that's not all! It's also necessary to know a few more practical things: what the principal applications do, and how the customers view the service of which those in the data center are so proud.

When the performance analyst has proper preparation, knowledge, good tools, support, operational discretion, and an open mind, no performance problem should long remain a mystery. Whether it can be fixed may depend on other considerations. We'll look at some of them in the final chapter.

# 12

# Application Tuning

In many installations, the last area to be influenced by the data center's performance staff is the set of production application programs that to a great extent justify the existence of the data center. Those responsible for such programs are in departments with names like Management Information Systems or Applications Development.

Typically, these departments are separate from the data center organization through the director or vice-president level of management, so sharing of common goals and cooperation do not arise naturally out of organizational proximity.

## 12.1. Open-shop Workloads

As urgently as production application programs need performance analysis and optimization, nonproduction or "open shop" batch and TSO may need such attention even more. A machine whose basic workload is business-related must be managed very carefully if it is also to accommodate such applications as engineering design, scientific data reduction and analysis, or econometric modeling.

Typically, those who run such programs never finish them—they never really become production programs. They are tweaked here and there, adjusted to different cases of interest, or run with more or less data or for more or fewer iterations. More than most "commercial" programs, these *numerically intensive* applications can be disruptive to systems, especially if they are written by professional engineers, scientists, or statisticians who happen to be amateur programmers.

CPU utilization is not the problem; it's easy to manage dispatching priority properly. Rather, numerically intensive programs can put tremendous stress on the processor storage resource when they exhibit poorly planned storage reference patterns. The techniques mentioned under "virtual storage" later in this chapter can be tried (or suggested to the program owners).

## 12.2. Application Performance Vulnerabilities

Almost any performance management action taken by the data center staff can be undone by implementation or installation choices for applications. It is unlikely that anyone gets up one fine day and says, "I'm going to mess up the CICS production system." What's more likely is something like one of the following:

- A "portable" packaged application is installed without examining the data definitions and JCL and adapting them to installation standards.

- A new program has been written, compiled, and installed with unchanged default parameters for I/O and storage use.

- An unoptimized prototype has been placed in production.

- A new production program has been "promoted" without removing debugging code (completely).

- A new version has been installed *via* STEPLIB.

- Input or transaction volume has grown to the extent that formerly efficient code has become inefficient today.

- An obsolete policy of volume ownership has forced inappropriate DASD volume sharing, creating inescapable contention among related applications.

- An upgraded system environment has failed to deliver its potential throughput or performance improvement because the new facilities cannot be used by old programs without change.

It is clear that these circumstances involve no malicious intent; some of them represent lack of care in areas that don't appear (to the application programmer) to be important. Most, however, are simple instances of the application developers not having "system" knowledge that the systems or performance staff thinks of as self-evident.

A system programmer can hardly avoid staying current with current hardware or operating system developments. On the other hand, application programmers are much more concerned with the target areas of their applications and do not normally receive detailed information on new system developments or capabilities. Organizational separation contributes to the lack of information flow.

## 12.2.1. Vendor application packages

If an applications group depends heavily on vendor-supplied application packages, it is almost inevitable that those packages have attributes that contribute strongly to inefficiency:

- They are designed to be portable across many levels of system environment, so that packaging, data set and data base definitions, and use of system services tend to be at a "least common denominator" level.

- They are implemented to satisfy functional needs primarily, and are not particularly optimized for performance.

- They are designed to be reliable and therefore are not implemented to assume the risk of using relatively new and untried features.

- They are designed for generality and therefore are not optimal for a particular installation's needs.

## 12.2.2. Turf wars

Data center performance analysts or specialists are usually staff people in their own departments. They are even more organizationally remote from applications developers. To be effective in getting the applications staff to change JCL, options, schedules, or even *code*, the performance person cannot rely on organizational authority. A person in such a position must cultivate the art of *influence*—getting others to take action because they perceive it to be in *their* best interest, not because someone in authority said so.

Effectiveness in building and using influence is based on trust, credibility, and respect. Techniques that help to build and rehabilitate a a data center's reputation with its customers in general, are just as necessary and effective when trying to get only a few of them to accept recommended changes.

# 12.3. Internal Inefficiency

First, we'll look at common examples of inefficiency in how resources are used by application programs. These programs may run as batch jobs, as TSO commands, or as transactions in IMS or CICS or some other transaction-processing system.

## 12.3.1. CPU

An application program can be inefficient in its CPU utilization pattern for many reasons. Some are cited above: forgetting to remove tracing or debugging options, or failure to employ maximum optimization options. Other possibilities are:

- using "roll-your-own" sorting routines instead of using efficient standard sort algorithms or advanced data base techniques that reduce the need for sorting

- ignoring standard optimization techniques, such as removing invariant code from inner loops, using early-decision logic optimized to path frequency, and "unrolling" function calls within inner loops. Although advanced compilers can do some of these things automatically, "efficient" assembly language programs must be hand-optimized. The sheer volume of assembly language source code, the difficulty of imposing structure on existing unstructured code, and the considerable egos of many assembly language programmers make it unlikely that such techniques will be applied to many programs written in that language.

- failing to use efficient alternatives to expensive CALLs on library routines or system services

- failing to recognize vectorizable algorithms and to use vector processors when available

- using inefficient and disruptive techniques such as scheduling SRBs in order to communicate across address spaces, instead of using cross-memory services

- failing to follow-through to production on programs developed according to a modular discipline. When such programs are promoted to a production status, linkage code that externalizes the modular design should be removed; the program should be "collapsed" to an "encapsulated" state once it is ready for production.

## 12.3.2. Virtual storage

We've already mentioned the use of STEPLIBs as a source of virtual storage inefficiency. Especially in an MVS/ESA environment, STEPLIBs should be reserved for infrequently run programs only. Because LINKLIST libraries are no longer automatically authorized, one of the stronger justifications for STEPLIBs is invalidated.

## 12.3.3. Real storage

Three design principles, first enunciated in the early 1970s, are still valid guidelines for ensuring optimal use of real storage:

- **Locality of Reference**—Code and data needed for a transaction should be kept together. If code is separated from data (for instance by using data spaces in MVS/ESA), two concentrations are OK.

- **Validity of Reference**—Having to plow through a series of wrong data items before finding the right one violates this principle.

- **Minimum Working Set Size**—Data should be used in such a way that local, valid references are grouped in time frame, as well as in virtual storage.

These principles are violated frequently. Some examples:

- Wrong-way tables: When all of the data for an application subsystem fits in a few pages of storage, the layout of data tables is not a matter of great concern. Suppose, however, that the volume handled by the subsystem has expanded to the point where data tables take up 500 pages. If the tables are organized functionally (all "A"s followed by all "B"s, etc.) a particular transaction or thread may touch 60 or 70 pages. If, on the other hand, the data tables are "turned sideways" so that each transaction's or user's data is contiguous, the storage reference pattern is significantly improved. By violating "locality of reference," "minimum working set size" is violated as well. Correcting one will correct the other.

- Inefficient search logic: In pioneering programs in the System/360 era like the FORTRAN H compiler, chained searching of large dictionary structures was a state-of-the-art technique. In a static real-memory environment, chained searching can be very efficient, compared to simple linear searching. In a virtual storage environment, however, it's poison.

  Chained searching is the classic violation of "validity of reference." Binary searches or other hashing algorithms are faster for large tables and use less real storage. Linear searches remain very efficient for small tables.

- Wrong-way arrays: A classical problem in translating programs from FORTRAN to PL/1 was the need to understand the difference in array storage layout. FORTRAN arrays are stored in column-major order, while PL/1 arrays are in row-major order. The original basis for this need was to deal with esoteric considerations like converting EQUIVALENCE in FORTRAN to overlay defining in PL/1.

A much more practical need exists in virtual storage systems. Regardless of the programming language, an array has a natural storage order. If a program uses the elements of that array in some order other than its natural order, its working set will be larger than necessary. Very much like the case of wrong-way tables, changing the order of array references (or of array definition) to make the most frequent reference pattern the natural array storage order will serve to minimize working-set size. Especially with vector processors, establishing correct array reference order is an optimization technique with no down-side considerations.

To localize the effects of programs with inefficient storage reference patterns, the technique of *negative storage isolation* described in Chapters 8 and 11 may be used. Of course, it must be fitted to the problem at hand. A program calculating eigenvalues without the use of sparse matrix techniques may have a 1-second working set of 10,000 pages and a 10-second working set of 60,000 pages. Specifying an ordinary level of storage isolation like PWSS=(0,2000) might cause such a program to page-fault continuously and never complete. A more appropriate storage isolation of PWSS=(0,10500) for such an address space might cause a modest paging-delay elongation of the job while freeing the rest of the system from page stealing.

## 12.3.4. Input and output

Perhaps advice under this heading will cease to be needed when system-managed storage is fully evolved and widely and fully implemented. For now, we still need to identify sources of I/O inefficiency other than contention.

### Sequential Data Sets

Knowledgeable experts including Siebo Friesenborg of IBM and Dr. H. W. (Barry) Merrill of Merrill Consultants have been say-ing for years that small block sizes for sequential data sets are inefficient. Consider the consequences of small block sizes:

- Inefficient device space utilization: Especially on IBM 3380s, data bytes per track decline dramatically with small block size.[1]

- Reduced data transfer rate: This is a direct consequence of reduced track capacity and fixed rotational speed, and leads to high response time per logical record.

- Disruptive CPU overhead: The high I/O rate associated with small block sizes causes at least two state switches per I/O, with increased CPU time disabled for interrupts and under lock. Every other address space in the system pays the price of increased CPU delay.

- Increased storage occupancy: With lower effective data transfer speed, programs take longer to run, increasing real storage use.

Merrill has recommended consistent use of the maximum block size supported on the device. With such block sizes, all four of the factors cited above take on their most efficient values.

When sequential data sets are managed with generous buffering and optimal (maximum) block sizes, data transfer is usually overlapped with processing, so the slow speed of DASD does not significantly influence processing speeds.

## Randomly Accessed Data

Randomly accessed data sets and data bases present a different challenge. In a transaction-processing environment, there is no way for the transaction to "do something else" while the I/O necessary to complete a transaction proceeds. When I/O predominates in such an application or subsystem, performance improvement can come from avoiding I/O, or from making it faster.

I/O can be avoided by application design or redesign. Many applications fail to make full use of available virtual storage, performing I/O to repeatedly read small tables or other data

---

1   Chapter 2 has a full discussion of this point.

areas instead of bringing them into virtual storage once and letting SRM and RSM manage the data. Such practices are common in "portable" applications that must run in several different operating system environments of differing storage architectures and sizes. When larger data aggregates (external data sets or data bases) are involved, basic design principles like validity of reference are just as effective in avoiding explicit I/O as they are in avoiding paging.

If there is significant re-reference activity in the aggregate of data used by an application, the use of cache controllers can bring about significant I/O response-time improvement. As cache devices such as the IBM 3990 Model 3 mature and grow in maximum cache sizes, restrictive cache planning considerations ease; often whole strings of triple-density 3380s are cached.

For data having very concentrated reference patterns, and in applications with extremely stringent response time targets, pure solid-state devices offer ultimate response time for channel-attached DASD. As SSDs have become obsolescent for improving the performance of paging subsystems, they have found new uses as conventional I/O devices for solving special performance problems.

More extensive redesign of applications will bring about further improvements as they move fully into the MVS/ESA environment, making effective use of data spaces (overcoming virtual storage limitations), hiperspaces (for scratch pad and large temporary data aggregates), and data-in-virtual (for large permanent data aggregates with sparse reference patterns).

IBM's DB2 relational data base system, and applications built on DB2, can take full advantage of many of ESA's new storage options.

## 12.4. Internal Contention

In the previous section we looked at efficiency of application programs and systems independent of contention. When there is contention, we must determine whether it is caused externally or internally. External contention is found by methods described in Chapter 11. Tools such as Impact Analysis, found in some products of Candle Corporation, will also reveal self-contention, usually for I/O devices.

Self-contention is often found in applications or subsystems when multiple data sets are on the same device. A frequent cause of such data set placement is a DASD management policy based on "volume ownership." The emerging trend to system-managed storage substitutes a much less restrictive volume pooling concept and allows the specification of desired performance characteristics as part of data set definition. As such subsystems evolve to include workload performance data in their criteria for data placement and continued residence, I/O device contention should migrate to the least important workloads on the system, subject to the capabilities of the configuration.

Another cause of self-contention, this time for the CPU, is a program organized with multiple tasks or multiple communicating address spaces running in a system without enough CPUs to support the level of simultaneity designed into the program. There is no contention if the internal multiprogramming is of functions not usually invoked concurrently. When there is active internal CPU contention, most performance monitors can't reveal it, since execution states are determined for the whole address space rather than for tasks, and the "waiting for CPU" execution state is subordinate to "using CPU."

## 12.5. Practical approaches to cooperation

The organizational tensions that often exist between the data center and the applications staff are not eased when a performance analyst makes a vague "suggestion" that a particular application program is the cause of poor response time, as opposed to something in the way the system is managed. The more detailed the analysis, the more specific the recommendation can be, and the more likely that it will be accepted. Results of execution-state analysis and direct contention analysis can be easily understood by application developers or subsystem maintainers, and corrective responses are clearly suggested by the kind of information presented.

It is difficult for someone without specific responsibility for an area to make credible recommendations for change in that area. A cool, factual, limited, and respectful approach is much more likely to be successful than the kind of emotional and confrontational scene often engendered by a service crisis. This advice may sound obvious and superficial, but ego involvement can often drive people out of control, particularly when solid facts are not available when required.

Therefore, get the facts! When a manager rages that Accounts Receivable came up late for the last two days, the last thing needed is confirmation that the problem did indeed occur. What is required to defuse the situation is a clear explanation of why the batch update was late (what caused it?) and a credible plan to avoid it in the future. (Credibility is compromised already because the problem should have been identified and headed off the day before.) Workload-oriented data collection tools, preferably with contention analysis capabilities, are essential for this task. Real-time alerts based on overdue production batch could have made remedial action possible within whatever buffer might have been available. It takes far more factual data, credibility, and presentation skill to calm down an irate manager than to put a plan and procedure in place to deal with late batch jobs.

## 12.6. Summing Up

How much is it worth to practice successful performance management in MVS? Hardware acquisition can be avoided or deferred; performance can be made acceptable and consistent; perhaps most important, though, the human resources formerly devoted to creating useless reports, making accusations, and finding fault can be directed to productive tasks.

# Glossary

*Author's note*: The definitions in this glossary are those assumed in the text and are my own; they are reasonably consistent with standard definitions. Terms in this glossary are in general those not contextually defined in the text or those for which an extended discussion seemed necessary. For a term not found here, the first reference found in the index should supply a contextual definition. Another book in this series, *MVS: Concepts and Facilities*, by Robert H. Johnson, also has an extensive glossary with useful alternate points of view for some terms. The ultimate reference for IBM's view of SRM-related terms and functions is the current edition of *Initialization and Tuning* for the system under consideration.

\* (asterisk) used in storage isolation specifications to indicate maximum value; used in objectives to signify linear interpolation.

## A

**ABEND** ABnormal END, the condition that occurs when a program terminates by issuing the ABEND Supervisor Call (SVC 13), or is terminated because of an unexpected program check or other condition that MVS cannot handle. A common consequence of an ABEND is a dump.

**above the line** addresses above 16 megabytes; in MVS/370 the term meant real storage in the extended addressing range. In MVS/XA and MVS/ESA it refers to the extended virtual areas. The significance of "above the line" in MVS/370 was the need to move I/O buffers "below the line" before START I/O [FAST] could be issued. In XA and ESA, virtual storage below the line is the area threatened by virtual storage constraint; moving code and data above the line by making program changes is the way to relieve such constraint.

**absolute address** the lowest level of central storage addressing in a processor complex in basic mode, or within a single logical partition. An absolute address is not adjusted by prefixing or translated by dynamic address translation, and is the object of a CCW address. There is an unnamed lower level of addressing in logically partitioned mode; only the preferred partition has logical absolute addresses corresponding to physical absolute addresses.

**absolute storage**   central storage accessed through absolute addressing.

**access control system**   system designed to define, control, and report on [attempted] access of users (jobs, TSO sessions, individual users of transaction processing systems) to resources, most often data sets, transactions, terminals, or other entities defined to the access control system. Examples are IBM's RACF and Computer Associates' ACF2 and Top Secret.

**access method**   part of an operating system providing the interface and device-driving code between high-level I/O requests (e.g. GET, PUT, READ, WRITE) and I/O devices as seen by the I/O supervisor (IOS). Access methods translate logical record requests to the physical data locations, create channel programs and convey them to IOS for execution, manage retries of unsuccessful I/O, and manage queued requests and buffers.

**access register**   in ESA, a register activated in access register (AR) mode to supply (indirectly) the segment table origin for data operands paired with the same-numbered general register used as a base register. The general register supplies the base address within the data space or address space designated by the segment table found by means of the access register.

**account number**   a character string assigned to an address space by the positional "account" field in a JOB statement or in the TSO UADS or equivalent source maintained by an access control system. The account number or a substring of it may be used as a basis for performance group assignment in the ICS, in MVS/XA and MVS/ESA systems.

**accounting data**   a more precise designation for **account number**.

**active I/O**   an execution state in which the workload is waiting for completion of an input or output operation while not dispatchable in another task. Active I/O is usually considered to be a productive state, but it also represents a tuning opportunity, since most sequential I/O can and should be overlapped with instruction execution.

**activity rate** a measure of throughput in work units per second. Tracking throughput is one of the essential functions of performance management.

**actuator** mechanism of a direct-access storage device (DASD) that moves the arm which in turn carries the read and write recording heads and associated electronics, by extension the arm itself and the assembly of arm[s] and disk[s] that corresponds to a single device address or device number in a DASD subsystem.

**actuator-level buffering** use of a small cache or buffer holding a track's worth of data to eliminate variable rotational delay (RPS miss) in DASD. The term is a trademark of Storage Technology Corporation.

**address space** a linear range of virtual storage addresses from 0 through the architecturally defined maximum for a given system. Each work unit (job, started task, TSO session, subsystem) is synonymous with at least one address space. An address space in MVS is defined by a segment table, its associated page tables, and several control blocks, notably the ASCB. It contains a common area and a private area. Address space layouts may be found in Chapter 3.

**addressing mode** the means by which the address parts of an instruction (base, displacement, optional index) are combined with other information to yield an absolute address. Absolute addresses are direct references to absolute storage. Real addresses may be altered by prefixing before being treated as absolute. Virtual addresses are translated to real addresses by dynamic address translation. Cross-memory mode uses a secondary segment table origin to initiate dynamic address translation for operands of certain instructions. Access register mode uses access registers to dynamically select segment table origins for each operand reference accessed through a base register. The final choice, independent of the others, is between 24-bit and 31-bit address generation.

**AFC** See **AFQ**.

**AFQ** Available Frame Queue, sometimes AFC for Available Frame Count. The queue is the ordered set of frames available for assignment by the Real Storage Manager, the count is the number of such frames in the queue.

**ALB** Actuator-Level Buffering.

**alert** an exception message, particularly one that is displayed on an operator's console.

**allegiance** set of electronic states denoting the association of channel, control unit, [device controller,] and device, for the duration of an I/O operation. Allegiance is established during unoverlapped protocol time and disbanded during overlapped protocol time.

**ALLOCATE command** TSO equivalent of the JCL DD statement, completes the late binding of DD-names in program references to physical I/O resources, usually the TSO terminal or data sets on DASD.

**allocation** set of operating system services to make associations between programs and I/O resources. Allocation establishes the required connections when specific resources (such as catalogued data sets) are needed, and additionally selects the resources to be assigned when the request is nonspecific, as for a temporary data set or a tape drive.

**allocation recovery** series of console messages and responses when the I/O resources called for by a program (usually a batch job step) are not all available. A series of device numbers (device addresses in MVS/370) is presented to the operator, who is expected to make a selection from among them. When allocation recovery is invoked, for other than tape units being switched between systems, a missing data set is often the cause and the operator dialogue is unlikely to succeed.

**alternate path** a redundant I/O connection from device through [device controller,] control unit, and channel to a CPU. In MVS/370, alternate paths provided enhanced availability at the cost of performance degradation. In XA and ESA, DASD supporting dynamic pathing provides benefits in both availability and performance from dynamic pathing. Up to four active paths are supported in some device subsystems.

**analytic model** a mathematical representation of a physical system (in this case a computer under MVS) that takes account of processing times, delays, and queues in accounting for or predicting the performance of the physical system.

**AOBJ** the use of an objective to control the MPL of a domain, in which the average service rate received by each address space in the domain is the independent variable of the objective.

**APF** Authorized Program Facility.

**APG** Automatic Priority Group, an obsolete IPS parameter to set the dispatching priority within the original restricted MVS APG. AN APG specification in IEASYSxx sets the high-order hexadecimal digit of the priority; the APG specification in the performance period in the IPS sets the low-order digit. The use of the APG parameter is incompatible with current SRM facilities for controlling dispatching priority.

**APG range** range of high-order hexadecimal digits of true dispatching priority subject to assignment by the DP, IOP, PVLDP, and TSDP IPS keywords. The range and its implicit mapping are set by the APGRNG keyword.

**APGRNG** IPS keyword to set the **APG range** controlled by the IPS.

**API** Application Programming Interface, a set of rules and conventions, possibly including service routines and macro definitions, that allow independent programs to communicate with the programming "owning" the API. An access method is an example of an API.

**application programming interface** See **API**.

**AR** access register; also the **addressing mode** that makes use of access registers.

**architecture** the highest level of logical design for a computing system or family of such systems, defining such elements as the instruction set, the objects operated on by the instructions, exceptions and their manifestation as interrupts, and reserved facilities. An architecture usually spans more than a single product family and may include features or facilities to be released at a future time. Current engineering designs may thus contemplate extensibility to a fuller implementation in the future.

**archive** to copy data for safekeeping and possible future use for recovery to another physical embodiment, usually from DASD to tape.

**array** data aggregate in which each element is of the same type and size.

**array storage layout** representation in storage of an array, the essential matter of concern being the order in which elements are stored. If the order of use or reference approximates the order of storage, the working set of the program making use of the array is minimized.

**ASCB** Address Space Control Block, the principal MVS data area defining the attributes of an address space.

**ASID** Address Space IDentifier, a number denoting the position of a pointer to an address space's ASCB in an array called the ASVT (Address Space Vector Table). The ASVT and ASID are architecturally defined in the various levels of System/370, XA, and ESA so that microcode-assisted routines may aid in speeding up key MVS functions that manipulate ASCBs.

**ASM** Auxiliary Storage Manager, the MVS component responsible for controlling and initiating I/O to and from page and swap data sets.

**ASM queue** queue of pending I/O requests managed by the ASM.

**ASN** Address Space Number, an engineer's or architect's synonym for ASID.

**asymmetric device attachment** in System/370, the attachment of an I/O device to only one channel set of an MP system.

**ATTACH** the MVS service, or its invoking macro-instruction or SVC, that creates new tasks.

**authorized program facility** (APF) the means for designating libraries as eligible to contain authorized programs which are granted the authorized status during execution. A program is designated as authorized by setting the AC bit in its directory entry to 1, usually by action of the Linkage Editor. An authorized program fetched from an authorized library is permitted to issue otherwise restricted SVCs, in turn giving it the ability to gain privileged states and protect keys giving it access to any part of the system.

**automated operations** replacement of human operator activities with programmed operations, with the purpose of eliminating repetitive tasks, performing selected activities without human intervention, simplifying complex tasks, and interpreting the message stream and reducing its volume, thereby enabling the operator to make constrained decisions and reducing the likelihood of operator error.

**automatic priority group** See **APG**.

**auxiliary storage** the set of page and swap data sets.

**Auxiliary Storage Manager**  See **ASM**.

**auxiliary storage shortage**  condition detected by the SRM in which the supply of unused auxiliary storage slots falls below a predetermined threshold.

**Auxiliary Storage Shortage Swap**  swap-out initiated by the SRM in response to an auxiliary storage shortage.

**auxiliary storage slot**  unit of measure of auxiliary storage; a slot is the same size as a frame or a page, 4096 bytes.

**availability**  portion (usually expressed as a percentage) of scheduled service time during which a computing system or service is fully usable by its customers. Tracking availability is one of the essential functions of performance management.

**available frame count**  See **AFQ**.

**available frame queue**  See **AFQ**.

# B

**back-end**  completion stage of a process that is partially asynchronous. Back-end I/O processing, for example, occurs in the I/O second-level interrupt handler after the channel-end and device-end interrupts are received by the CPU.

**backing**  real resources used to materialize virtual resources; pages are backed by frames of real storage. The term has a somewhat different meaning in real storage hierarchies—the higher-level, smaller, faster, more expensive storage element is fully backed by the slower, cheaper, and more abundant lower level. In some cache I/O subsystems, such as the IBM 3990 Model 3 with the Fast Write feature, non-volatile storage at the higher level is used to defer backing.

**backup jobs**  batch jobs used to preserve the content of essential data resources in archives.

**balanced methodology**  performance management approach making optimum use of service data, resource data, bottleneck data, and contention data.

**balanced system**  system configuration with adequate but not excessive resource in all key hardware areas: CPU, central storage, expanded storage, channels, control units, and devices. A balanced system when loaded to capacity will show a similar degree of constraint in all resource areas. The term (but not the definition) was originated and popularized by Ray Wicks of the IBM Washington Systems Center.

**Base Control Program**  that part of an MVS system other than the JES and DFP.

**batch**  workload consisting of discrete *jobs*, managed up to initiation and after termination by the JES.

**Batch Message Processor**  batch job making use of IMS data base facilities, often used for report creation, mass inquiries, or bulk updates to data bases.

**batch window**  time period during which essential batch jobs must be completed. Such jobs are often not compatible with online service, either by demanding exclusive access to critical resources or by causing such high activity rates that online service would be unacceptably slow.

**BCP**  See **Base Control Program**.

**binary search**  search technique in which the ordered list denoting the items to be searched is successively halved, discarding the half not encompassing the item's identifier. The technique is efficient if the list contains only identifiers; if the items are large and constitute the list that is searched, the principle of validity of reference is violated, and working set size (for internal searches) or I/O time (for external searches) may be excessive.

**binding**  process of resolving symbolic references to data by associating physical resources with the references. *Early* binding is efficient but limits flexibility; *late* binding requires more effort and more formally defined interfaces but preserves maximum flexibility.

**block multiplexing**  I/O technique in which a portion of a path (notably the channel) may be processing more than one request at a time. Only one request at a time may be connected through the entire path; other requests are disconnected. In block multiplexing, data transfer proceeds without interruption. Byte multiplexing is a lower speed technique in which the data stream is shared among active low-speed devices.

**block multiplexor channel** channel capable of block multiplexing.

**block paging** alternate name for paging using the contiguous slot allocation technique.

**block size** size in bytes of the unit of physical data transfer in an I/O operation.

**BMP** See **Batch Message Processor**.

**bottleneck analysis** performance monitoring technique that identifies execution states of a workload, leading to a table or histogram of frequency of each state. A bottleneck is a state that prevents the workload from achieving its service goal; identification and easing of bottlenecks is a key part of performance management.

**buffer** area of storage that contains a physical record or block. Optimum use of buffers is a trade-off between I/O avoidance and excessive use of virtual storage. Buffers use fixed real storage during I/O operations.

**byte** smallest unit of addressable data in central storage. In current IBM architecture, a byte is eight bits.

# C

**cache** in a storage hierarchy, a small unit of fast storage that contains the active data elements otherwise found in a larger unit of slower (less expensive) storage. Examples of caches include the high-speed buffer associated with a CPU and the storage in a cached DASD control unit.

**cache control unit** an I/O control unit with a cache. Tape and DASD control units are most often augmented with caches.

**cache controller** See **cache control unit**.

**cache device** strictly, an I/O storage device with a built-in cache; in common usage, a device connected to a channel through a cache control unit.

**capacity management** art of planning and implementing sufficient (but not excessive) computing capacity to enable an establishment's data processing needs to be met. See also **balanced system**.

**capture ratio** ratio of CPU use which can be accounted for in CPU (TCB and SRB) service accumulation, divided by absolute CPU use in the same time interval. Uncaptured time is often accounted for by multiplying captured service by the reciprocal of the capture ratio. Capture ratios differ by types of workload, so such correction may not be equitable.

**CAT** See **Criteria Age Table**.

**catalog** data set containing at minimum the locations (volume-IDs) of other data sets. For VSAM data sets, the catalog also contains comprehensive information about the data set. Catalogs also contain alias pointers to other catalogs which in turn contain entries for data sets whose names begin with the string that forms an alias pointer. Active catalogs form a hierarchy topped by one master catalog.

**catalogued** data set that may be found through a search of catalogs beginning with the master catalog.

**catalogued procedure** misnomer for a set of predefined JCL statements contained in a library (partitioned data set) known to the JES. The library need not be a catalogued data set since it is allocated to JES at startup time. A catalogued procedure is invoked by simply specifying its name in a JCL EXEC statement. If the procedure contains symbolic parameters, the actual parameters to be substituted are supplied in the invoking JCL.

**CAW** Channel Address Word.

**CCW** Channel Command Word.

**CEC** **central electronic complex**, now usually known as a processor complex.

**central electronic complex** the set of CPUs, channels, and auxiliary elements that constitute the resources of a computing system other than channel-attached I/O devices.

**central storage** real storage in which instructions and data reside. The term was introduced when expanded storage was introduced, to denote the subset of real storage that is not expanded storage.

**chained searching** search technique in which data elements are unordered but have identifiers that are in a sequence linked by pointers to the next element and optionally to the preceding element. Chained structures are easy to build with minimum data rearrangement but often expensive to search. For large chained structures a preliminary search through a "thumb index" will enable only a portion of the structure to be searched. Sequential searching through a large chained structure violates the principles of validity of reference and minimum working set size.

**channel** part of a computer system that performs input/output operations, linking central storage with I/O devices, as specified by channel-command words. An I/O operation is initiated by a CPU instruction, which designates the starting point for the channel operation to commence. The channel then proceeds independently, asynchronously with the CPU, until its sequence of command words ends. When the last I/O operation of the sequence ends, the channel causes an interrupt in the CPU. Even though a channel may not be fully independent of the CPU (as in the cycle-stealing channels of the IBM 4381), the series of operations is conceptually followed.

**channel-command word (CCW)** control word similar to an instruction, designating an I/O operation to be performed, the data address in absolute storage that is to be used, the number of bytes to be transferred, and bits designating options to be invoked for the operation.

**channel program** series of CCWs defining an entire logical sequence of I/O operations and linked together by means of the command-chaining option bit in each CCW but the last.

**channel-to-channel adapter (CTC)** a pseudo-device that enables two CECs to be connected together using a channel of each complex. Systems connected this way are sometimes known as loosely coupled multiprocessors. CTC connections are fast and efficient, but can cause high channel utilizations leading to delay of other I/O using that channel.

**CI** contention index; also, in VSAM, control interval.

**CKD** Count-Key-Data.

**coincident usage** an imprecise approach to contention analysis in which a resource in contention is identified, followed by identification of its users in the time span of interest. Within that set of users is the one causing the contention. The main value of this approach is to rule out non-contenders.

**combined algorithm** MPL adjustment algorithm based on combined consideration of demand paging rate, CPU utilization, and page delay time. The combined algorithm is not recommended for use in current MVS systems.

**common area** the area of virtual storage whose segments are in each address space's segment table, thus addressable from any address space.

**common page-in delay** delay state of an address space waiting for resolution of a page fault in the common area, from either the PLPA or CSA page data set.

**console automation** See **automated operations**.

**contention analysis** performance analysis technique in which the focus is on a workload of interest, and the data gathered identifies other workloads using resources for which the workload of interest is waiting.

**contiguous slot allocation** the use of a local page data set for page-out of a group of related pages (such as a swap-out group) assigned to contiguous slot locations within a single cylinder of the data set. "Contiguous slot," sometimes called block paging, was introduced as a Small Programming Enhancement (SPE) prior to the release of MVS/SP 1.3, then incorporated into that release. Contiguous slot makes the channel programs of local page data sets as efficient as those of swap data sets; for 3380 devices they are more efficient. The combination of contiguous slot and extended swap has all but made swap data sets obsolete.

**control register** one of a set of special registers included in every IBM system architecture since the introduction of System/370. Control registers contain control bits denoting the modal states of certain features (as a logical extension to the Program Status Word), mask bits selecting which of certain system elements are active in a particular context, ASIDs, and addresses. Control registers are not visible to problem-state programs. Some are loaded explicitly with the LOAD CONTROL instruction and others are loaded implicitly as selected conditions occur during normal program execution. In general, control registers are of no significance to ordinary (problem-state) programs; their content may be inspected using the STORE CONTROL instruction, itself a privileged (supervisor state) instruction.

**controlled variable** in MVS, a measurable quantity that is controlled by the SRM. Such quantities as CPU utilization, page fault rate, available frame count, and unreferenced interval count (UIC) are subject to SRM control. The value of a controlled variable is worthless as an indicator of system activity or capacity when it is in a controlled range. If, for instance, MPL adjustment tends to keep CPU utilization between 95 and 99 percent on average, a utilization of 85 percent indicates a surplus of CPU capacity, but a utilization of 97 percent simply means that MPL adjustment is effective.

**count-key-data** IBM's basic large system DASD architecture, in which data tracks have no intrinsic format, but are formatted to reflect actual data stored. Each block or physical record is of variable length and consists of a *count* field identifying the record and specifying its size, an optional *key* field, and a *data* field, with gaps between the fields and following the block. In contrast, DASD in smaller systems uses a newer fixed block architecture (FBA) in which the device is preformatted in fixed-length blocks much as are hard disks in personal computers.

**CPU delay** state of an address space ready to use a CPU but not sufficiently high on the dispatching queue to receive service in a measurement interval or sample.

**CPU overcommitment** having more address spaces in the multiprogramming set than the CPU[s] can service. If central storage can accommodate all such address spaces with acceptably low paging delay, the lowest-priority address spaces can receive service when a sufficient number of higher-priority address spaces are even temporarily non-dispatchable. If CPU overcommitment can be tolerated, throughput can be maximized.

**CPU queueing** CPU delay, usually as described in an analytic model.

**CPU, well-ordered** a system in which address spaces with high dispatching priority use relatively short bursts of CPU service, with the length of the service burst increasing as priority decreases. This ideal picture is rarely attained and is compromised by the high-priority global SRB activity engendered by I/O completions.

**criteria [*sic*] age** criterion used to determine eligibility of a class of page for movement to expanded storage. Current migration age is always considered, augmented in certain categories by UIC or think time.

**Criteria Age Table** table containing all criteria ages.

**cross-memory addressing** See **addressing mode**.

**cross-memory mode** attribute of an address space making use of cross-memory services, or the target of such services, or using secondary addressing mode.

**cross-memory services** set of MVS services enabling use of the PRO-GRAM CALL and PROGRAM TRANSFER instructions to allow address spaces to invoke, synchronously, functional code in other address spaces.

**CSA** common service area or common storage area, the common area.

**CSA page data set** the second-named page data set in an MVS system. It is used only for page-outs of common area pages. PLPA pages are not included unless the PLPA page data set is too small to contain all such pages.

**CTC** See **channel-to-channel adapter**.

**CTC ring** configuration of CTC connections supporting the GRS function across multiple MVS systems.

**cutoff RV** an address space's workload recommendation value at zero service rate, as determined by its objective.

# D

**DASD** Direct-Access Storage Device[s], disk storage.

**DAT** Dynamic Address Translation.

**Data Control Block** MVS control block or its defining macro-instruction, the internal (to a program) representation of a data set.

**data management** portion of MVS responsible for handling input and output operations at the level above physical device management; the major portion of the Data Facility Product (DFP) now part of each MVS system.

**data set** IBM terminology for an externally manageable unit of data, often called a *file* in other systems. A data set is contextually defined as the entity described by a DSCB on DASD, as a physical file on magnetic tape, as the portion of the JCL data stream following a "//SYSIN DD *" or "//SYSIN DD DATA" statement, or as a SYSOUT data stream.

**data set control block (DSCB)** data area on a DASD describing the location, content, format, and size of a data area on that device. DCSBs exist in several formats, the most common being the Format 1 DSCB describing a nonVSAM data set. The DSCB is the generalization of the file label or directory entry of other systems.

**data set organization (DSORG)** physical format of a data set on its containing medium. DSORGs include *physical sequential*, *partitioned*, *direct*, and *VSAM*.

**data set, linear** type of VSAM data set used to back a data-in-virtual object or a scroll hiperspace.

**data space** MVS/ESA variant of an address space containing no common segments, therefore a full two gigabytes of private space. Data in a data space is addressable only in access register (AR) mode and cannot be executed as instructions.

**data stream** data organized as a continuous stream of bytes, given meaning as individual data fields by the program reading or writing it. The concept of *stream I/O* originated in FORTRAN and was further formalized in PL/1. The contrasting type is called *record I/O*, consisting of discrete records of fixed or variable size.

**data windowing services** set of services provided in MVS/ESA to make hiperspaces and data-in-virtual objects accessible to programs written in high-level languages.

**dataset** non-IBM spelling of *data set*.

**DCB** Data Control Block.

**DCC** Disconnected Command Chaining.

**default** behavior of a system in the absence of specification or control information—what the system will do on its own.

**default parameter** values assigned to a control variable if no value is communicated to the system.

**defragmentation** process of consolidating and coalescing data sets on DASD to make each data set occupy a single contiguous extent. For data sets that can contain internally unused and unusable space ("gas"), "defragging" usually includes "degassing" as well.

**degradation analysis** performance monitoring technique that samples and breaks down the time taken by a process into its component parts, classifying each sample into the appropriate state, and accumulating data to produce a table of state frequencies. The data so collected may be displayed in various forms. Other names for degradation analysis include *execution state analysis, bottleneck analysis*, and *response time component analysis*.

**delay state** state found in degradation analysis in which the workload of interest is not receiving service because it is waiting for access to a resource that is not currently available [to it].

**demand paging** in the SRM, the sum of nonswap, non-VIO page-ins and page-outs; in common parlance, page-ins caused by page faults. This is a case in which the SRM term is contradictory to common understanding.

**detected wait** a wait (without the LONG parameter) that exceeds a duration limit set by the SRM. Address spaces sustaining detected waits are candidates for swap-out. At this writing , the duration limit is eight SRM seconds or two seconds, whichever is shorter.

**device utilization** the average (mean) portion of a time interval during which the device in question was found to be busy—the target of a currently active I/O operation. Devices are either busy or not busy, but utilization can be any value from 0 to 100 percent.

**DFHSM** current name of IBM's Hierarchical Storage Manager, a data management extension that handles archiving, backup, and migration of data among levels of a storage hierarchy.

**DFP** Data Facility Product; See **data management**.

**DFSMS** Data Facility-Storage Management Subsystem; that part of MVS/ESA that implements system-managed storage.

**direct access storage device** DASD.

**disconnect** time in the execution of a channel program in which disconnected command chaining is initiated.

**disconnected command chaining (DCC)** the capability of an I/O device (through its control unit) to break its connection with the channel, allowing an operation that does not require data transfer to proceed without tying up the channel. DCC allows block multiplexor channels to be used for multiple concurrent DASD operations, since the time such a device is disconnected usually far exceeds its connect-time.

**disk** the IBM way to spell the word for a thin, circular spinning (usually magnetic-coated) object found in a DASD. Non-IBMers and (especially) anti-IBMers make it an article of religious faith to spell the word *disc*.

**DIV** Data-in-Virtual.

**DSCB** Data Set Control Block.

**DSORG** Data Set Organization.

**dual processors** computer configuration typified by larger models of the IBM 4381 in which two processors (CPUs) share common storage and each have a complement of attached cycle-stealing channels. Such a configuration is not physically partitionable and, in MVS/XA and MVS/ESA environments, does not intrinsically provide the independent channel subsystem of those architectures. The channel subsystem is simulated through microcode but "channel set" considerations are still necessary in system planning.

**dyadic** computer configuration in which two processors share common storage and an independent channel subsystem. Such a configuration is not physically partitionable.

**dynamic path reconnect (DPR)** ability of a DASD subsystem (control unit or storage director, string controller, and device) to re-establish an I/O connection after completion of a disconnected operation through any available storage director to any available channel connected to the initiating system. DPR is not supported in MVS/370, requiring the path-definition facilities of the XA or ESA channel subsystem.

**dynamic pathing** DASD subsystem facility consisting of two parts, dynamic path selection and dynamic path reconnect.

# E

**engineering embodiment** physical realization of an architecture, usually defining a system or product-family of systems; it may not implement all of the architecture or the full extent of the quantitative limits of the architecture. For instance, XA defines 2 gigabytes as its maximum real (central storage); no model of the 308X product family had more than 128 megabytes.

**enqueue lockout** condition in which a serially reusable resource controlled by the ENQueue service is held by a work unit that will not let it go. A typical cause is when the holder of the exclusive ENQ in turn requires another resource held by yet another work unit. The root problem is often known as a *deadly embrace*, but that term normally refers only to the symmetrical situation. (There are exactly two affected work units and each has what the other wants.) Other work units (usually each is a separate address space) are merely locked out.

**ES** Expanded Storage.

**ESA** Enterprise System[s] Architecture.

**exception analysis** monitoring technique in which states or quantities observable within a system are continually compared with acceptable states or values. When a deviation is found, an *exception* is said to exist. The monitor may display a message describing the exception on a terminal associated with it or on the system console, store the exception data on a data set, send it to SYSOUT, or take any of several other possible actions. Depending on the type of data examined, the monitor may be performing system availability analysis, service delivery analysis, response time analysis, elapsed time analysis, and so on.

**execution-state analysis** See **degradation analysis**.

**expert system** branch of artificial intelligence known also as a rules-based system. Elements include a *knowledge base*, describing the rules by which decisions are to be made, and an *inference engine*, a program that will follow the rules in any knowledge base to yield unambiguous conclusions. Expert systems are usually driven in a *consultation* by a human user; some expert systems gather data from performance monitors to make recommendations aimed at improving system performance.

**extent** contiguous portion of a DASD containing all or part of a data set. A data set with multiple widely distributed extents tends to be inefficient in random-access performance.

**externalize** to make a portion of a system subject to change or control without requiring knowledge of internal structure. MVS's OPT parameters prior to MVS/SE2 were limited and system changes were often made by changing the values in internal control blocks. Many of those values were externalized—became OPT parameters in MVS/SE2 and subsequent releases, thus reducing the exposure to MVS integrity.

**externals**  parts of a system subject to control by parameters or commands; also the descriptions of such parameters and commands.

# F

**fencing**  early name for storage isolation.

**fragmentation**  See **defragmentation**.

**frame**  the unit of real storage, 4096 contiguous bytes beginning at a real storage address divisible by 4096, the same size as a page.

**front-end**  the portion of I/O processing preceding the issuing of the instruction initiating the I/O; see **back-end**.

# G

**GETMAIN**  MVS service routine and its invoking SVC; allocates virtual storage upon program request. In MVS/ESA, GETMAIN (as well as its companion deallocation service FREEMAIN) has been superseded by a more comprehensive STORAGE service, rather that expanding GETMAIN to deal with allocation of storage in data spaces.

**GRS**  Global Resource Serialization.

**GTF**  Generalized Trace Facility.

**GUIDE**  an association of users of IBM large systems. GUIDE , and a similar association called SHARE, contribute to the development and refinement of IBM hardware and software through technical conferences and exchanges, as well as a formal requirements process.

# H

**happy values**  obsolescent name for SRM's MPL adjustment parameters, from the notion that the SRM is "happy" and therefore not about to change the MPL if each measured value is within its specified range.

**hashing algorithm**  data structure algorithm that distributes data according to some function of its key value so that searching the structure approximates ideal validity of reference. Simple hashing algorithms (such as assigning each letter of the alphabet to its own area) lead to numerous collisions and the need for supplementary local tables; more complex algorithms may require very large virtual filing cabinets.

**head of string**  control point of a DASD subsystem usually contained in the "A-box" of the string. Since the string controller is part of a DASD path, it represents a site of contention and queueing, usually called "head-of-string delay." In some past devices, the actuators physically present in the A-box may have had slightly less protocol delay and some priority in processing concurrent requests. The differences today are negligible at most.

**high-speed buffer (HSB)**  fast storage associated with the instruction fetch and processing elements of a CPU: a cache. For example, a CPU with a 15-nanosecond cycle time would have to take three idle cycles while waiting for data or instructions from a 60-nanosecond memory element. If the data and instructions are asynchronously staged into a 15-nanosecond HSB, CPU operations could proceed without the inserted delays. Correctly sizing an HSB is a classical exercise in cost/performance analysis.

**HSM**  See **DFHSM**.

**hypervisor**  a control program whose only function is to facilitate the running of other control programs or operating systems. IBM's PR/SM is a hypervisor embodied in hardware and microcode. VM is a somewhat compromised hypervisor because it supports numerous functions that allow virtual machines to communicate with it, in recognition of practical performance realities. A "pure" hypervisor insulates its various subordinate operating environments from one another; to the extent that it approximates an operating system that benefit is diluted.

**I**

**ICS**  Installation Control Specification, the IEAICSxx member of SYS1.-PARMLIB, used to assign address spaces to performance groups.

**IDAW**  Indirect Data Address Word, a logical extension to a CCW that specifies data address and count; it may contain a 31-bit address and was the means of enabling MVS/370 to support I/O to real storage addresses exceeding 16 megabytes.

**image processing** form of data processing in which digitized images of actual documents are stored and manipulated in order to save transcription time and avoid transcription error. Large potential cost savings are offset by very high computer resource requirements. The image of a typewritten page may require 50,000 bytes to store; as text it may take 3000.

**Indirect Data Address Word** See **IDAW**.

*Initialization and Tuning* IBM publication, in a different edition for each version of MVS, that specifies (or points to) the operating parameter choices for an MVS system.

**Installation Control Specification** See **ICS**.

**Installation Performance Specification** See **IPS**.

**Interval Service Value (ISV)** duration, expressed in service units, during which a transaction may not be considered for exchange swap, and in which the swap recommendation value for the address space is kept at the cutoff value.

**IPL** Initial Program Load; hardware-defined operation leading to the reinitialization of an MVS system.

**IPS** Installation Performance Specification.

**ISPF** Interactive System Productivity Facility, fullscreen text interface to TSO and a great contributor to TSO's acceptance.

**ISV** See **Interval Service Value**.

# J

**JCL** Job Control Language.

**JES** Job Entry Subsystem. In response to MVT's deficiencies at managing job sequencing, printers, and input data streams, two rival subsystems were designed and implemented primarily by customers with IBM support at only the local level. Both were eventually acquired by IBM. The Houston Automatic SPOOLing Priority system (HASP) eventually was made into JES2; the Attached Support Processor (ASP) became JES3. As the two JESs converge in function and performance, they are more and more distinguished primarily by their mutually incompatible control languages. The time may yet come when there is only one JES, but it probably won't be soon.

**JES2**  JES2 started out as the smaller, faster, simpler JES. It hs since grown in functionality so that most of what JES3 can do is found now in JES2, perhaps with extensions built on its numerous exits. See also **JES**.

**JES3**  JES3 began as the high-function JES for multi-system environments and with complex batch job streams requiring dependency scheduling. JES3 performance now rivals that of JES2. See also **JES**.

**job control language (JCL)**  Control statements that define a batch job, started task, or subsystem, existing in 80-byte fixed-length records or *card images*.

**Job Entry Subsystem**  See **JES**.

**jobstream**  sequence of batch jobs. Usually the term refers to a related sequence or *suite* of jobs that accomplish a single business purpose. For example, a General Ledger jobstream might consist of 30 or more individual jobs with sequential dependencies to be controlled by a production control staff or an automated job management system.

# K

**K**  in scientific and engineering notation the quantity 1000; in binary-based computing systems the quantity $2^{10}$, or 1024.

# L

**late binding**  See **binding**.

**latency**  the mean minimum rotational delay of any angular position on a DASD track; generally estimated as one-half of the rotational period.

**linear searching**  simplest data searching technique in which the element to be matched is compared with the corresponding part of each stored data structure. If the list is ordered, a miss requires an average search of one-half of the data extent; for an unordered list a miss requires a full element-by-element search, the worst-case violation of validity of reference. Linear searching requires no set-up; therefore if the setup time of a more efficient search method is greater than the time needed to traverse the list (or half if ordered), linear searching may be an appropriate choice. The bad reputation of linear searching comes from its fixed time requirement per element; more efficient methods have a fixed setup time and a variable time component that is less than proportional to the number of elements. Once the crossover point (the number of elements at which competing methods have equal search times) is passed, linear searching becomes increasingly costly in both execution time and working-set size.

**LLA** in MVS/XA, *Linklist Lookaside Area*, an address space that contains the directories of LINKLIST libraries, used to avoid outboard searching for load modules. In MVS/ESA, *Library Lookaside Area*, a service employing data spaces through VLF services to contain directories and load modules of selected LINKLIST libraries, used to avoid both searching and Program Fetch I/O.

**locality of reference** design principle and common property of programs; instructions and the data they use tend to be tightly clustered, whether the data is in virtual storage or on DASD. The clustering is both spatial and temporal; temporal clustering is sometimes called *temporality of reference*. If the implementation environment does not enforce locality of reference it may be necessary to enforce it as a design principle, to ensure minimum working set size for internal data and minimum access delay for external data.

**"loved one"** a workload that is economically significant to the business unit operating a data center; therefore it is closely watched and rescued if it is headed for trouble.

**LPAR** Logical PARtition in a PR/SM environment.

**LRU** Least Recently Used, page stealing strategy which assumes that a page not recently referenced is not likely to be referenced again soon. For programs exhibiting strong locality of reference, this is usually a sound assumption. There are, however, many instances in which LRU is counterproductive. If a transaction-processing subsystem serves a large population with little commonality in the transactions they invoke, the correct strategy may be to discard the pages of a transaction as soon as it is completed. This "MRU" (Most Recently Used) strategy resembles swapping more than LRU page stealing. The original studies that resulted in LRU's becoming the standard page replacement strategy may need to be reexamined with today's workloads.

# M

**M** in scientific and engineering notation the quantity 1,000,000; in binary-based computing systems such as the ones that support MVS, the quantity $2^{20}$, or 1,048,576.

**M/M/1** queueing model which assumes an exponentially distributed arrival rate (first "M"), exponentially distributed range of service times (second "M"), and a single server ("1"). M/M/1 is a useful model because it is mathematically simple and does match well to some common delay scenarios in data processing. As with any model, the scenario under consideration should be carefully checked against the assumptions of the model before using it.

**main storage** old name for storage internal to a computing system as opposed to DASD or tape. The term evolved to *real storage* when virtual storage came in, then to *processor storage* in preparation for the announcement of expanded storage, and finally to *central storage* when expanded was announced.

**maximum PWSS** storage-isolation parameter designating the maximum value an address space's target protected working set may reach. This is also the central storage frame count above which the address space is subject to preferred page stealing. A limited maximum PWSS should be specified *only* when preferred page stealing is desired.

**MC** MONITOR CALL instruction.

**MDF** Multiple Domain Facility, Amdahl Corporation's name for a hardware hypervisor providing multiple system images on a single processor complex. It preceded IBM's PR/SM in the marketplace.

**megabyte** See **M**; 1 M bytes.

**microcode** a level of programmed operation beneath the architecturally-defined "Principles of Operation" interface. In most of today's systems, hardware provides a low-level machine not generally seen by the operating system; the power-on reset process initiates loading (from an internal storage device) and execution of microcode to initialize the hardware to be, for instance, a 3090-280S in LPAR mode. At some other activation, one side of the 280S could be the equivalent of a 180S in ESA mode, the other a 180S in 370 mode. Microcode programming (microcoding) is usually considered to be an engineering discipline, but the required skills are exactly those of a very flexible assembly language programmer. Underlying engineering designs may have seemingly arbitrary word sizes, and "instructions" that perform complex compound operations. Microcode also provides support for extended operation codes available to operating system (supervisor state) code to perform functions such as creating an MVS address space.

**migration**  movement of pages from one medium to another. Migration is used to move long-unreferenced pages from a device high in a storage hierarchy to one at a lower position. It was first used in VM's predecessor, CP/67, in the days of IBM 2305 fixed-head files (drums), moving pages from the few slots on the expensive drums to relatively unlimited cheaper storage on DASD. In MVS/XA and MVS/ESA, migration moves pages from expanded storage to auxiliary storage. Just as in the CP or VM case, expanded storage migration requires frames in central storage as I/O destinations for incoming pages and origins for outgoing pages. Migration is triggered by internally-maintained thresholds of migration age.

**migration age**  measure of activity in expanded storage. The migration age for a page in expanded storage is approximately the number of seconds since it was referenced. Lower migration ages are usually correlated with higher contention for expanded storage pages. In this way, migration age in expanded storage resembles unreferenced interval count (UIC) in central storage. Overall migration age is used to determine which pages are sent to expanded storage, and individual pages' migration age determines which is to be selected for migration.

**MIPS**  millions of instructions per second, a measure of CPU power. However, all instructions are not alike, and IBM in particular does not generally release MIPS data for its products. Bare measures like MIPS tend to ignore important CPU performance factors including storage and I/O bandwidth, microcoded assists for operating systems and key programs, concurrency, and the power of individual instructions.

**MLPF**  Multiple Logical Processor Facility, National Advanced Systems' name for a hardware hypervisor providing multiple system images on a single processor complex. MLPF is similar in functional capability to IBM's PR/SM.

**MP**  multiprocessor.

**MPL** multiprogramming level, the number of address spaces resident in central storage at any given time; also the number of address spaces of a particular kind or in a particular domain.

**MPL delay** delay state in which an address space is swapped out and ready to be swapped in, but the SRM cannot increase the MPL in its domain to allow the address space to be swapped in. MPL delay is also known as "out and ready" time.

**MSO** (1) component of service unit accumulation based on Main Storage Occupancy; (2) service definition coefficient (SDC) in the IPS establishing the weight of MSO service units in the overall service unit quantity; (3) coefficient in the OPT determining the extent to which storage load balancing is allowed to bias swap recommendation values.

**MSPP** milliseconds per page, a statistic used for MPL control in the default OPT.

**MSS** Mass Storage Subsystem, the IBM 3850 and its associated devices, control units, and microcode. MSS was an early attempt to minimize the use of manually mounted tape reels in data centers. The subsystem provided virtual DASD materialized on demand on a relatively small number of real DASD units. The backing storage for the virtual data was a special tape cartridge; large numbers of such cartridges were stored in a "honeycomb" array, and fetched and loaded by a robotic mechanism. The device never achieved sufficient success to justify follow-on development, so its support of only virtual IBM 3330s became marginal when 3350s became standard, and inadequate when the 3380 entered the marketplace.

**MTTW** Mean Time to Wait; the average CPU service burst in an address space between successive WAIT SVCs. The ranking of address spaces in inverse order of their MTTWs is one means of adjusting dispatching priorities.

**Multiple Domain Facility** See **MDF**.

**multiprogramming** method of operating a computing system so that multiple workloads are concurrently active. When one workload gives up its use of the CPU by entering the WAIT state, another workload can be dispatched. In earlier times, batch multiprogramming exploited I/O waits; in current systems, multiprogramming exploits the "think time" of terminal users as well.

**multiprogramming level** See MPL.

**multiprogramming set** the set of address spaces that constitutes the MPL.

**multitasking** the possibility of multiprogramming within a single address space. The ATTACH SVC creates an additional dispatchable unit (task), independent of the task that created it.

**MVM** original name for MVS, Multiple Virtual Memories.

**MVT** most complete version of OS/360, Multiprogramming with a Variable number of Tasks.

# N

**negative storage isolation** use of storage isolation with a low maximum PWSS to designate an address space as a preferred source for page stealing.

**nonswappable** address space not eligible for swap-out. Many started tasks that run in authorized state simply make themselves nonswappable by issuing the appropriate SYSEVENT SVC. Others become nonswappable by means of an entry in the Program Properties Table, and any address space operating in cross-memory mode is nonswappable by definition.

**nucleus** the permanently resident portion of MVS, encompassing the I/O supervisor, the various resource managers (ASM, RSM, SRM, ...), interrupt handlers, and the most essential service routines. The "horizontal splitting" made possible by cross-memory services complicates the definition. ENQ/DEQ services used to be in the nucleus, but now these services are provided by GRS in a separate address space.

# O

**operator** person responsible for directing the activities of a computing system. Key operator tasks include [initiating] system startup and shutdown, observing and replying to messages displayed at the system console, entering commands to deal with unusual circumstances, mounting and demounting tapes, and loading and removing printer paper. All of these tasks except those dealing with printer paper are candidates for automation. Automated tape libraries and console automation programs are redefining the operator's job away from performing mundane tasks and towards high-level decision-making. Paper-handling is becoming less important as more high-quality page printers are installed at the point of need rather than in the central computer room.

**OPT** abbreviation for "optimizer," an early name for the SRM. Also, usual designation for the IEAOPTxx member of SYS1.PARMLIB.

**out-and-ready** condition of an address space that is swapped out and ready to run, but cannot be swapped in because the MPL in its domain will not allow a unilateral swap-in and there is no candidate in the domain eligible for an exchange swap. With a suitable exchange swap candidate, several swap analysis cycles may go by until the exchange swap can be performed, because of the low priority given to exchange swapping in swap analysis.

**overinitiation** pejorative name for the condition in which the aggregate MPL of batch jobs is less than the number of active batch jobs. In fact overinitiation is a prerequisite to effective MPL management.

**overlapped processing** characteristic of a computing system in which I/O operations proceed concurrently with CPU processing. Independently operating channels make overlapped processing possible. Overlapped processing in turn makes multiprogramming and multitasking possible.

**override** to substitute a selected value for the default value of a parameter.

# P

**page** *n.* 1. the unit of virtual storage, 4096 contiguous bytes at a starting address divisible by 4096; 2. the unit of expanded storage, 4096 bytes designated by a single page number; *v.* to move pages between slots of auxiliary storage and frames of central storage; usually the movement from auxiliary to central (page-in) is of interest.

**page fault** an interrupt caused by a page-translation exception, signifying that the page is not shown to be occupying a frame of central storage. A page fault usually results in a page-in; when the required page had been selected for page-out but not yet removed from central storage, the page fault can be resolved as a *reclaim* in minimum time.

**page movement** the transfer of pages between central and expanded storage; also the movement of frames from central storage above 16 megabytes to and from addresses "below the line," used in MVS/370 to allow ordinary I/O (without IDAWs) to proceed.

**page stealing** activity initiated when the Real Storage Manager (RSM) has allocated a frame and finds that the available frame count has fallen below the current MCCAFCLO threshold. The condition is also triggered in conjunction with a swap-in when the required number of frames would put AFC below MCCAFCLO. SRM selects the frames to be reassigned, first taking frames from storage-isolated address spaces with frame counts above their PWSS maximums, then taking frames from storage-isolated address spaces with more frames than their current targets as well as other address spaces and the common area, in descending order of UIC. SRM sends any required page-outs to the auxiliary storage manager (ASM).

**PARMLIB** partitioned data set (SYS1.PARMLIB) containing the externally specifiable parameters of MVS and some of its subsystems. *Initialization and Tuning* contains a description of each member of SYS1.PARMLIB.

**partitioned data set (PDS)** data set organization (DSORG) consisting of a directory and a set of members resembling individual sequential data sets. A PDS is often known as a library.

**partitioning, physical** the act of dividing a computer system into two (or more) independent computer systems. Physical partitioning requires separate components from power supplies on up. IBM systems and compatibles capable of running MVS support (to date only) two-way physical partitioning if appropriately configured in "two-sided" configurations.

**path** an I/O connection between a CPU and a device consisting of a channel, control unit, and device controller, if applicable, as well as the device.

**PEND** in XA and ESA, the time spent by the channel subsystem waiting for a path to become available. PEND time is often associated with shared DASD contention.

**pending-out queue** set of pages destined to be moved to expanded storage in FIFO order, as central storage is needed. The queue includes single pages (as from page steals and requested page-outs) and groups of pages (VIO windows, trims, and swap groups), which are moved as groups.

**physical sequential**  data set organization (DSORG) in which logical records (defined by use in a program) are organized in (often larger) physical records (defined to optimize device performance) and read or written in strict order from the beginning to the end of the data set.

**physical swap**  movement of the trimmed working set of an address space between central (real) storage and auxiliary storage. Although a processor storage swap is also a physical phenomenon, the term is used only for the swap involving the use of auxiliary storage.

**PLPA**  Pageable Link Pack Area, part of the common area, also including EPLPA in MVS/XA and MVS/ESA, containing **reenterable** load modules that may be used (in place) by any address space. There is also a Fixed Link Pack Area, containing modules that may not sustain page faults and therefore are ineligible for page stealing.

**PLPA page data set**  the first-named page data set in an MVS IPL, containing only pages of the PLPA. Since the PLPA is read-only, the PLPA page data set is preserved across IPLs and is rewritten only when the CLPA option is specified for the IPL.

**portable application**  application program or system written so it can be executed on several different kinds of computer systems. In general, portable applications trade off ease of implementation for environments other than the first for less-than-optimal performance in each environment. Of necessity, they must use a "lowest common denominator" of system facilities and services in order to be portable. Implementors or vendors of such applications must often devote substantial expense to improving performance, reliability, integrity, and flexibility in particular environments, in response to customer requirements. IBM's Systems Application Architecture (SAA) is designed to improve the portability of applications across the various IBM "platforms" while minimizing the need for compromises in the interest of portability.

**PPT**  Program Properties Table, an MVS data area specifying names of programs that are to enjoy various forms of privilege.

**preferred page stealing**  page stealing incurred by storage-isolated address spaces holding more frames than the maximum PWSS for the current performance period. See also **negative storage isolation**.

*Principles of Operation* IBM publication defining hardware data structures and organization, instruction set, and related interpretations and relationships for a computer system or family of systems.

**processor storage** central storage and expanded storage; all storage accessible to a processor.

**Program Fetch** service routine in the MVS nucleus that loads programs from libraries into virtual storage. In ESA, Fetch also loads programs from the LLA data space. Program loading is more complex than simply reading in a module; programs are generally relocatable and internal references to addresses must be adjusted relative to the loading address of the module. The principal SVCs serviced by Fetch are those for ATTACH, LINK, LOAD, and XCTL.

**Program Properties Table (PPT)** See **PPT**.

**Program Status Word (PSW)** in System/360, the 64-bit (double-word) representation of the current state of the CPU. In System/370, XA, and ESA, the PSW still contains the current instruction address and various mode and mask settings, but to capture the full status of the CPU requires the content of several control register fields as well. The PSW does not exist as a viewable object except when stored as the result of an interrupt. When the interrupt occurs, the PSW is created and stored at one of six reserved addresses according to the interrupt type, and a new PSW is fetched from a corresponding reserved address. A PSW at any double-word address is made the current PSW when it is the object of the LPSW (LOAD PROGRAM STATUS WORD) privileged instruction.

**PSW** See **Program Status Word**.

**push-out** the process of moving the trimmed working set of an address space from central storage to expanded storage, thus completing a processor storage swap-out.

# Q

**QSAM** See **queued sequential access method**.

**queued sequential access method** access method for physically sequential data sets or members of PDSs which accepts (PUTs) or provides (GETs) logical records one at a time. QSAM handles synchronization, blocking, and buffering without the need for problem program direction.

**quiesce** series of actions to prepare an address space for swapping; the principal task is to ensure that all pending I/O is completed.

# R

**re-reference** subsequent reference to data that was previously used. Re-reference to pages is what keeps their UICs low and thus protects them from stealing. Re-reference to blocks or tracks in a cache control unit prevents that data from being destaged to the backing device. In active TSO populations with some degree of storage constraint, re-reference to pages trimmed in the last few swaps accounts for about 60 percent of page faults. The use of storage isolation for TSO in such a case reduces TSO page faults dramatically at the low cost of moving a few more pages in the swap group. Re-reference frequency is the measure of locality of reference.

**real frame replacement** See **page stealing**.

**reclaim** See **page fault**.

**reconnect** the activity in the progress of an I/O operation following the successful completion of a disconnected command or series of commands; the device controller and storage director re-establish connection to the CPU through a channel. In System/370, reconnect could occur only on the original channel through which the operation began; in XA and ESA, any channel physically connected to the CPU and storage director or control unit may be used.

**reenterability** property of a program in which multiple concurrent activations may proceed without interference. In systems such as MVS, based on OS/360, reenterability was easy to achieve because programs generally acquire storage from the operating system (via the GET-MAIN SVC) for work areas and I/O buffers, and do not carry around such data in load modules so that program size and loading time can be minimized.

**reenterable** attribute of a program that possesses the property of reenterability. The attribute is indicated by a bit in a load module's PDS directory entry.

**reentrant** [*sic*] common alternative designation for *reenterable*. This word is etymologically incorrect, having the plain meaning in other contexts of an entity that re-enters itself. In a program, this would be a loop.

**region** in OS/360 MVT, a contiguous portion of real storage in which a program executed. The size of the region was a *de facto* limit on the aggregate size of all GETMAINs of the program in the region and all of its subordinate programs. In SVS, the storage became virtual, but *region* still functioned the same way. In MVS, the region became an address space of 16 megabytes, later two gigabytes in XA and ESA. Region size would appear to have no meaning. However, the page tables needed to map a full address space are sufficiently large that it is desirable to limit their extent if the full potential is not needed. Hence an MVS parameter and the REGION= specification in JCL or at LOGON allows a limit to be stated, separately in XA and ESA for both storage below 16 MB and above the line. The REGION limit in MVS retains the consequence of the MVT definition. It is the limit on the amount of virtual storage obtainable in an address space.

**resource-oriented point of view** approach to performance management that focuses on quantities measurable for hardware and operating system resources, such as CPU and channel utilization, paging rates, and queue lengths.

**RM1** interval at which SRM collects data, the SRM second.

**RM2** interval at which SRM summarizes the data collected at RM1 intervals and decides whether to adjust the system's MPL. In MVS/370, RM2 was fixed at 20 seconds, but in MVS/XA and MVS/ESA it becomes smaller as the power of the processor complex increases.

**RSM** Real Storage Manager.

**rule of thumb (ROT)** method of making performance management decisions, based on comparing resource values with a set of values deemed to be acceptable. Deviations of the measurable values from the ROTs is taken to signify a performance deviation, irrespective of workload indicators such as response time. This method of performance management sounds absurd, but it is all too close to what MVS does for itself by default.

# S

**scale-up problem**  performance problem that comes about when a workload volume increase makes formerly acceptable performance unacceptable. In particular, an algorithm that was efficient for low volume becomes noticeably inefficient for high volume.

**SCP**  System Control Program, one of two designations introduced on June 23, 1969, when IBM "unbundled" software and services from hardware, thus creating the mainframe software business. Originally, SCPs were provided at no cost with the hardware and Program Products were available at a fee. As MVS evolved through MVS/SE to MVS/SP, this distinction was lost, and today's counterparts to SCPs are not free.

**sequential data set**  See **physical sequential**.

**SHARE**  See **GUIDE**.

**slot**  unit of auxiliary storage, a 4096-byte physical record on a page data set.

**SMS**  System-Managed Storage, the use of hardware and software in MVS/ESA to automate the DASD Management or Storage Management functions usually found in an MVS installation. These functions include space allocation, data set placement, backup, recovery, and archiving or migration of inactive data to less expensive media. SMS in ESA also supports the use of performance considerations in determining data set placement, if only at initial allocation time. The part of DFP in MVS/ESA that implements SMS is called DFSMS.

**SRM summarization interval**  See **RM2**.

**SRR**  Serially Reusable Resource.

**Status Switch[ing]**  Transition from problem state to supervisor state caused by an interrupt. Status switching is an expensive and disruptive operation because it interrupts the flow of instruction processing, causing the Translation Lookaside Buffer (TLB) and the CPU's High Speed Buffer to be purged either explicitly or implicitly as other virtual storage areas are used. Recent changes in MVS and the hardware it runs on, including the improved PROGRAM CALL facilities in ESA and use of the TEST PENDING INTERRUPT instruction, seek to minimize the need for status switching.

**Storage Management Subsystem** See **DFSMS** and **SMS**.

**SVC** the SUPERVISOR CALL instruction, used by a program to request service from the operating system. A code imbedded in the instruction designates the service to be performed; register contents and data addressed through the registers give the details of the request.

**swap group** in systems without expanded storage, the set of pages that are both swapped out and swapped in. With expanded storage, only the primary working set is swapped in from expanded, and the term does not apply except for direct swaps to auxiliary storage.

**swap trim** form of page stealing just prior to swap-out, reducing the frame count of the address space down to the swap group or trimmed working set. Swap trim is aggressive by default; it can be moderated (the swap group expanded) by specifying storage isolation for performance periods (such as first period TSO) to be protected from page stealing.

**synchronous delay** delay to a workload that is caused by the workload itself. For instance, an address space that initiates an I/O operation on a uniprocessor without entering a WAIT state will inevitably be delayed by the back-end processing when the I/O request is completed. Even with a relatively inactive CPU, the address space will be found in the "waiting for CPU" execution state for a portion of its active time proportional to that kind of activity.

**system-managed storage** See **SMS**.

# T

**target control keyword** means of defining the contention index of a domain, one of the keywords FWKL, AOBJ, and DOBJ; mutually exclusive with the use of domain weight.

**target MPL** the current number of address spaces that the SRM will allow to be resident in a given domain.

**target multiprogramming level** See **target MPL**.

**target working set** the number of frames held by an address space that will be protected from normal page stealing when storage isolation is specified in its current performance period definition.

**TCAS** Terminal Control Address Space, an address spaced invoked during the TSO LOGON process, used to create the address space that will eventually become the TSO session.

**Terminal Monitor Program (TMP)** the facilitating, service-providing environment that defines a TSO session. TSO was conceived as a generalized interface in which the TMP could be replaced to meet special needs, but in practice, the IBM-supplied TMP is used as is.

**tetradic** a CPU configuration in which four processors share storage and a channel subsystem. To the date of writing, no such system has been announced.

**think time** time during which a user of a terminal-based system is either reading or interpreting the screen content, keying in data without hitting the ENTER key, thinking about the screen and the session, or doing something else entirely. In MVS, it is strictly defined for TSO as the interval between two SYSEVENTs—Terminal Input Wait and User Ready. The recent think time history of an address space is used in the decision process for logical swapping and for swapping to expanded storage.

**TMPL** See **target MPL**.

**TPI** TEST PENDING INTERRUPT, an instruction used in MVS/XA and MVS/ESA to allow a processor (CPU) to "pick off" and process a pending I/O interrupt without leaving the I/O interrupt handler. Doing so eliminates a subsequent interrupt and the corresponding disruption to instruction processing caused by status switching. The extent to which TPI is successful is used by the SRM to control the number of processors enabled for I/O interrupts.

**transaction-oriented measurement systems** data collector which captures data reflecting the completion and history of each transaction in a given environment, for later analysis and reporting.

**trimmed working set** set of frames remaining as part of an address space after swap trim.

**tuning** performance management activity with the purpose of removing known inefficiency or restoring inadequate service to an acceptable level. In the context of "buy, steal, tune, or accept," to "tune" is to change programs to be more efficient or to change installation choices (such as block sizes) to improve the operation of one workload without penalizing another.

# U

**UADS** User Attribute Data Set, a data set containing identity and control attributes for TSO users.

**UCB** Unit Control Block, data area in MVS describing the nature and current state of an I/O device. There are as many UCBs as defined devices. When a device is found busy in attempting to start an I/O operation, the queue of requests awaiting the device is associated with the UCB.

**UCBBSY** bit in the UCB indicating, when set to "1" that an I/O operation is currently active on the device.

**UIC** Unreferenced Interval Count, measure of activity in central storage. The UIC for a frame is approximately the number of seconds since it was referenced. Lower UICs are usually correlated with higher contention for central storage frames, although it is possible for a workload with a large and stable working set to drive a system's UIC close to zero with little or no contention.

**unattended operation** See **operator**.

**unblocked data set** a data set in which the physical record or block is the same size as the logical record. Unblocked data sets with small block sizes, especially heavily used sequential or partitioned data sets, usually represent a system-wide performance problem.

**uncaptured time** See **capture ratio**.

**under-initiation** See **over-initiation**.

**Unit Control Block** See **UCB**.

# V

**V=R** attribute of an address space whose virtual addresses are required to match its real addresses. Pages of such an address space cannot be stolen, and the address space cannot be swapped. V=R was used heavily in the infancy of MVS, when it was feared that the burden of I/O address translation would cause incorrect operation of certain critical I/O devices, or that the dynamic address translation process was not to be trusted. V=R has all but disappeared except for some specialized hardware diagnostic programs.

**virtual=real**  See **V=R**.

**VLF**  Virtual Lookaside Facility; in MVS/ESA, used to store named objects such as load modules or TSO CLISTs in data spaces, to save the I/O associated with repeated use.

# W

**WAIT**  SVC to suspend the execution of instructions in an address space until an expected event occurs. The usual mechanism is to define an Event Control Block (ECB), which is the object of the WAIT macro-instruction. Some other process (for instance another active task in the address space) will later issue the POST macro with the ECB as its object, to signify that the WAIT is completed. Most WAITs are not invoked directly by a problem program but are the implicit conse-quence of I/O or other service requests.

**WAIT state**  state of a CPU when it has no work to do. The accumula-tion of wait state time is the complement of CPU utilization.

**workload-oriented point of view**  performance management ap-proach based primarily on the measurement of service delivered by the workloads of interest, with corrective action initiated when a service target is missed

# Index

## About the Author

Stephen L. Samson is an executive consultant with Candle
Corporation in Los Angeles, California, one of the world's
largest vendors of performance management and
productivity software for the environment. As a
programming architect with IBM, Samson was involved
with the early development of MVS. Since then, he has
worked with the operating system as a technical support
manager, performance management specialist, and
consultant.